I Was a Teenage JFK Conspiracy Freak

Also by Fred Litwin

Conservative Confidential

I Was a Teenage JFK Conspiracy Freak

Fred Litwin

Copyright © 2018 by Fred Litwin

All rights reserved. No part of this publication may be reproduced in any form or by any means without the prior written permission of Fred Litwin.

Excerpts from Secrets of a Homicide: The JFK Assassination © 1995-2018 Dale K. Myers. Reprinted with permission from Dale K. Myers.
Internet: www.jfkfiles.com
Dealey Plaza Map ©2018 by Gene Thorp, Cartographic Concepts Incorporated, www.mapmanusa.com.

First North American edition published in 2018 by NorthernBlues Books

Cover design by Kathleen Lynch
Edited by Michael J. Totten

Manufactured in the United States and Canada on acid-free paper

FIRST NORTH AMERICAN EDITION

Litwin, Fred
I Was a Teenage JFK Conspiracy Freak

ISBN: 978-0-9948630-2-7

0123456789

Dedicated to John McAdams and Paul Hoch

There have been many people bold enough to tell us the truth about the JFK assassination. But John McAdams and Paul Hoch have gone above and beyond the call of duty by instructing us how to evaluate evidence, how to think about documents, and how to use logic and reason to think clearly about what actually happened. All students of the JFK assassination owe a debt of gratitude to John McAdams and Paul Hoch.

Fred in Dealey Plaza standing next to the pedestal where Abraham Zapruder shot his famous film.

Fred Litwin

I Was a Teenage JFK Conspiracy Freak is Fred Litwin's second book. (You can find updates and pictures at conspiracyfreak.com.) In 2015, he published *Conservative Confidential: Inside the Fabulous Blue Tent*, detailing his journey from left-wing anti-nuclear activist to Conservative Party campaigner.

Fred has also written articles for the *National Post*, the *Ottawa Citizen*, the *Toronto Sun*, *C2C Journal*, *iPolitics*, and the *Dorchester Review*.

In 2000, he founded NorthernBlues Music, a cutting-edge blues label. The company has released over 70 CDs and garnered 12 Juno Award and more than 40 Blues Music Award nominations. In 2007, Fred started the Free Thinking Film Society to showcase films on liberty, freedom and democracy. The Society has shown over 100 films and also organizes book launches and panel discussions.

Contents

Prologue		11
Introduction		15
1.	The People of the Books	37
2.	Jim Garrison's Excellent Homosexual Adventure	75
3.	I Was a Teenage JFK Conspiracy Freak	101
4.	Oliver Stone's Excellent Homosexual Adventure	120
5.	A Conspiracy Too Big?	143
6.	Did the CBC Solve the JFK Assassination?	169
7.	The Quest for the Holy Document	193
Postscript		215
Acknowledgements		221
For Further Information		225
Notes and Sources		233

Prologue

On November 22, 1963, President John F. Kennedy flew from Ft. Worth, Texas, to Dallas. It was the second day of a trip designed to shore up his political standings and to heal rifts in the state Democratic Party. The day before, the presidential party was in San Antonio and Houston. The Dallas plan was for a motorcade through the city, a luncheon speech at the Trade Mart, and then a flight to Austin.

Initially, it looked like it would rain but the skies cleared by midmorning and there was no thought of using the "bubbletop" which would shield Kennedy from the weather. Kennedy sat next to his wife Jackie in the back seat, and the Governor of Texas, John Connally, sat in front with his wife Nellie. Secret Service agent William Greer drove and agent Roy Kellerman sat next to him.

The motorcade left Love Field at 11:50 am (CST) and proceeded downtown. The crowds were enthusiastic and Kennedy stopped the motorcade twice to greet people. It then proceeded on Main Street, a major east-west road and turned right on Houston Street. One block later it turned left on to Elm Street so that it could take an exit for the Stemmons Freeway which would take them to the Trade Mart.

At 12:30 pm, as the motorcade made its way down Elm Street, shots rang out. Kennedy's hands moved up toward his neck and Governor Connally was hit in the back. A few seconds later, a bullet hit Kennedy in the head and he moved back and to the left. The motorcade sped off to Parkland Memorial Hospital.

A team of doctors frantically treated Kennedy and they observed a small wound in the front of Kennedy's throat and a massive head wound.

Dealey Plaza
November 22, 1963

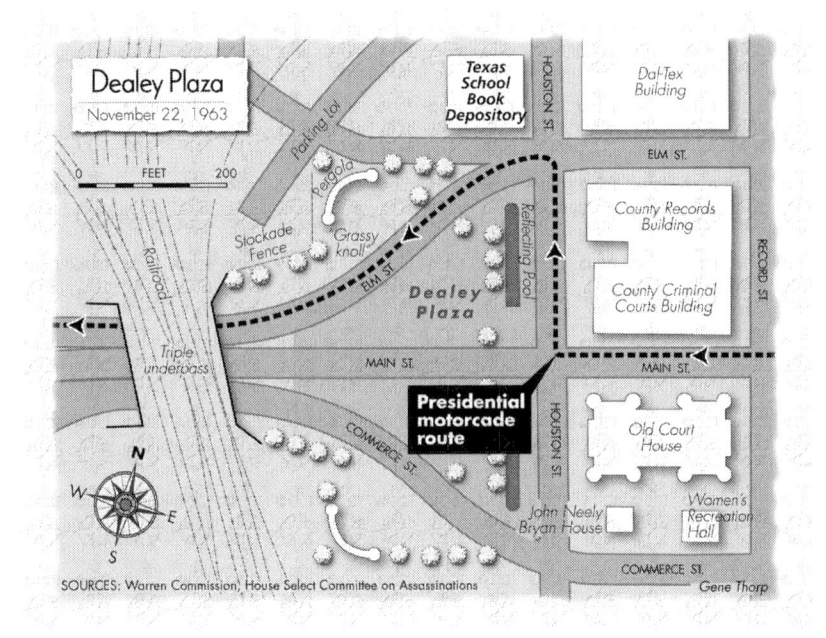

At 1:00 pm, they pronounced Kennedy dead and last rites were performed. Governor Connally was treated for wounds in his chest, wrist, and thigh.

It didn't take long for the Dallas police to centre their activity on the Texas School Book Depository (TSBD) as the source of the shots. They searched the building and found a rifle hidden amongst book cartons on the sixth floor as well as three spent cartridge cases at the southeast corner window.

Lee Harvey Oswald worked at the TSBD and was missing after the assassination. He had taken a bus and taxi to his rooming house. He picked up his revolver and left his house at 1:00 pm. About 15 minutes later, police officer J.D. Tippit was killed about nine-tenths of a mile away.

Right after the shooting, the manager of a shoe store, Johnny Brewer, saw a man stop in the entranceway of his store as a police car whizzed by. After the car left, the man stepped away and was followed by Brewer. He ducked into the Texas Theater without buying a ticket. Brewer pointed this out to the cashier who then called the police.

Police officers approached Oswald in the theatre. He pulled his gun and struck a policeman in the face. The officers then handcuffed and brought him to police headquarters. For two days, Oswald denied he was the assassin. On Sunday morning, the 24th of November, nightclub owner Jack Ruby killed Oswald just as he was about to be taken to the county jail.

On November 29th, 1963, President Lyndon Johnson set up a commission to investigate the assassination and named Earl Warren, the Chief Justice of the US Supreme Court, as chairman. On September 24th, 1964, the commission submitted its report concluding that Lee Harvey Oswald killed JFK and that they could not find any evidence of a conspiracy. Jack Ruby was convicted of killing Oswald and years later won an appeal for a new trial (based in the inadmissibility of some testimony and the requirement of a new venue). He died in January of 1967 just as they were to set a date for his re-trial.

Introduction

When I first started telling friends that I was writing about the JFK assassination, I received some strange reactions. Just about everybody I talked to looked puzzled and then asked whether there was "really something to that, no?" Was there a second gun? What about the movement of Kennedy's head? How could Oswald have fired that fast? Will we ever know the truth? They had no detailed understanding of what happened, or what didn't happen, but they suspected that something was amiss.

There was a real thirst for more information. I remember one Wednesday calling my synagogue to reserve a couple of spots at an upcoming Shabbat dinner. I spent about 20 minutes talking about the assassination with the office manager. Tell me more about Jack Ruby. He was Jewish, right? I couldn't get off the phone.

It's been over fifty years since the JFK assassination and people still aren't sure about what happened.

When I told most people that there was no conspiracy and that just about every issue could be easily explained, they just smiled. The conspiracy narrative was so deeply embedded that there was nothing I could say to relieve their doubts.

It's actually not that surprising.

Thousands of JFK conspiracy books have been published. College campuses have been inundated with speakers spouting poppycock about plots, treachery, and ultimately power in America. Oliver Stone's 1991 fantasy film *JFK* exposed millions to unadulterated nonsense about a supposed cabal at the highest level of the U.S. government. And the Canadian Broadcasting Corporations' (CBC) premier documentary television series, *The Fifth Estate*, repeatedly pushed the craziest theories about the assassination.

It was narrative by slow percolation. And there's nothing new about this at all.

The *New York Times* printed a steady stream of communist propaganda by their Soviet correspondent Walter Duranty in the 1930s. The 1932 Pulitzer Prize was awarded to Duranty for a series of 13 articles in 1931. He relied totally on Soviet sources and never quoted a single ordinary Russian. How else could he have written "Enemies and foreign critics can say what they please. Weaklings and despondents at home may groan under the burden, but the youth and strength of the Russian people is essentially at one with the Kremlin's program, believes it worthwhile and supports it, however hard be the sledding."

Duranty even denied there was a famine in Ukraine, writing in 1933 that "any report of a famine in Russia is today an exaggeration or malignant propaganda." He added that "but—to put it brutally—you can't make an omelet without breaking eggs."

Malcolm Muggeridge, reporter for the *Manchester Guardian*, went to Ukraine in 1933 and reported that "the population is starving…cattle and horses dead; fields neglected; meager harvest despite moderately good climatic conditions; all the grain that was produced taken by the government now no bread at all, greatest liar of any journalist I have met in fifty years of journalism."

That didn't stop *The Nation* (a leading left-wing magazine) from honouring the *New York Times* and Walter Duranty in 1933, writing that his reporting was "the most enlightened, dispassionate dispatches from a great nation in the making which appears in any newspaper in the world." None of this fooled George Orwell—he put Duranty's name on a list of writers considered to be unacceptable (too favourable to Stalinism) for the British Foreign Office Information research department. Besides Duranty's name, Orwell noted that he was a "sympathiser only."

Indeed, in Orwell's 1942 essay, "Looking Back on the Spanish War," he wrote that "Early in life, I had noticed that no event is ever correctly reported in a newspaper, but in Spain, for the first time, I saw newspaper reports which did not bear any relation to the facts, not even the relationship which is implied in an ordinary lie…and I saw newspapers in London retailing these lies and eager intellectuals building emotional superstructures over events that had never happened. I saw, in fact, history being written not in terms of what happened but of what ought to have happened according to various 'party lines.'"

He added that he often had "the feeling that the very concept of objective truth is fading out of the world. After all, the changes are that those lies [about the Spanish civil war], or at any rate similar lies, will pass into history." Norman Mailer coined the term 'factoid' in 1973 to refer to pieces of information that are accepted as true but which are not true. Combine a small number of factoids and you have the beginnings of a false narrative.

Thus, the propagandist and the conspiracy theorist both exploit their specious narratives to the same end—convincing people of something that is just plain untrue.

There are quite a few factoids about the JFK assassination; that the motorcade route was changed; that CIA operatives E. Howard Hunt and Frank Sturgis were in Dallas on November 22nd; that a Mauser, and not a Mannlicher-Carcano, was found on the Sixth Floor of the Texas School Depository; that Jack Ruby knew Lee Harvey Oswald; that Oswald was standing in the doorway of the TSBD during the assassination and could not be the gunman. And so on and so forth. Those who care about the truth are always in a rearguard action debunking all sorts of nonsense.

A good example of a Canadian factoid, ultimately used in a false narrative, relates to the 2009 "attempted" visit to Canada by George Galloway, the ridiculous 'pro-peace' Labour MP from the UK. When the Canadian High Commission learned that he might be going to Canada, they invited him in for an interview. They wanted to discuss his deliverance of funds to Hamas, an organization on the Canadian terrorist list. He passed on the interview, flew to the United States, and made it appear that he had been turned back from the border. Galloway didn't even try to enter the country. He then appeared on the George Stroumboulopoulos show, *The Hour*, on the CBC on March 30, 2009, via video hookup and wasn't even questioned about his dubious claims.

On the July 8, 2015, CBC show *Power & Politics*, host Rosemary Barton had a discussion with veteran journalist Terry Milewski. They talked about a Senate Committee Report on the fight against radicalization and the need to ban extremists from entering the country.

Barton: Who's on the list? Anyone the Minister doesn't like?

Milewski: Remember the case of the British very left-wing MP George Galloway banned from Canada because basically the then-immigration Minister Jason Kenney didn't want him.

The CBC repeated this factoid in September, 2017, in an article about an MP junket to China. A Conservative MP, Candice Bergen, was denied a travel visa when she refused to fill out portions of the application form. The organizer of the trip, Senator Joseph Day, told Bergen that "China had the right to decide who to let in." When she suggested to the CBC that Canada would not do the same to an elected official, the CBC added that "There was, in fact, a lot of controversy in 2009 when the Canadian Border Services Agency denied entry to George Galloway, then a British MP."

The 'Galloway factoid' can now be used to portray the Conservative Party as being hostile to free speech, or as an example of how Canada can keep 'elected officials' out of the country. Take your pick.

Of course, no one was better using rare factoids to push a fiction than Noam Chomsky, the MIT linguistics Professor turned demi-god of the left.

Chomsky covered for the Pol Pot Communist dictatorship in Cambodia and its massacre of over one million Cambodians. In his book, *The Political Economy of Human Rights*, co-authored with Edward Herman, he noted that in Cambodia there was "on the one hand, oppression, regimentation and terror; on the other, constructive achievements for much of the population." To downplay the massive forced evacuation of Phnom Penh, Chomsky and Herman quoted from a Khmer Rouge sympathetic newspaper,—*News from Kampuchea*,—that claimed the march out of Phnom Penh was voluntary. Chomsky and Herman disputed mass executions and said that "analyses by highly qualified specialists ... who have concluded that executions [by the Khmer Rouge] have numbered at most in the thousands."

Another factoid is that George W. Bush lied about Weapons of Mass Destruction in Iraq. And you don't have to take Jon Stewart's or Michael Moore's word for it—Donald Trump said in the 2016 election campaign that "I want to tell you, they lied. They said there were weapons of mass destruction. There were none. And they knew there were none."

The Bush administration did not lie. Certainly, the intelligence was wrong, Saddam did not have WMDs. But was there any evidence to support the mantra, 'Bush lied, People died'? Did George Bush force the intelligence agencies to 'alter' the evidence?

In 2004, The Commission on the Intelligence Capabilities of the United States Regarding Weapons of Mass Destruction was established to investigate what really happened. Here is their conclusion on the politicization of the intelligence:

Finally, we closely examined the possibility that intelligence analysts were pressured by policymakers to change their judgments about Iraq's nuclear, biological, and chemical weapons programs. The analysts who worked Iraqi weapons issues universally agreed that in no instance did political pressure cause them to skew or alter any of their analytical judgments.

Few people will read the 619-page report. And, even if they did, it would just be dismissed as mere government propaganda.

So, fake news and false narratives are nothing new. What is new is the rise of social media on the Internet. You no longer have to rely upon exotic sources, you can make them up out of the blue. And you can have them up on an Internet news site in minutes. I first noticed fake news in 2013 when the Syrian civil war raged and Bashar al-Assad used chemical weapons in two opposition-controlled areas in the Damascus suburb of Ghouta. The death toll ranged from 281 to 1,729 people.

Right from the start, there were claims that Assad was not responsible. One group, Veteran Intelligence Professionals for Sanity (VIPS), wrote a letter to President Barack Obama saying that "the most reliable intelligence shows that Bashar al-Assad was NOT responsible for the chemical incident that killed and injured Syrian civilians on August 21." They claimed the attack was a "pre-planned provocation by the Syrian opposition."

Rush Limbaugh used the letter on his radio show. Michael Moore put it up on his website (he has since removed it, but you can see the link on his Facebook page dated September 7, 2013), and the letter was given coverage by World Net Daily, an ultra-conservative news aggregator. Then it was picked up by none other than Pamela Geller, the pin-up girl for the counter-jihad. On September 13, 2013, Geller published an article entitled

"Syria: Nerve gas points to Obama-backed jihadists as WH Chief of Staff Admits they don't have evidence Assad carried it out."

There were three basic sources for the letter. The first was Michel Chossudovsky's Global Research—a Canadian website that is known for its wacky conspiracy theories—which ran the article, "Did the White House Help Plan the Syrian Chemical Attacks?" *Foreign Policy* noted that the author, Yosef Bodansky, was "an ally of Bashar's uncle, Rifaat al-Assad — he pushed him as a potential leader of Syria in 2005."

The other two were Alex Jones' InfoWars and Daily Kos. But the latter two got their information from a website called *Mint Press News*.

EXCLUSIVE: Syrians In Ghouta Claim Saudi-Supplied Rebels Behind Chemical Attack
Rebels and local residents in Ghouta accuse Saudi Prince Bandar bin Sultan of providing chemical weapons to an al-Qaida linked rebel group.
by Dale Gavlak and Yahya Ababneh

INFOWARS — THE ALEX JONES RADIO SHOW
RADIO SHOW   NEWS   VIDEOS   STORE   TOP STORIES   BREAKING NEWS   CONTACT   SUBSCRIBE

EXCLUSIVE: SYRIANS IN GHOUTA CLAIM SAUDI-SUPPLIED REBELS BEHIND CHEMICAL ATTACK
AUGUST 30, 2013

Dale Gavlak and Yahya Ababneh
Mint Press News
August 30, 2013

2ND AMERICAN REVOLUTION FOURTH OF JULY

Mint Press News is a website run by the Muhawesh family in Minneapolis. They are Khomeinists—sympathetic to Iran and Syria and hostile to Saudi Arabia. The editor's father-in-law studied under an ayatollah for five years in Iran. The site is "super anti-Israel" and asserts that the Palestinian territories are an "open-air prison."

The *Mint Press News* article ran on August 29th, 2013. One of the co-writers, Yahya Ababneh, claimed to have assignments in "Jordan, Syria,

Lebanon, Saudi Arabia, Russia and Libya for clients such as *Al-Jazeera, Al-Quds, Al-Arabi, Amman Net* and other publications." A *Buzzfeed* article by Rosie Gray said that in 2013 he was in Iran studying for his master's degree. The co-writer, Dale Gavlak, asked that her byline be removed.

The article claimed that "certain rebels received chemical weapons via the Saudi intelligence chief, Prince Bandar bin Sultan, and were responsible for carrying out the dealing gas attack." The allegations were never verified and *Mint Press News* had to issue a disclaimer: "*Some information in this article could not be independently verified.*" The UN's detailed investigation ultimately confirmed that the Assad regime was behind the attack.

Not surprisingly, the Russians pushed the story and it was cited by the *Voice of Russia* and *RT*, and then by Vladimir Putin himself. Iran's *Press TV* also cited the article. Filmmaker John Pilger and Guardian senior editor Seumas Milne (now an aide to UK Labour Party Leader Jeremy Corbyn) also referenced the article.

Mint Press News was in the news again in 2016 when it published an article, "Media Blackout as Millions of Muslims March Against ISIS in Iraq." There was indeed a march but it had nothing to do with ISIS—it was Shiite Muslims marching in Arbaeen, an annual event that honours a Muslim martyr. The article went viral on Facebook where it was listed as one of their trending stories. Other alternative media sites picked up the story.

It turns out that the original source for the story was the *American Herald Tribune* (AHT), yet another website whose aim is to "inspire action and advocacy on human rights, social justice, media, spirituality and religion, contemporary history, youth issues and more." The editor-in-chief of the AHT is Anthony Hall, a Canadian Professor at the University of

Lethbridge who was suspended in 2016 for Holocaust denial and a series of articles suggesting there was a Zionist connection to 9/11.

Today, *Mint Press News* says it uses the "lens of social justice and human rights" in its reporting. If you look at their current reporters, you'll find Ramona Wadi, who writes about the "ramifications of settler-colonialism" and the "United Nations as an imperialist organization"; Caleb Maupin, who "was part of the Occupy Wall Street movement from its early planning stages" and who "participated in the voyage of Iran Shaheed Rescue Ship, attempting to deliver humanitarian aid to Yemen with the Red Crescent Society of the Islamic Republic of Iran"; Joe Catron, who "has written frequently for *Electronic Intifada*" who "co-edited the *Prisoner's Diaries: Palestinian Voices from the Israeli Gulag*"; Eric Draitser, who is a regular contributor to *RT* and *Press TV*; Vanessa Beeley, a "Member of the Steering Committee of the Syria Solidarity Movement [a pro-Assad organization] and a "volunteer with the Global Campaign to Return to Palestine."; Mikala Reasbeck, an editor for "*Xinhua Press Agency's* news desk" and who regularly appears in the *China Daily*; and Kevin Zeese, who serves on the "steering committee for the Private Manning Support Network" and is on the advisory board of the "Courage Foundation that advocates for Edward Snowden and other whistleblowers."

Quite a lens for social justice!

And that's not the last of the VIPS. In July of 2017, they released another memo claiming that the 'Russian hack' of DNC emails was an inside job. This story was picked up by *The Nation*, now a mouthpiece for Russian propaganda, and then, in turn, by Rush Limbaugh on his website and radio show, and then of course, on Alex Jones' *InfoWars*.

Op-eds now sometimes run on the front page of newspapers, and not only do opinions masquerade as news, you can make any sort of claim you want. In January, 2014, a columnist for the *Globe & Mail* claimed that polls of Afghans show that they "increasingly favour the Taliban over NATO and its own chosen regime." How many people checked actual surveys? *National Post* columnist Terry Glavin did and found just the opposite, that "since 2009, there has been decreasing support for armed opposition groups." Sanjar Sohail, editor of Afghan daily Hast-e-Sohb, told Glavin that "I don't know how anyone can rationally justify such illogical and fact-absent claims."

And, once you stop caring about the truth, it's just a short hop, skip and a jump to conspiracy theory. Warren Hinckle, editor of left-wing Ramparts magazine in the 1960s, wrote, "...conspiracy theories, unlike old soldiers, never really fade away; someone is forever coming along to give them a fresh coat of paint." Now the political right has caught on to the JFK conspiracy and they've brought out the primer. After all, they like to talk about the "deep state," and a JFK conspiracy plays into their theories of a malignant, out-of-control government.

Lew Rockwell, Ron Paul's Congressional chief of staff from 1978-1982 and contributing editor of many of Ron Paul's racist newsletters, now runs a website (lewrockwell.com) that has published hundreds of ridiculous articles on the JFK assassination. No topic is too crazy for Rockwell—the strange deaths of witnesses; Zapruder film alteration; JFK's phonied-up autopsy; JFK murder was an inside job; LBJ had JFK killed. He'll even publish kook authors like former-wrestler-turned-politician Jesse Ventura.

Another bizarre website that has recently started running silly JFK articles is the pseudo-military veterans site veteranstoday.com. Not nearly as popular as Lewrockwell.com (ranked 19,105 in the United States), the site is virulently anti-Israel, regularly runs 9/11 truther stories, and is a partner organization to *Press TV*—the press arm of the Iranian government.

I Was a Teenage JFK Conspiracy Freak   25

And Alex Jones' *InfoWars* has also gone down the JFK rabbit hole. In December 2012, Judyth Vary Baker appeared as a guest to promote her book, *Me and Lee*. Baker professes to have been the mistress of Lee Harvey Oswald while he was living in New Orleans. She claims they were involved in a plot to kill Castro using some sort of "cocktail" that would infect his immune system. Other people involved included David Ferrie (you'll read more about him in Chapter Four) and orthopedic surgeon Mary Sherman. Oswald went to Mexico City to deliver the poison to someone who would deliver it to Cuba. The handoff never happened and the mission moved to killing Kennedy. Oswald intentionally missed Kennedy while the other conspirators killed him.

It's a great story but the only thing missing is evidence. Baker did work at the Reily Coffee Company where Oswald worked as a labourer, cleaning and oiling the machines. There's no evidence they even met, nor can Baker supply evidence for any other part of her story.

Lest we make fun of Alex Jones, it's good to be reminded of what happened in Toronto when Judyth Vary Baker visited in 2011. She was invited to speak at the Toronto Women's Bookshelf and the Conspiracy Culture Shop to help celebrate what would have been Lee Harvey Oswald's 72nd birthday.

▶ THE STAR ◀

News · GTA

Lee Harvey Oswald's lover tries to clear his name

By **KATIE DAUBS** Staff Reporter
Mon., Oct. 17, 2011

The *Globe & Mail* actually ran an entire interview with Baker. She told the *Globe* that she "was sick of the lies that have been told about

Lee" and that she "can't go to the United States for my family's safety and for mine." She was "hopeful that people will hear my story and understand that Lee was actually someone that tried to save the President." Of course, "one of her sons isn't talking" to her and "he thinks I might have helped Lee kill the President." What does she believe happened in 1963? "A coup occurred in the United States" because Kennedy was "no good." She wanted people to know that Oswald "was someone who liked people, who loved children and cared about his country." He "knew that if they couldn't kill Castro in time that they would turn and kill Kennedy. Oswald acted to penetrate this group as a spy." Baker decided to go "public with this story because of love."

The *Toronto Star*, to their credit, actually talked to John McAdams who runs the best JFK conspiracy debunking website. Baker also appeared on the Michael Coren show on *Sun News* and on the CTV morning television show.

While in Toronto, Baker headed over to the Conspiracy Culture Shop for a 72nd birthday party for Lee Harvey Oswald, where she "cut the handcuffs apart" on the cake. The Conspiracy Culture shop is run by Patrick Whyte and Kadina Yu and was opened in 2006 to remedy "the limited availability of alternative media found in corporate-controlled mainstream bookstores." Customers can find books on 9/11, flying saucers, Sasquatch, the Illuminati, and the occult, and you can even buy supplements like Glacial Blue Tooth Oil there.

A few days later, Sydney White, a self-described investigative reporter who lectures weekly at her free seminar, Studies in Propaganda, at the University of Toronto, was invited to attend a "celebration" family dinner with Baker. During the dinner, Baker spurted out, "I think my gum is bleeding." White reported that "she put her finger in her mouth and brought out a pointed piece of glass." She took out another piece of glass and they called an ambulance to take her to the hospital where "she was immediately taken to the triage room." Whatever happened at that dinner, Sydney White wasn't fooled—it was nothing less than the "attempted murder of *Lee and Me* author Judyth Vary Baker.

rense.com

Attempted Murder Of 'Lee and Me' Author In Toronto
In Revenge And Physics, Time Does Not Exist
By Sydney White
10-30-11

The incident was bizarre enough but it got even more bizarre when Judyth took issue with White on a blog post. She wrote that "Sydney White published the incident without checking with me for details and also kept the glass pieces...she immediately believed it was a murder attempt...I NEVER assume such a thing and always try to find other explanations first."

In November 2017, White was a guest on CKUW in Winnipeg where she claimed that "Israelis gassed and cremated the victims of the Sept. 11, 2001 terror attacks and accused Jewish businessman Larry Silverstein (who leased the World Trade Centre) of making 'billions' on the massacre." She also referred to the United States as "Zionist America" and "accused Jewish bankers of instigating and funding the Russian Revolution." White also told listeners that "a Toronto newspaper banned coverage of her talks" because "the owners of the publication are Zionists."

The dalliance of the right with the JFK assassination continued in 2016 when Presidential candidate Donald Trump charged that Ted Cruz's father, Rafael Cruz, helped Lee Harvey Oswald hand out pro-Castro leaflets in New Orleans in 1963. This story initially ran in the *National Enquirer* and Trump repeated it on *Fox & Friends*. The story was just plain wrong. The man helping Lee Harvey Oswald was most probably recruited from the Louisiana State Employment Service. It's hard to believe that he was Rafael Cruz who was decidedly anti-Castro by 1963. Of course, *InfoWars* ran with the story.

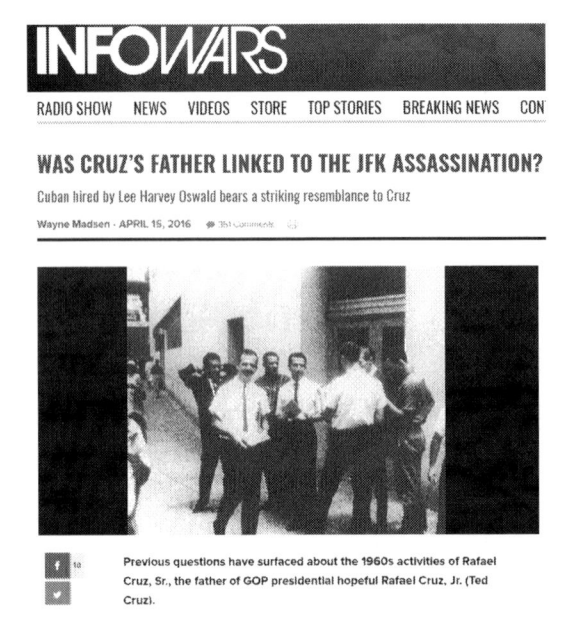

INFOWARS

RADIO SHOW   NEWS   VIDEOS   STORE   TOP STORIES   BREAKING NEWS   CON

WAS CRUZ'S FATHER LINKED TO THE JFK ASSASSINATION?
Cuban hired by Lee Harvey Oswald bears a striking resemblance to Cruz

Wayne Madsen - APRIL 15, 2016

Previous questions have surfaced about the 1960s activities of Rafael Cruz, Sr., the father of GOP presidential hopeful Rafael Cruz, Jr. (Ted Cruz).

But if you think that Trump's statement was ridiculous, how about this from Barack Obama? An article from the February 17th, 2017, edition of *The Nation*, "Are We Witnessing a Coup Operation Against the Trump White House?" included this amazing statement: "A few years ago into Barack Obama's presidency, supporters asked at a fundraiser, 'Where's our progressive foreign policy, Mr. President?' Obama's reply: 'Do you want me to end up another JFK?'" It's not clear if this is a credible quote (I could not find any other sources for it), but it speaks to the mindset of a large segment of the left.

For instance, former London mayor Ken Livingstone told *The Independent* newspaper in March, 2018, that the intelligence agencies killed Kennedy. "Governments all over the world do terrible things. Often to their own people. Look at Kennedy. Kennedy didn't trust his own military." Livingstone claimed that, after the Bay of Pigs, Kennedy was "starting to distance himself from the military." And we were all lied to: "The surgeons who were in Dallas when the body was brought in to the hospital were absolutely clear. He had been shot from behind and he had also been shot from the front. And that was all suppressed." Livingstone resigned from the UK Labour Party in May of 2018 after years of charging that Hitler supported Zionism.

It looks like Livingstone and, if not Obama, then others at *The Nation*, fell for the Oliver Stone narrative that JFK would have withdrawn from Vietnam and would have ended the Cold War. Yup, if not for the assassination, we'd be living in nirvana. It's a favourite meme on the left side of the spectrum. In May, 2018, Netflix launched a four-part series on Robert Kennedy's run for the White House. His assassination is presented in the same way—first, as the result of a conspiracy, and second, Kennedy was on the verge of solving all of our problems and had to be killed.

And now we come to the point where the conspiracy theorist Oliver Stone is now a propagandist for Vladimir Putin.

To showcase his admiration, Stone released *The Putin Interviews* in June 2017, a series of four interviews with the dictator on *Showtime*. Masha Gessen, author of *The Man Without a Face: The Unlikely Rise of Vladimir Putin*, says the series answers the question many Americans have been asking, namely, "How can a powerful, wealthy American man [Trump] hold affection for the tyrannical, corrupt leader of a hostile power?" She noted there are five conditions necessary for such affection and all are exhibited in the Stone interviews: ignorance, a love of power and grandeur, shared prejudice, an inability or an unwillingness to distinguish fact from fiction, and moral neutrality. Michael Weiss, an expert on Syria, noted on Facebook that "Putin was caught showing Oliver Stone footage of American aircraft bombing the Taliban in Afghanistan, which he passed off as his own forces hitting ISIS in Syria."

Stone, of course, believes that Russia did not interfere with the 2016 American election. He says, "It's very close to the Kennedy report. This will harden the anti-Russia policy we've been taking for years…And it's very dangerous, because now we've got to go to war with Russia. It's the same mentality that locked in on the Kennedy case." When he went on *The Late Show with Stephen Colbert* to publicize his interviews, the audience could barely believe what they were hearing. Actor T.J. Miller was on the show and he couldn't help tweeting exactly what happened.

T.J. Miller ✔ *@nottjmiller . 19m*

Oh my fucking god. Oliver Stone just jaw droppingly praised Vladimir Putin and talk down to @stephenAtHome asking if he knew what WikiLeaks

T.J. Miller ✔ *@nottjmiller . 19m*

…was. My god. He implied put in never killed anyone and our own intelligence agencies planted malware…good. God. He's fucking crazy.

T.J. Miller ✔ *@nottjmiller . 18m*

The audience was boo'ing and laughing at him. The entire @ColbertShow audience was aghast. Fucking nightmare. He said Israel meddled—

T.J. Miller ✔ *@nottjmiller . 17m*

In our election more than Russia. He's a lunatic. He made every wrong move you can make. He didn't know his audience, he snapped at them.

T.J. Miller ✔ *@nottjmiller . 10m*

Colbert became visibly aggressive & he very well should have. Oliver stone was hardly cogent in his points—was dodging & weaving like Hilary.

T.J. Miller ✔ *@nottjmiller -. 9m*

Wow. I can't believe all that just happened. You HAVE to tune into @ColbertShow show tonight. IT WAS VERY MUCH INSANE. I mean this is bad.

T.J. Miller ✔ *@nottjmiller . 5m*

Oliver Stone just payed the biggest egg ever on @Colbertshow

It's official

He laid an egg. In the truest definition of the expression.

The confluence of conspiracy theorist-turned propagandist is not just a function of the left. Roger Stone, one of Donald Trump's chief supporters, was probably the source of that silly *National Enquirer* story on Ted

Cruz's father. That was pure propaganda to help the campaign, but he has a history as a conspiracy theorist. His 2013 book, *The Man Who Killed Kennedy: The Case Against LBJ*, argued that then Vice-President Lyndon Johnson was the mastermind behind the JFK assassination.

The only way Stone can build such a case is by relying on a series of factoids. Stone regurgitates an old story—that Lyndon Johnson told Madeleine Brown, his supposed mistress, at a party at the home of rich oil man Clint Murchison the night before the assassination that "after tomorrow those SOBs will never embarrass me again. That's no threat. That's a promise." Supposedly, guests at the party included J. Edgar Hoover, Richard Nixon, former Chairman of the Chase Manhattan Bank John McCloy, and H.L. Hunt, the rich Texas oilman.

Journalist Hugh Aynesworth points out in his scathing review of Stone's book in the *Washington Times* that "Murchison hadn't been in Dallas in more than two years." He notes that "further investigation showed that on the evening of Nov. 21, 1963, Hoover was in Washington, Brown was in Houston, McCloy never left New York, and Nixon, who was in Dallas that night, was seen by several reporters near midnight at a function with Pepsi-Cola Corp. bigwigs at the Baker Hotel in downtown Dallas." And Lyndon Johnson was in Houston until 10:00 pm that night when he then flew to Ft. Worth. A photo shows him at the Texas Hotel at 11:50 pm and Aynesworth notes that that was "at least two hours from where Murchison actually was."

Many years ago, Aynesworth confronted Brown about her story and she told him, "I don't care if you believe me or not. A lot of people do and I've sold a lot of books."

Stone repeats many other factoids in his book. He believes JFK assassination witnesses have died mysteriously; that Johnson changed Kennedy's Vietnam policies; that Lee Harvey Oswald knew Jack Ruby; that

Oswald was a CIA pawn; that Oswald was an FBI informant; that security procedures were purposely scaled back in Dealey Plaza, that conspirators planned the motorcade route; and that Oswald was a poor shot. Stone also throws in the anti-Zionist conspiracy theory that Lyndon Johnson coordinated with the Israelis in the sinking of the USS Liberty in 1967. And, of course, the Robert Kennedy assassination was a conspiracy as well. As Hugh Aynesworth writes, "If a reader doesn't let facts get in the way, it could be an interesting adventure."

Stone's story was picked up by the *Daily Caller*, —a conservative news and opinion website founded by Tucker Carlson. Their story was then picked up by InfoWars.

INFOWARS

RADIO SHOW   NEWS   VIDEOS   STORE   TOP STORIES   BREAK

ROGER STONE: LBJ HAD KENNEDY KILLED

MAY 10, 2013   0 Comments

Patrick Howley
Daily Caller
May 10, 2013

From there, Roger Stone went to *Fox News* and his first stop was an appearance on *Fox & Friends*.

FOX & FRIENDS BLOG · November 4th, 2013

'The Man Who Killed Kennedy' by Roger Stone

Fox News

Of course, Sean Hannity couldn't resist, so Stone was a guest on his show on November 13th, 2013. He was treated with kid gloves and there was no pushback against any of Stone's ridiculous accusations. Stone was also interviewed by Glenn Beck and Larry King (on his show Larry King Now which is carried by *RT*, the Russian propaganda channel).

In late 2017, when President Donald Trump decided to keep some JFK files secret (see Chapter Seven), Stone knew this was because of "an effort by "deep state" policies to cover their "asses." He went on *InfoWars* to plead his case with Alex Jones and they both "painted the intelligence community as part of a secret group trying to exert its authority over the government and democracy."

INFOWARS
RADIO SHOW   NEWS   VIDEOS   STORE   TOP STORIES   BREAKING NEWS   CONTACT

WHAT IS THE DEEP STATE HIDING ABOUT THE JFK HIT?
The upcoming release of documents related to the JFK assassination has the establishment scared
Owen Shroyer & Roger Stone | War Room · OCTOBER 24, 2017   💬 46 Comments

Guess who agreed with Roger Stone about the "deep state?" None other than Oliver Stone. A conspiracy carved in stones.

Oliver Stone on Release of JFK Assassination Files: 'Trump Got Rolled' by 'Deep State' (Guest Blog)

"As with everything else in the 'Deep State,' the Chief Priests told him, 'You can't do that,'" the filmmaker writes
Oliver Stone | November 15, 2017 @ 9:30 PM

So there you have it. The left could never face the fact that a Castro-loving Marxist killed John Kennedy. Now the right can't accept it—because it was really the "deep state." And the left could never face the fact that an Israel-hating Palestinian killed Robert Kennedy. Now the right can claim RFK wanted to expose the "deep state" and thus had to be eliminated.

The JFK assassination has become a metaphor for politics. You can tell lies; you can spin incredibly ridiculous stories; you can make outlandish claims that are grounded in complete falsehoods; and there will still be people who believe and quote your every word.

But, truth matters. Lee Harvey Oswald killed JFK[1]. There was no conspiracy. End of story.

---

1   We will never know exactly why Oswald killed Kennedy. Jean Davison, author of *Oswald's Game*, offers a persuasive explanation. Oswald most probably read the New Orleans *Times-Picayune* story of September 9, 1963 in which it was reported that Fidel Castro said that if US leaders "are aiding terrorist plans to eliminate Cuban leaders, they themselves will not be safe." Oswald had made attempts to infiltrate anti-Castro groups in New Orleans and he might have been aware of plots against Castro. In late November 1963, it was announced that Kennedy's motorcade route would pass right in front of the building in which he worked. Strictly by chance, Oswald was able to strike a blow for the revolution.

One

The People of the Books

The 888-page Warren Report was presented to President Lyndon Johnson on September 24, 1964, and made public three days later. Two months later, the Warren Commission published fifteen volumes of testimony from more than 500 witnesses and eleven volumes containing 3,154 exhibits, most of which were referenced in some way in the report. These 26 books would become religious texts for the critical community.

You can still find the 26 volumes for sale on eBay but you'll probably have to pay about 2,000 dollars for the luxury of rummaging through the books in your own home. Fortunately, their contents have long since been digitized and are available for free on the Internet.

Critics pored over the Warren Report and checked its citations in the 26 volumes. They started finding small inconsistencies, which is not surprising when you have over 20,000 pages of evidence. Every deviation, no matter how minor, between the Warren Report and the 26 volumes was discussed, analyzed, and ultimately written about. Norman Mailer said that volumes were "a species of Talmudic text begging for commentary and further elucidation." Josiah Thompson, a second-wave researcher, went further, noting that "There's a fantastic way in which the assassination becomes a religious event. There are relics, and scriptures, and even a holy scene—the killing ground. People make pilgrimages to it."

When I first went over to researcher Ian Griggs' house on the outskirts of London back in 1994, I noticed that he was a proud owner of the 26 volumes. He stored them in a special location just outside his kitchen on a bottom shelf and up on top he had a small podium. Every morning, he picked a book at random and conducted a short reading. Perhaps some new nugget of information or some new interpretation would come to him. I don't know how long it took him to complete the entire cycle of evidence.

This is the story of the people of the books.

The early critics of the Warren Report were mostly on the left and had a paranoid view of politics. Right from the start, they believed in a conspiracy and that Lee Harvey Oswald was completely innocent. They formed a small network sharing the latest discovery and they argued like crazy. Warren Hinckle, editor of *Ramparts* in the 1960s, wrote that "like feuding Democrats, hardly a one of the sleuths ever had a nice thing to say about another one." And if you deviated from the party line, you would be expelled. Edward Jay Epstein was booted from the inner circle when he wrote that he believed that Oswald was one of the assassins.

So, here are the early 'buffs:'

Vincent Salandria was a lawyer in Philadelphia. He viewed Kennedy as a "rich and privileged Cold Warrior" who had acted "irresponsibly in the Bay of Pigs and in the Cuban Missile Crisis." When he heard the news that Kennedy had been killed, his first thought was that the "admirals were involved in it." His paranoia started after Pearl Harbor, which Salandria believed that "was President Roosevelt's duplicitous device to eliminate the powerful neutralist sentiment in our country while thrusting us into the war."

Harold Weisberg, a former Senate Committee staffer who was ultimately fired from his job, knew right from the start "that the assassination of JFK had to have been a conspiracy" and that "high-ranking government officials had resolved to prevent an honest investigation." Weisberg once sued the government for $300,000 because he said military helicopters and sonic booms were scaring his chickens on his small farm. Prior to the assassination, Weisberg "was developing a book about the dangers of excessive noise." Now he also had a calling.

In New York City, Sylvia Meagher, an analyst for the World Health Organization, wrote that "never for one moment could I believe LHO guilty; and every shifting version of events only reinforced my conviction that we had not had the truth." She felt that "few people who have followed the events closely—and who are not indentured to the Establishment—conceive of the Kennedy assassination as anything but a political crime."

Maggie Field, a housewife in Los Angeles, was just as convinced of a conspiracy. "My first words were, 'Well, they really got him, just as if he were a sitting duck!' and I have never changed my opinion." She told Calvin Trillin that she was "convinced that it was a political conspiracy and I was convinced that Oswald was not the assassin." Shirley Martin, another housewife in Hominy, Oklahoma, wrote to Sylvia Meagher that "the Kennedy's were moving (as fast as they dared) in the directions we wanted. As it was, the movement went too fast. He had to be killed." She felt that Oswald was innocent and was a "fall guy for an unknown and undefined conspiracy."

Raymond Marcus, a small business owner in Los Angeles, believed "that something important and evil had happened and was happening to our country; that the official story was a lie of monumental and historic proportions."

And Penn Jones Jr. ran a small newspaper in Midlothian, Texas, a town about 25 miles southwest of Dallas. He had noticed that a witness to the Tippit murder had been shot and a brother of a witness had also been shot. Jones wrote that "with the mounting list of these deaths, the likelihood grows that these people have been systemically and skillfully eliminated."

But the most important of the early critics was Mark Lane, a former New York State Assemblyman, who, immediately after the assassination, wrote a "Defense Brief for Oswald." After being rejected by all major publications, it was picked up by the left-wing *National Guardian* on December 19th, 1963. Lane tried to rebut the allegations raised by Dallas District Attorney Henry Wade in his press conference after Oswald's arrest. But Wade had made his comments when information was still coming in. And Lane had not yet been to Dallas and hadn't spoken to a single witness. So there's not much hard information in Lane's article. Nonetheless, Lane argued that "if Oswald is innocent…then the assassin of President Kennedy remains at large."

Shirley Martin read Lane's brief and sent it to Marguerite Oswald, the mother of the accused assassin Lee Harvey Oswald. She also phoned Marguerite and said, "Here was Richard Coeur de Lion riding to the rescue in the form of a stouthearted New York lawyer." Mrs. Oswald then contacted Lane and asked him to represent her son before the Warren Commission. Lane had all the ammunition he needed and was off to the races. He had found a way to squeeze into a national conversation. The Warren Commission turned him down, but Lane had his meal horse.

Marguerite Oswald was a bit of a nut. She was estranged from her son and was surprised on the day of the assassination to learn that he had a second daughter. Right after the assassination, reporter Bob Schieffer of the *Fort Worth Star-Telegram* drove her to the police station. "She was a very peculiar person and she immediately began to talk about how nobody would feel sorry for her, they'd feel sympathy to his wife and they would give her money. She was completely obsessed with money. She expressed no remorse about the president being killed."

Mark Lane rented a theatre in New York City and started lecturing nightly on the assassination. The New York *World-Telegram* reported on one of his lectures and wrote, "It doesn't matter to Lane that they [the Warren Commission] can supply evidence that Oswald was the killer. They have their truth, and he has his."

On February 18, 1964, Mrs. Oswald was also on the speaker's list. She told the crowd, "Everybody has sympathy for Mrs. Kennedy. Doesn't anybody feel sorry for me? I've had enough misery." The early critics loved her and started calling her "Mama." Her son had defected to the Soviet Union in 1959 and she was convinced that he was an agent of the government. "He never did tell me why he went to Russia. I have my own opinion. He spoke Russian, he wrote Russian, and he read Russian. Why? Because my boy was being trained as an agent, that's why." And she had loads of other strange opinions. "President Kennedy was a dying man. So, I say it is possible that my son was chosen to shoot him in a mercy killing for the security of the country."

Harold Feldman wrote a fawning portrait in *The Realist* entitled "The Unsinkable Marguerite Oswald." He wrote that there was "not a trace of cautious ambiguity, not a second of hesitation in the warm courtesy that carried within it only a faint suggestion of loneliness." Salandria added that "She was a very bright woman and most determined to demonstrate that Lee was a patriot and a hero." The Ft. Worth Council of Churches set up a fund for Marina Oswald and her children with none of the money going to Mrs. Oswald. Feldman wrote that "the reason is obvious enough. Marina cooperates."

That first weekend, Salandria discussed the assassination with his brother-in-law, Harold Feldman. He believed that "Oswald will probably be killed. And they'll get a Jew to do it, because they always involve a Jew in these things." Salandria then replied that "If Oswald is killed this weekend by a Jew, then we must look for a WASP conspiracy." He felt that a "Jewish killer would frighten the Left and dampen the interests of normally left-leaning Jews in thinking critically about the assassination."

On Sunday, November 24th, Oswald was killed by Jack Ruby. "That's the Jew," said Salandria.

He was also skeptical about Lee Harvey Oswald, who had been involved in a variety of left-wing causes. When Oswald returned to the US in 1962 because of his disillusionment with life in the Soviet Union, he turned his focus to Cuba. He started a one-man chapter of the Fair Play for Cuba Committee in New Orleans and handed out pro-Castro leaflets on the streets. He also subscribed to two communist newspapers, *The Militant* (a publication of the Socialist Worker's Party) and *The Worker* (official publication of the CPUSA).

To Salandria, this was all suspicious. "It was apparent to me that no legitimate leftist straddles so many diverse political fences in a fractionalized American left." Oswald was not a "genuine leftist" and was perhaps connected to U.S. intelligence. He told his students that "the CIA may have killed Kennedy."

The two started collecting articles on the assassination and paid "special attention to those articles they felt indicated Oswald might have some kind of connection to U.S. intelligence." Their joint article, "Oswald and the FBI," was published in *The Nation* on January 27th, 1964. They wrote that the Warren Commission "must tell us if the FBI or any other government intelligence agency was in any way connected with the alleged assassin." Rumours had been circulating that Oswald was an FBI informant, but it ultimately turned out that *Houston Post* reporter Lonnie Hudkins had just made up the story (see Chapter Three for a fuller discussion).

One of their pieces of evidence that Oswald had some connection to intelligence agencies were letters he had written to the Fair Play for Cuba Committee in New York. Oswald was a notoriously bad speller, but these letters were perfect. Feldman and Salandria wondered if "it is reasonable to suppose that Oswald did not compose them, at least not without help." What they did not know was that *The New York Times* had corrected Oswald's spelling, thus accounting for the contrast in his letters.

Many of the early buffs would spend time in Dallas trying to find and interview witnesses. They could be bothersome and it's not surprising that many witnesses were reluctant to speak.

Shirley Martin visited the home of Ruth Paine where Oswald's wife Marina had lived before the assassination. Mrs. Paine told the FBI that Martin had called on the telephone "many times and has written almost daily letters to Mrs. Paine all along the same line, looking for inconsistencies in the case and seeking to find out why Oswald shot President Kennedy if such was the case." For her part, Martin felt that "there were microphones hidden in the Paine home tape-recording their conversations." When she interviewed Acquilla Clemmons, a witness in the Tippit murder, she had her daughter hide a tape recorder in her purse. Martin went on to interview more than 50 witnesses and she sent all of her tapes to Mark Lane.

One of the early controversies of the assassination was a picture taken by James Altgens, a photographer for the Associated Press, which showed Kennedy right after he had been hit, along with the front entrance of the Texas School Book Depository in the background. One of the people standing at the entrance looked like Lee Harvey Oswald, although it was actually another worker, Billy Lovelady. One of the critics, Jones Harris, hired a photographer to take Lovelady's picture. He spent three weeks trying to get a photo but Lovelady caught on and called the police. Shirley Martin also wanted a picture. She hired a private investigator but he also could not get a suitable picture. So she turned to her two children. They hung around the loading dock of the Texas School Book Depository and actually got pictures of Lovelady, but they were unusable.

The first two books on the JFK assassination were published before the Warren Report. Carl Marzani, an Italian-American communist who received money from the Soviet Union (although this was not known at the time), published Joachim Joesten's book, *Oswald: Assassin or Fall Guy*, in the summer of 1964. The book, dedicated to Mark Lane, charged that "the assassination of the President was a military-type operation with firing from the both front and rear." He claimed that the CIA, the FBI, the Dallas Police, and a group of right-wing Texas oil tycoons conspired to kill Kennedy. Hugh Aynesworth, a reporter for the *Dallas Morning News* reviewed the book and wrote, "If you would listen to this one, he would have you thinking that Lee Harvey Oswald was a polite little misunderstood youth who just got mixed up in the wrong company... poor little Lee Harvey was the victim of a ruthless plot headed by Dallas police leaders, District Attorney Henry Wade and his staff and a few 'bad guys' from the FBI. Joesten further states that Oswald was an agent of both the FBI and the CIA (how's that for a 24-year-old who couldn't spell 'wrist'?)."

The other major book was *Who Killed Kennedy?* by Thomas Buchanan, published first in England in the spring of 1964 and then in the United States. He believed the assassination was organized by those same Texas oil tycoons who were incensed that Kennedy was going to eliminate the oil-depletion tax allowance. Buchanan wrote the assassination "was provoked, primarily by fear of the domestic and international consequences of the Moscow Pact: The danger of disarmament which would disrupt the industries on which the plotters depended and of an international détente which would, in their view, have threatened the eventual nationalization of their oil investments overseas."

The buffs found an ally in M.S. Arnoni, a Polish Jew who had survived the Holocaust and who ran *The Minority of One*, a small magazine based in New Jersey. Arnoni might have been the first person to raise the issue of why Kennedy had been killed. In the March 20, 1964, issue, he wrote an open letter to Earl Warren asking, "Could it be that there was a criminal plot not only against the person of John F. Kennedy but also against his attempts to bring the Cold War to an end?"

In the September, 1964, issue, a few weeks before the Warren Report was released, Arnoni published an article by Bertrand Russell, "16 Questions on the Assassination," which was really written by Ralph Schoenman, his personal secretary, although it noted that Russell "was indebted to Mr. Mark Lane…for much of the information in this article."

Russell charged that witnesses "involved have disappeared or died in extraordinary circumstances." The Warren Commission was "utterly unrepresentative of the American people" and that Gerald Ford was a "leader of the local Goldwater movement." More importantly, Russell wrote that the "six panels of inquiry" of the Warren Commission were not charged to deal with "the question of who killed President Kennedy." This was all entirely not true. As we shall soon see, there was nothing nefarious about any of the deaths. It was entirely irrelevant if Gerald Ford supported Barry Goldwater. And the first panel of the Warren Commission had the mission of determining the basic facts of the assassination.

Another false claim in the article was that "at the last minute the Secret Service changed a small part of their plans so that the President left Main Street and turned into Houston and Elm Street." The motorcade *had* to turn onto Elm Street so it could take an exit to the Stemmons Freeway which would have taken them to the Dallas Trade Mart for Kennedy's speech.

Russell issued a statement accompanying the article which said, "Mark Lane's evidence comprises one of the most remarkable documents I have seen and is an unanswerable indictment of the Government's attempt to suppress the truth and conceal the circumstances of the death of the President. There has never been a more subversive, conspiratorial, unpatriotic or endangering course for the security of the United States and the world than the attempt by the United States Government to hide the murderers of its recent President."

The Warren Report was released to the public on September 24, 1964 concluding that Lee Harvey Oswald killed Kennedy and that the Commission could find no evidence of any conspiracy. The buffs were incensed. Salandria said, "The Report confirmed for me that the cover story was totally unbelievable" and that it was "a fabric of transparent lies that could never withstand disinterested analysis." He added that if the public accepted the Warren Report, "it would mean that 1984 was with us and our experiment with democracy was ended…I couldn't live in a society that could pull a swindle of this kind." Harold Weisberg said the Commission was "whoring with our history." Penn Jones wrote that "the only way you can believe the Warren Report is not to read it." Raymond Marcus said it was "the most massively fraudulent document ever foisted on a free society."

I.F. Stone, one of America's most important left-wing journalists, was horrified by the reaction to the Warren Report. He devoted most of the October 6, 1964 issue of *I.F. Stone's Weekly* to "The Left and the Warren Commission Report." Stone believed that the "Commission has done a first-rate job, on a level that does our country proud and is worthy of so tragic an event. I regard the case against Lee Harvey Oswald as the lone killer of the President as conclusive."

I. F. Stone's Weekly

VOL. XII, NO. 33   OCTOBER 5, 1964   WASHINGTON, D. C.   15 CENTS

The Left and the Warren Commission Report

All my adult life as a newspaperman I have been fighting, in defense of the Left and of a sane politics, against conspiracy theories of history, character assassination, guilt by association and demonology. Now I see elements of the Left using these same tactics in the controversy over the Kennedy assassination and the Warren Commission Report. I believe the Commission has done a first-rate job, on a level that does our country proud and is worthy of so tragic an event. I regard the case against Lee Harvey Oswald as the lone killer of the President as conclusive. By the nature of the case, also.

They Finally Listed Rightists

"When the special file [in the Protective Research Section of the Secret Service] was reviewed on Nov. 5 [for the President's trip], it contained the names of no persons from the entire Dallas-Ft. Worth area, notwithstanding the fact that Ambassador Stevenson had been abused by pickets in Dallas less than a month before . . . (pps. 432-3).

"Since the assassination, both the Secret Service and the FBI have recognized that the PRS files can no

He criticized Russell's statement about a "subversive, conspiratorial, unpatriotic or endangering course…" Stone wrote, "This assumes instead of proving. It is slander, not controversy." Stone believed that the implication of a conspiracy to kill Kennedy and a conspiracy to cover up the facts to be "monstrous charges, and cannot honorably be made on the basis of surmise. Russell's American advisers have fed him not evidence but misstatement and poppycock."

Stone felt that Russell's attack on the makeup of the Commission was "demonology, and this is what so often has been used against the Left. Demonology is the notion that because a man disagrees with you politically, he must be impervious to honor, duty, patriotism, and mercy—in short a demon." Stone himself had disagreed with Commission member Allen Dulles over the years, "but I would not impute to him or any other member of the Commission conduct so evil as to conspire with the secret services to protect the killers of a President. This is also to assume that Chief Justice Warren, whom the right hates for his decisions protecting Negroes and radicals, would be a party to a conspiracy to protect a cabal of rightist assassins."

Joachim Joesten's book, *Oswald: Assassin or Fall Guy,* also came in for scorn from Stone. Joesten had written that the CIA could not countenance the end of the Cold War and "thought of Kennedy as a traitor. And traitors are executed." Stone found this "libelous in the extreme. It implies that Allen Dulles would be a party to killing Kennedy and hushing up the truth because he lost his job after the Bay of Pigs. Such charges, as sloppy as they are wild, are dishonorable and dissolve the fabric of society. They seek to destroy a man's reputation on the basis of evil surmise and guilt by association…The Joesten book is rubbish."

He also didn't like Thomas Buchanan's book, *Who Killed Kennedy?* Stone wrote that "Buchanan names an oilman he calls Mr. X. This imputes murder to a man whose views we dislike, and does so without any evidence of any kind." He concluded that "people who believe such things belong in the booby-hatch."

Stone wrapped up his issue by saying that this was all an "insane morass of paranoid conjecture, and those who remain in it even after the Warren report are either unscrupulous or sick." *The Nation* also praised the Warren Report saying that "the Commission did its work well; the report is an admirable document, and the Chief Justice, his associates and the staff merit the praise they have received."

Raymond Marcus was "appalled" by Stone's newsletter. He wrote Stone a letter saying "I read, first with disbelief, then with growing shock and anger, your diatribe against freedom of thought and expression" and wondered how he had been "stricken so blind and arrogant." His seven-and-a-half-page letter to Stone went unanswered. In September 1966 Marcus found himself in Washington D.C. and he phoned Stone at his home. He asked for a meeting, but Stone yelled into the receiver: "I DON'T CARE ABOUT THAT ASSHOLE CASE."

But to many people you weren't a proper leftist if you didn't understand the "right-wing" plot to take over America and the huge coverup. Todd Gitlin wrote in *The Sixties: Years of Hope, Days of Rage* that there was "a huge cultural disbelief that an event so traumatic and vast in its consequences could be accounted by a petty assassin." Raymond Marcus hoped that if people became aware of the fraud in the Warren Report, "they'll start to demand other answers. Maybe they'll ask about the Rosenbergs, Hiss, the whole Cold War. Maybe we can get clean and whole. But if this stays down, there's no hope."

In November 1964 the Warren Commission published its 26 volumes of evidence consisting of 20,000 pages of testimony, depositions of witnesses, and exhibits. The Government Printing Office sold 1,442 sets at a price of $76. The buffs finally had what they were waiting for—and they could peruse all the evidence in the luxury of their own home.

Penn Jones bought fifteen sets of the hearings and exhibits. He kept two sets at home and one at the office. He wrote that "we are so grateful for the many answers in the twenty-six volumes of testimony. The answers are there for those who are willing to dig." Maggie Field bought three sets. Shirley Martin was eager to "have my toys." Harold Weisberg bought two sets—one as a working copy and one to preserve. When Sylvia Meagher got her set, she was "wildly excited." Every day she took one volume to work. She started to "list what is now a long series of deliberate misrepresentations, omissions, distortions, and other defects demonstrating not only extreme bias, incompetence, and carelessness but irrefutable instances of dishonesty." The 26 volumes became her life and she told a friend, "I am trying to exclude everything in the way of a social life."

The buffs had a field day.

Raymond Marcus was amazed by the contradictions between the Warren Report and the 26 volumes. "How the hell could they—here's their own evidence, how could they do this? And, on the other hand, we'd say, Gee, we're sure glad they put that stuff in there." Vincent Salandria wrote a friend, "They make such easy pickings, that I keep worrying whether we were meant to dine on them."

Then the books started coming out. Harold Weisberg's *Whitewash*; Mark Lane's *Rush to Judgment*; Edward Jay Epstein's *Inquest*; Raymond Marcus' *The Bastard Bullet*; and Penn Jones' *Forgive My Grief*. Sylvia Meagher published a subject index to the Warren Commission volumes of evidence.

The two books with the biggest impact were *Inquest*, which focused on the working of the Warren Commission, and *Rush to Judgment*, Lane's defense brief for Oswald. *Rush to Judgment* was on the *New York Times* bestseller list for 29 weeks. Calvin Trillin wrote in the *New Yorker* that *Inquest* was "generally considered the single greatest contribution to making criticism of the Report respectable." But Epstein angered many of the critics because he thought that Oswald was one of the assassins.

And it wasn't just books. *Ramparts* announced in its November, 1966, issue that "In the last eight months, a team of RAMPARTS editors, aided by researchers and trained investigators, has read, re-read, catalogued and analyzed the 26 volumes of the Warren Report." They concluded "that the weight of evidence indicates the existence of more than one assassin."

Despite the seriousness of their effort, there were some lighter moments at *Ramparts*. Warren Hinckle remembers "One of the most horrific experiences of my life was when a dogged female sleuth trapped me in the men's room, where I was sitting in the loo in a particularly compromised and gaseous state the morning after a long evening of drinking. She lounged against the urinal, lecturing me for half an hour through the stall door about the conspiratorial significance of Oswald's having shaved off all his pubic hair."

Amongst mainstream publications, *Life* magazine asked for a new investigation largely based on John Connally's assertion that he was hit by a separate bullet than had hit Kennedy. This would imply a second assassin because Oswald would not have had time to fire two shots in such a short period.

David Welsh wrote in *Ramparts* that the critics were "doing the job the Dallas police, the FBI and the Warren Commission should have done in the first place."

Well, not exactly. The authors of the Warren Report were honourable men who conducted an honest investigation and reached the right answer. They had no idea that a wave of skepticism was about to hit them. After all, who could ever believe that Earl Warren, one of the great Chief Justices of the Supreme Court, would mislead the nation?

In fact, the Warren Commission made two egregious errors.

First, they did not have expert forensic pathologists examine JFK's autopsy X-rays and photographs. A proper medical report could have forestalled all the questions about the locations of the wounds, the directions of the shots, and perhaps offered a medical explanation for the backward movement of Kennedy's head.

Second, they should have hired photographic experts to dissect the film shot by Abraham Zapruder, a Dallas dress manufacturer. Had they brought in a variety of scientists, they could have found the flip of Connally's lapel in frame 224 which would have helped confirm the theory that one bullet hit both Connally and Kennedy (also known as the single-bullet theory). They could have noted the slight forward movement of Kennedy's head in frame 313, as well as the forward dispersal of brain matter indicating a shot from behind.

Despite these flaws, the evidence led them to the only possible conclusion—that Lee Harvey Oswald was the lone assassin. And the evidence was overwhelming. For instance, on the morning of the assassination, Oswald left his wedding ring and $170 for his wife Marina on the bedroom dresser, and he brought a long bulky package to work. His rifle was stored in Ruth Paine's garage (where his wife was staying) and when the FBI visited after the assassination, lo and behold, the rifle was gone.

After the assassination, he was the only warehouseman missing. He went back to his rooming house to pick up his revolver and then killed police officer J.D. Tippit. Many witnesses identified Oswald unloading his pistol and running away from the scene. One expert concluded that one of the four bullets recovered from Tippit's body matched the revolver found in Oswald's possession when he was arrested; another expert said they all "could have been" fired from his gun; the expended cartridge cases matched Oswald's gun to the exclusion of all other weapons. The rifle found on the sixth floor of the Book Depository was bought by Oswald; fibres found on the rifle matched Oswald's shirt, although they could have come from another identical shirt; two bullet fragments found in the limousine and the cartridge cases found in the sniper's nest matched his rifle "to the exclusion of all other weapons"; Oswald's right palm print was found on the rifle barrel; and his fingerprints were found on the bag used to carry the rifle to work.

Faced with this massive amount of incriminating evidence, the critics could only chip away at the margins. One of Mark Lane's standard operating procedures was to selectively quote from witness testimony. The second chapter of *Rush to Judgment*, "Where the Shots Came From," claimed that "Of the 90 persons who were asked this important question and who were able to give an answer, 58 said that shots came from the direction of the grassy knoll and not from the Book Depository Building, while 32 disagreed. Thus, almost two-thirds of those who expressed an opinion supported the evidence given by Miss Mercer, Bowers, Price, Holland and Weitzman."

One of his favourite witnesses was Lee Bowers, who was in a 14-foot railroad tower behind the grassy knoll during the assassination. Just before the shots, he saw three cars enter the area behind the picket fence on the grassy knoll and two men standing near the fence. Lane quotes Bowers telling the Warren Commission that "something occurred in this particular spot which was out of the ordinary, which attracted my eye for some reason, which I could not identify."

> Mr. Ball: You couldn't describe it?
>
> Mr. Bowers: Nothing that I could pinpoint as having happened that –"

Lane charges that the Warren Commission lawyer, Mr. Ball, purposely cut off Bowers before he could answer. But Lane leaves out the first part of Bowers answer quoted above: "I just am unable to describe rather than it was something out of the ordinary, a sort of milling around, but something occurred…"

In addition, Lane does not mention that Bowers testified that the two men "gave no appearance of being together, as far as I know." One of the men remained there after the shooting and Bowers was unsure about the other man because he "was too hard to distinguish from the trees." The men did nothing suspicious.

All of this is enough for Lane to conclude that Bowers supported shots fired from the front. But he omits this part of his testimony before the Warren Commission:

Bowers: I heard three shots. One, then a slight pause, then two very close together. Also, reverberation from the shots.

Mr. Ball: And were you able to form an opinion as to the source of the sound or what direction it came from, I mean?

Bowers: The sounds came from either up against the School Depository Building or near the mouth of the triple underpass.

Mr. Ball: Were you able to tell which?

Bowers: No; I could not.

Mr. Ball: Well, now had you any experience before being in the tower as to sounds coming from various places?

Bowers: Yes; I had worked this same tower for some 10 or 12 years, and was there during the time they were renovating the School Depository Building, and had noticed at the time the similarity of sounds occurring in either of those two locations.

Mr. Ball: Can you tell me now whether or not it came, the sounds you heard, the three shots came from the direction of the Depository Building or the triple underpass?

Bowers: No; I could not.

> Mr. Ball: From your experience there, previous experience there in hearing sounds that originated at the Texas School Book Depository Building, did you notice that sometimes those sounds seem to come from the triple underpass? Is that what you told me a moment ago.
>
> Bowers: There is a similarity of sound, because there is a reverberation which takes place from either location.
>
> Mr. Ball: Had you heard sounds originating near the triple underpass often?
>
> Bowers: Yes, quite often. Because trucks backfire and various occurrences.

Dealey Plaza was an echo chamber which made it hard for witnesses to determine the direction of the shots. This was corroborated by Abraham Zapruder, although you wouldn't know it from *Rush to Judgment*. Lane wrote that Zapruder believed the shot came from the front because "A Secret Service interview report stated, 'According to Mr. Zapruder, the position of the assassin was behind Mr. Zapruder.'" But Lane omits this part of his testimony which explained his reasoning:

> Mr. Liebeler: Did you have an impression as to the direction from which these shots came?
>
> Mr. Zapruder: No, I also thought it came from back of me. Of course, you can't tell when something is in line—it could come from anywhere, but being I was here and he was hit on this

line and he was hit right in the head—I saw it right around here, so it looked like it came from here and it could come from there.

Mr. Liebeler: All right, as you stood there on the abutment and looked down into Elm Street, you saw the President hit on the right side of the head and you thought perhaps the shot had come from behind you?

Mr. Zapruder: Well, yes.

Mr. Liebeler: From the direction behind you?

Mr. Zapruder: Yes, actually—I couldn't say what I thought at the moment, where they came from—after the impact of the tragedy was really what I saw and I started and I said—yelling, "They've killed him"—and I assumed that they came from there because as the police started running in back of me, it looked like it came from the back of me.

Mr. Liebeler: But you didn't form any opinion at the time as to what direction the shots did come from actually?

Mr. Zapruder: No.

Mr. Liebeler: And you indicated that they could have come also from behind or from any other direction except perhaps from the left, because they could have been from behind or even from the front.

> Mr. Zapruder: Well, it could have been—in other words, if you have a point—you could hit a point from any place as far as that's concerned. I have no way of determining what direction the bullet was going.
>
> Mr. Liebeler: Did you form any opinion about the direction from which the shots came by the sound, or were just upset by the thing you had seen?
>
> Mr. Zapruder: No, there was too much reverberation. There was also an echo which made a sound all over. In other words that square is kind of—it had a sound all over.

Lane does admit that "there is some evidence that one or more shots may have been fired from the Book Depository" but that "it is considerably less compelling than the evidence suggesting that shots came from behind the fence." So it is not surprising that Lane omits the testimony of Bob Jackson, a photographer who was in the motorcade that afternoon in Dallas.

> Mr. Jackson: And, as we heard the first shot, I believe it was Tom Dillard from Dallas News who made some remark as to that sounding like a firecracker, and it could have been somebody else who said that. But someone else did speak up and make that comment and before he actually finished the sentence we heard the other two shots. Then we realized or we thought that it was gunfire, and then we could not at that point see the President's car. We were still moving slowly, and after the third shot the second two shots seemed much closer

together than the first shot, than they were to the first shot. Then after the last shot, I guess all of us where just looking all around and I just looked straight up ahead of me which would have been looking at the School Book Depository and I noticed two Negro men in a window straining to see directly above them, and my eyes followed right on up to the window above them and I saw the rifle or what looked like a rifle approximately half of the weapon. I guess I saw, and just as I looked at it, was drawn fairly slowly back into the building, and I saw no one in the window with it. I didn't even see a form in the window.

Mr. Specter: What did you do next?

Mr. Jackson: I said, "There is the gun," or it came from that window. I tried to point it out. But by the time the other people looked up, of course, it was gone and about that time we were beginning to turn the corner.

Other witnesses also saw a gunman in the sixth-floor window which forces Lane to try and impugn their testimony. He can't face the fact that there were absolutely no witnesses to gunmen on the grassy knoll or behind the wooden picket fence. The *only* place where witnesses saw a gun was in the sixth-floor window of the Texas School Book Depository.

Lane is also misleading on the medical evidence. In his chapter, "The Gauze Curtain," he writes, "none of the doctors who examined the President in Dallas observed in the rear of his head a 'smaller hole' to which the Commission alluded as the entrance point." Quite true, but the

Dallas doctors did not see the entrance wound because they didn't turn Kennedy's body over—they were far too busy trying to save Kennedy's life.

And Lane also completely misrepresented the witnesses in the J.D. Tippit murder. He writes that "The statements of 13 persons are said by the Report to form the basis of its reconstruction of the Tippit killing and the flight of Tippit's assailant. However, only two of the 13 saw the shooting." Quite right, but he neglects to tell readers that two witnesses, Virginia and Barbara Davis, saw Oswald run across their lawn after the murder and unload the shells from his gun (which of course matched the revolver found in his possession).

The 26 volumes also contained some really strange witness reports and the critics uncritically accepted them. Take, for example, the story of Carroll Jarnagin, published by the Warren Commission as Commission Exhibit 2821 in volume 26 of the Evidence and Hearings. Penn Jones took material from this exhibit and published it in his *Midlothian Mirror* newspaper which was then re-published in *Ramparts* and in his book.

Jarnagin was a Dallas lawyer with a healthy imagination. In December, 1963, he sent a letter to the FBI stating that he had overheard a discussion at Jack Ruby's nightclub, the Carousel Club, on October 4, 1963. He was accompanied there by a stripper with the stage name of Robin Hood. He overheard a man with the name of H.L. Lee talking to Jack Ruby about killing Governor John Connally. After the assassination, he recognized H.L. Lee as Lee Harvey Oswald. With his photographic memory, Jarnagin furnished a complete transcript of the conversation.

Man who had been sitting alone: I'm using the name of H.L. Lee.

Ruby: What do you want?

Lee: I need some money.

Ruby: Money?

Lee: I just got in from New Orleans. I need a place to stay, and a job.

*****

Ruby: You'll get the money after the job is done.

Lee: How about half now, and half after the job is done.

****

Ruby: How do I know that you can do the job?

Lee: It's simple. I'm a Marine sharpshooter.

Ruby: Are you sure that you can do the job without hitting anybody but the Governor?

Lee: I'm sure. I've got the equipment ready.

Ruby: Have you tested it? Will you need to practice any?

Lee: Don't worry about that. I don't need any practice; when will the Governor be here?

Ruby; Oh, he'll be here plenty of times during campaigns.

Lee: Where can I do the job?

Ruby: From the roof of some building.

The transcript goes on for several pages. The FBI interviewed Jarnagin and their report is included in Warren Commission Exhibit 2821. He told them he first became aware that Oswald was part of the conversation on November 24 but he failed to report it until early December. He "had considered the possibility that his mind was playing a trick on him and that he imagined the conversation, but he stated that he had reached the conclusion that this was not true." He then told the agents that he had an alcoholism problem and that, on the night in question, he was drunk. He was also undergoing a divorce from his wife. Even so, "he still believes he could recall the events that occurred."

Jarnagin claimed that right after the conversation he had telephoned the Texas Department of Public Safety. FBI agents contacted them and they said they had never received such a call. In addition, Jarnagin's companion, Shirley Mauldin (aka Robin Hood) "overheard no conversation in the Carousel Club between Ruby and anyone, and she could recall no discussion regarding the shooting of the Governor of Texas."

The Dallas District Attorney's office administered a lie detector test and Jarnagin failed miserably. Dallas reporter Hugh Aynesworth recounts in his book, *Witness to History*, that one of his friends in December, 1963, had talked to Jarnagin. "He's told us other stories. One about LBJ we would have loved to believe, another about John Tower. The guy gets around, especially in his own mind."

Not surprisingly, Carroll Jarnagin was not mentioned in the Warren Report. Penn Jones left out of his report the fact that he was drunk at the time of the conversation and that his companion could not substantiate anything. Jarnagin told Jones that "he once made 100 on a college chemistry examination with many chemical formulas as answers. He said, "I made 100 on the test and I think I could recite the chemical formulas to you right now."

Jones wanted a "thorough investigation of the Jarnagin statement." Yet, had he read the Warren Report, he would have learned that Lee Harvey Oswald was on a bus on October 3 returning from Mexico City. He spent the night at the YMCA and on October 4 hitchhiked to the Paine residence where he spent the night. He could not have been in the Carousel Club that evening.

Mark Lane fell for a very similar story. Fort Worth *Star-Telegram* reporter Waldo Thayer told him that Bernard Weissman (author of an ad in the *Dallas Morning News* on the morning of November 22, 1963, denouncing Kennedy), police officer J.D. Tippit, and Jack Ruby met in the Carousel Club on November 14, 1963. Lane told the Warren Commission about this incident on March 4, 1964, but refused to name his source for the story. Lane wrote in his book, *Rush to Judgment,* that Thayer's informant "was a frequent visitor to Ruby's club—not because of the strip show but because of his involvement with one of the dancers." That sure sounds like Jarnagin.

When Weissman heard Lane make the allegation on a radio call-in show, he called in to confront him. "I know what you are trying to do. I think you are hunting for headlines. But you had been talking to some liar in Dallas who has been feeding you all this baloney about me. You are making all these allegations at the Town Hall and now on radio. And you have never taken the trouble to contact me. My name has been in the paper. It is very well known where I live. I am in the phone book. You could have at least tried to contact me." Lane replied that, yes, he should have called him and that he would "recheck his facts" in Dallas.

Weissman called Lane several days later at his office and Lane made him an offer. He said "he would arrange for a public meeting, he would pay my transportation to Dallas to see this guy (Lane's source) as soon as he could arrange a meeting. And I have not heard from him since." All this didn't stop Lane from repeating the allegations in an entire chapter in his book. He did not mention Weissman's denials nor their discussions.

The story reappeared in 2008 when Dallas District Attorney Craig Watkins released several documents found in his office. One of them was a transcript of a conversation between Lee Harvey Oswald and Jack Ruby. The meeting seemed similar to the Jarnagin allegation—it had the same date, October 4, 1963, and some of the language was similar. But in this transcript the target was then-Attorney General Robert Kennedy. Watkins held a news conference to announce the documents and said, "It will open up the debate as to whether or not there was a conspiracy to assassinate the president."

A screen capture from The Guardian newspaper.

This generated big headlines, but seasoned JFK researchers realized his story linked back to Carroll Jarnagin's tale. Even Watkins' top assistant thought the transcript was perhaps part of a movie that Henry Wade, the DA in 1963, was working on. Wade discussed the movie, *Countdown to Dallas*, in letters found in the safe.

Penn Jones not only bought the delusions of Carroll Jarnagin, he also believed that witnesses were dying mysteriously. He began cataloguing the deaths in his *Midlothian Mirror* newspaper and in May, 1966, he published his first book, *Forgive My Grief*. *Ramparts* featured Penn Jones in its November, 1966, special issue dedicated to the assassination. They said that Jones "had made a singular contribution to uncovering the hidden facts of the Kennedy case." This was significant—*Ramparts* had a circulation in 1968 of 250,000, more than double that of *The Nation*.

Ramparts writer David Welsh spent some time with Jones in Midlothian and wrote that "His talk went like rabbit tracks, touching one by one of the thousand riddles of the Kennedy case—talks so bizarre that even an editor of cheap paperbacks would turn them down for lack of credibility." But not *Ramparts*, which "decided to check out of few of Penn's leads" and found that "it was always Penn Jones, his ear tuned to the Dallas gossip, who furnished the best leads."

Jones first big story was about a meeting at Jack Ruby's apartment the night of November 24, 1963. He wrote that "five persons were present for the meeting and three have died strangely." Two journalists were there—Bill Hunter of the Long Beach *Press-Telegram* and Jim Koethe of The *Dallas Times Herald*, and well as two lawyers, Tom Howard and C.A. Droby. Joining them was George Senator who had previously been Jack Ruby's roommate and who had rented an apartment next to Ruby's.

Hunter was killed in Long Beach on April 22, 1964, accidentally by another policeman; Tom Howard died of a heart attack a few months later; and Jim Koethe was supposedly killed by a karate chop in Dallas in September, 1964. Jones wondered if "Senator accidentally revealed something important that night." He then asked, "What went on in that significant meeting in Ruby's and Senator's apartment? Few are left to tell. There is no one in authority to ask the questions, since the Warren Commission has made its final report and has closed its investigation."

There were actually seven people at the apartment, including a photographer for the *Times-Herald*, William Allen, who shot some pictures. James Martin, a friend of Senator's, was also there. It wasn't really a meeting but just a bunch of newspapermen passing through the apartment. In the Hunter case, two officers were convicted of involuntary manslaughter. Tom Howard had been ill for quite a while and had been complaining of chest pains, and diabetes was a contributing factor in his death. Koethe was actually killed by strangulation, and not by a karate chop. In September, 1964, an ex-con was arrested for Koethe's murder. Police suspected it might have been during a homosexual liaison. Three of the other participants lived fairly long lives —C.A. Droby lived until 2011; James Martin died in 1996; and William Allen gave a talk at the Sixth Floor Museum in Dallas in 2014. None of them reported anything suspicious about that evening.

Mark Lane included this false story in his book. He faulted the Warren Commission for failing to "refer to the meeting in the Report, and the names of the two deceased reporters are not listed in its index." Lane believed that "powerful influences certainly did exist which tended to discourage testimony that did not conform to the accepted interpretation." Even worse, the "Commission did nothing to investigate or explain adequately the peripheral assaults, murders and threats."

Warren Hinckle said that "Lane had a tendency to grab bits of evidence like a sea gull swooping down to snap up a fish, swallowing it whole without taking the time to see if it was anything digestible."

Jones' obsession with the deaths of people associated with the assassination would take many silly turns. For instance, Earlene Roberts, the housekeeper at Lee Harvey Oswald's rooming house, died in 1966 from a heart attack at the age of 60, and an autopsy found huge calcium deposits. She also suffered from diabetes. But Jones considered her death suspicious because her sister was a real estate agent acquainted with Jack Ruby. He claimed that there was no autopsy but the certificate of death says otherwise.

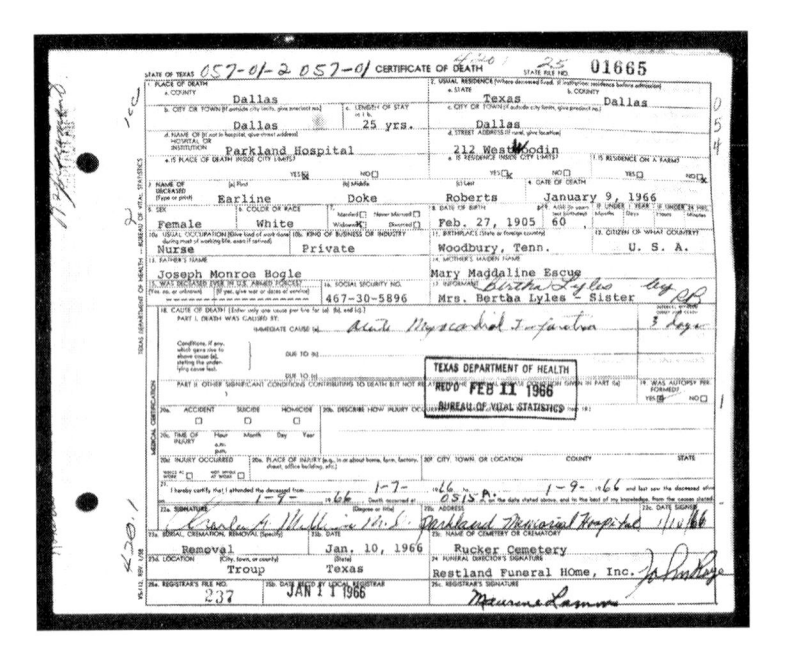

Hinckle claimed that the "mysterious deaths" issue "became an overnight sensation. *Ramparts* sold out and went back on the presses. Penn Jones found himself catapulted to the status of instant folk hero. Walter

Cronkite dispatched a film crew to Midlothian and devoted long segments of three consecutive newscasts to Penn Jones's big story."

Jones didn't stop there. He published more and more accounts of mysterious deaths. In his second *Forgive My Grief* book, the table of contents testified to his obsession: "Chapter 1. Deaths. Chapter 2. Deaths. Chapter 3. Deaths. Chapter 4. More Deaths. Chapter 5. And More Deaths." This silly story received some legitimacy with a London *Sunday Times* article in February, 1967. They consulted an actuary who calculated that the odds of the people dying on Jones' list was "100 trillion to one." That was enough to convince more serious researchers like Sylvia Meagher, who added a chapter on the deaths in her book, noting that "the deaths of many witnesses discussed here might also have remained unknown but for the indefatigable Penn Jones."

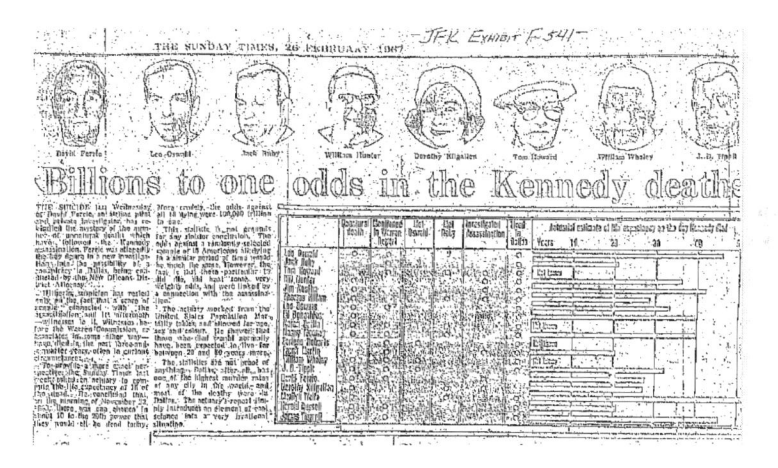

In May, 1978, the *Sunday Times* wrote a letter to the House Select Committee on Assassination admitting that their article was "based on a careless journalistic mistake and should never have been published." They figured out the odds to the wrong question—the actuary "was asked what the odds against fifteen named people were out of the population of the United States dying within a short period of time to which replied—correctly that they were very high. However, if one asks what are the odds against fifteen of those included in the Warren Commission index dying within a given period, the answer is, of course, that they are much lower. Our mistake was to treat the reply to the former question as if it dealt with the latter—hence the fundamental error in our first edition report, for which we apologize."

JFK Exhibit F-543

TIMES NEWSPAPERS LIMITED

Registered office: P.O. Box no. 7, New Printing House Square,
Gray's Inn Road, London WC1X 8EZ
Telephone 01-837 1234 Telex 264971 Registered no. 894646 England

008644

Mr. G. Robert Blakey,
Chief Counsel and Director,
Select Committee on Assassinations,
U.S. House of Representatives,
3331 House Office Building, Annex 2,
Washington, D.C. 20515,
U.S.A.

19th May, 1978

Dear Mr. Blakey,

Kennedy deaths statistics - The Sunday Times 26 February 1967

The Editor has passed me your letter of 25th April.

Our piece about the odds against the deaths of the Kennedy witnesses was, I regret to say, based on a careless journalistic mistake and should not have been published. This was realized by The Sunday Times' editorial staff after the first edition - the one which goes to the United States and which I believe you have - had gone out, and later editions were amended.

There was no question of our actuary having got his answer wrong: it was simply that we asked him the wrong question. He was asked what were the odds against fifteen named people out of the population of the United States dying within a short period of time, to which he replied - correctly - that they were very high. However, if one asks what are the odds against fifteen of those included in the Warren Commission Index dying within a given period, the answer is, of course, that they are much lower. Our mistake was to treat the reply to the former question as if it dealt with the latter - hence the fundamental error in our first edition report, for which we apologize.

None of the editorial staff involved in this story can remember the name of the actuary we consulted, but in view of what happened you will, I imagine, agree that his identity is hardly material.

Yours sincerely,

Antony Whitaker,
Legal Manager

While the early critics were deadly serious, two writers decided to add a bit of fun to the proceedings. Jacob Brackman and Faye Levine submitted a book review of a non-existent four-volume treatise of the Warren Report, "Time of Assassins," by Ulov G.K. Leboeuf, to *Ramparts*. Editor Warren Hinckle published the review without any indication of the fictitious nature of these 'books.'

Ephemera

BOOKS   ART   CINEMA   THEATRE   MISCELLANY

Books:

INQUEST by Edward Jay Epstein. New York: Viking. 224 pp. $5.
WHITEWASH by Harold Weisberg. Hyattstown, Md.: Harold Weisberg. 208 pp. $4.95. (paper)
RUSH TO JUDGMENT by Mark Lane. New York: Holt, Rinehart & Winston. 395 pp. $4.95.
TIME OF ASSASSINS by Ulov G. K. Leboeuf. Levittown, N.Y.: Ulov G. H. Leboeuf. 4 Vols. I: 495 pp., II: 387 pp., III: 691 pp., IV: 460 pp. $24.
OSWALD: PATSY WITHOUT PORTFOLIO by Leopold Zaftig. Vanitas. 29 pp. $.85.

Reviewed by Jacob Brackman and Faye Levine

ren Commission's 26 volumes, dedicated to a predetermined verdict of guilty for Lee Harvey Oswald. Unhappily, the works of the opposition have been little better. Edward Jay Epstein's *Inquest* is merely a legal-pedantic close analysis of the workings of the Commission (So what? one is inclined to ask), and Harold Weisberg's *Whitewash*, a literary-pedantic analysis of the Warren Commission's collection of red herrings. One had hoped that Mark Lane, in *Rush to Judgment*, would at last provide something more nourishing than his already familiar theory of Oswald's innocence. (Impeccable documentation of 72 unnatural deaths—including the Oswald bus driver, both police officers who accompanied Officer Tippit, and 14 newsmen who interviewed Jack Ruby—linked intimately to

Weisberg, Lane, Salandria, Cook. Ford, Buchanan, Yossarian, and Holmes—as well as all their first drafts—and spent six months with FBI officers as they gathered their information on biweekly forays to Jack Ruby's strip emporium. Furthermore, Leboeuf made an impressive collection of hitherto unexplored documents, including the Dallas-Irving 1960 tax assessor's records and 1960-1963 telephone directories, the ledgers for the month of November, 1963, and several Irving retail stores, including Hutchison's grocery (scene of the much-discussed milk and cinnamon roll purchases), the Sports Drome Range, the Ford-Lincoln agency, and the notorious Tsien-Huang's hand laundry.

The massive evidence in these four volumes bespeaks a scholarly patience

They noted that "During three years of painstaking research, Leboeuf read the Warren Commission's 26 volumes 13 times through, studied the published works of Epstein, Weisberg, Lane, Salandria, Cook, Ford, Buchanan, Yossarian, and Holmes—as well as their first drafts—and spent six months with FBI officers as they gather their information on biweekly forays to Jack Ruby's strip emporium. Furthermore, Leboeuf made an impressive collection of hitherto unexplored documents, including the Dallas-Irving 1960 tax assessor's records and 1960-1963 telephone directories, the ledgers for the month of November 1963 and several Irving retail stores, including Hutchinson's grocery (scene of the much-discussed cinnamon roll purchases), the Sports Drome Range, the Ford-Lincoln agency, and the notorious Tsien-Huang's hand laundry."

Leboeuf found evidence of five different Oswalds, "the four going by the name L.H. Oswell, H.L. Oswill, Lee R.V. Isabell, and Oswald Harby" and the evidence indicates that "Lee Harvey Oswald was the only one of the five who was not a crack shot; that it was L.H. Oswell, and not Oswald, who took the often-discussed trip to Mexico in September, he having the greatest resemblance to Lee Harvey among the four and being already known to a certain few Mexican girls…"

However, "it is only in Volumes III and IV that Leboeuf really pulls out the stops. It is only here, among the murky Exhibits of the gigantic Volume III (Exhibit 226, III:682: a James Beard cookbook from the pantry of Peggy Goldwater with a recipe for cinnamon rolls circled in red; Exhibit 252, III:654: a comic book retrieved from a Mexican house of ill-repute with the name "Oswell" scrawled on it), that the scrupulously academic reader might have occasional doubts over the unorthodox, even manic, spirit with which Leboeuf has conducted his investigations."

And, as for the actual conspiracy, well, Leboeuf "presents convincing new evidence linking a number of prominent millionaire conservatives, as well as a few beer, oil and birth control trusts, with the plot. The case for an inside job is persuasive, if not incontrovertible."

One bookstore in Manhattan received over 100 orders for the Leboeuf volumes in just the first day after the magazine appeared on the newsstand. The *Ramparts* switchboard "was besieged with long-distance calls from readers who couldn't find 'Leboeuf' in their local bookstores, and from hungry booksellers who wanted to stock such a hot item but couldn't raise the author and publisher in Levittown information." Over 300 people sent cheques directly to *Ramparts*.

Proving that the critics had no sense of humour, Sylvia Meagher wrote to *Ramparts* and said that the spoof was a "gratuitous and vicious attack on every researcher and critic of the Warren Report." She closed her letter noting that "For all your grandiose crusading against evil, the publication of that sordid lampoon places you in the same camp with the outright pornographers and other befouled merchants who are assassins of the human spirit." Raymond Marcus wrote that "I have just read with disgust the extremely unfunny and totally stupid bag of drivel by Brackman and Levine." He wondered why "valuable space was given to such worthless and malicious trash."

In the end, Warren Hinckle apologized to readers in the January, 1967, issue. But Hinckle took solace in the fact that Ulov Leboeuf and his four-volume epic, *Time of Assassins*, was mentioned in a November 20, 1966, *Boston Globe* article on the assassination.

the truth about
THAT DAY IN DALLAS

Wouldn't this be
the most appropriate monument
to President Kennedy?

Story by James S. Doyle and Stephen Zorn.
Photos by A.P. and U.P.I.

Kennedy - *Continued from Page 9*

but the evidence linking it to the assassination is not. A clean bullet, with remnants neither blood nor tissue, with negligible disfiguration and with a loss of original weight of no more than 2.5 grains, was found by a janitor on a hospital stretcher that may have been used for either Connally or Kennedy. The bullet had the markings of one fired from Oswald's gun, but experts were unable to reproduce such a clean bullet when they test-fired the gun into any substance firmer than cotton batting. Critics suggest the bullet was planted on the stretcher to frame Oswald. One critic of undetermined reliability, Ulov G. K. Leboeuf of Levittown, N.Y., suggests that the janitor who found this pristine bullet is a cousin-in-law of Jack Ruby, that the janitor's divorced wife is now living with an FBI agent, a munitions expert, who investigated Oswald before Kennedy's trip to Dallas. (Leboeuf, an Austrian educated sociologist, is the author of a four volume book, "Time of Assassins," which he has recently had published at his own expense.) Is all this unmitigated fancy? A new inquiry could easily determine the answer.

Two important books appeared in early 1967—Josiah Thompson's *Six Seconds in Dallas* and Sylvia Meagher's *Accessories After the Fact*.

Thompson had access to original transparencies of the Zapruder film at *Life* magazine and used it to develop an alternative scenario. He argued for three assassins. He figured that the time between the reaction of Kennedy and Connally was too short for one assassin to fire two shots. And the head snap meant that one assassin was firing from the grassy knoll in front. This was a very similar argument to the one in David Lifton and David Welsh's essay, "The Case for Three Assassins" in the January, 1967, issue of *Ramparts*.

Meagher's book was widely viewed as the most thorough of the critiques but, in many instances, she argued about minutiae. She questioned the link between Oswald and his rifle's ammunition clip; the uniqueness of his Mannlicher-Carcano's serial number; why Oswald would have his wife take photos of him and his guns; instances of 'two Oswalds'; the speed of the presidential limousine; and irrelevant questions about the rifle sling. And she had a whole chapter in her book on the mysterious deaths.

In the meantime, Mark Lane was crisscrossing the country promoting his book. He was the Michael Moore of his time—at college campuses, on radio and television and always ready with a comment. *Time* magazine claimed he was the third most popular speaker on campuses in the United States. In early September, 1966, Lane made his first appearance on the Mort Sahl show. Sahl was a wildly popular comedian—in fact, he was the first comic to ever grace the cover of *Time*.

The whole show was devoted to the assassination and Lane showed clips from the upcoming film of his book. At the end, Sahl told the audience, "It isn't any fun to awaken America now. It's like walking into a party—everybody's been drunk for 175 years, and you're getting the tab for the liquor."

From that point on, Sahl was hooked on the JFK assassination. Lane was on the show again in October, along with actors reading portions of the Warren Report. Sahl's biographer James Curtis wrote that "There was a concern at the station that his growing obsession with the killing, while energizing a core audience, was alienating more casual viewers." Sahl eventually lost the show and Curtis noted that "the conspiracy Sahl blamed for keeping him unemployed got conflated with the one he saw as being responsible for the death of the President." Sahl's earnings dropped from $400,000 per year in the early 1960s to just $19,000.

On January 23, 1967, Jack Dempsey's column in the New Orleans *States-Item* contained an intriguing item: "Did you know? At least five persons have been questioned by the District Attorney's office in connection with another investigation into events linked to the Kennedy assassination." This was the first mention that something big was going on in New Orleans. The *States-Item* broke the story wide open on February 17 with a major story by Rosemary James who revealed that DA Jim Garrison had spent $8,000 in public money investigating the JFK assassination.

That forced Garrison out into the open and he boasted that "There will be arrests. Charges will be filed and on the basis of these charges, convictions will be obtained." His prime suspect in the assassination, David Ferrie, died of natural causes on February 22. Two days later, Garrison claimed that "My staff and I solved the case weeks ago. I wouldn't say this if I didn't have evidence beyond the shadow of a doubt. We know the key individuals, the cities involved and how it was done." Mysteriously, he added that "The key to the whole case is through the looking glass. Black is white; white is black. I don't want to be cryptic, but that's the way it is."

On March 1, Jim Garrison arrested businessman Clay Shaw for conspiring to kill President John F. Kennedy.

That set off a stampede to New Orleans. Mort Sahl went right to Jim Garrison's home and introduced himself. He told Garrison, "I want to shake your hand," to which Garrison replied, "I hope you're available to do a lot more than that." He made Sahl an unpaid investigator and even gave him business cards. Harold Weisberg, Edward Jay Epstein, Raymond Marcus and Mark Lane all headed down south.

On March 29, 1967 Lane called into Sahl's radio show and told him that "I think I can say this, that the evidence is conclusive that no foreign power was involved, none at all, but a very powerful domestic force was involved in planning the events which culminated in the death of President Kennedy and that the persons that actually participated in the conspiracy and in the assassination are known to Mr. Garrison, to his staff, and now to me. The evidence is so conclusive, I believe, that when Garrison walks into that courtroom in New Orleans and presents it, and when the American people learn for the first time who planned the events, which culminated in the death of President Kennedy, they are going to be outraged, absolutely outraged, and shocked and stunned. Then I think that there are going to be some important, drastic changes in this country. There will have to be after that evidence is known."

It was an exciting time to be alive. The truth was finally going to be revealed.

Two

Jim Garrison's Excellent Homosexual Adventure

New Orleans played a big part in the life of Lee Harvey Oswald. He was born there in 1939, moved away at the age of six, moved back at the age of fifteen, and stayed there for two years before joining the Marines. He defected to the Soviet Union in 1959 and came back to the United States in 1962, living in Ft. Worth-Dallas. Oswald went back to New Orleans for five months in 1963.

He became politically active and started a one-man chapter of the Fair Play for Cuba Committee. He printed up pro-Castro leaflets and handed them out on street corners. Oswald also tried to infiltrate an anti-Castro group which ended up in a scuffle on a street corner when they discovered him distributing his literature. This got Oswald on the radio where he engaged in debates on Marxism and Communism. So it's not surprising that any investigation into the assassination would start in New Orleans.

In 1961, Jim Garrison was elected District Attorney of New Orleans. He was 41 years old, 6'6" tall, extremely good-looking, and had a charismatic and flamboyant personality. His first mission cracked down on vice in the French quarter (raiding gay bars) which generated a lot of positive headlines. It didn't take long for the city of New Orleans to fall in love with the "Jolly Green Giant."

Two days after the JFK assassination, Garrison's office got a tip from a local drunk and former felon, Jack Martin, about a possible New Orleans connection. Martin had a long-standing grudge against David Ferrie, a former Eastern Airlines pilot who had since lost his job because of homosexual advances on an underage teenager. Martin thought that Lee

Harvey Oswald's rifle looked similar to the one that Ferrie owned years earlier and that Ferrie had mentioned a short story about a presidential assassination. Martin watched the television coverage of the assassination and heard that Oswald had been a member of the Civil Air Patrol (CAP) when he was a teenager in New Orleans. Martin also knew that Ferrie had been in CAP and this was enough to send him to the telephone.

Ferrie was questioned by the FBI and the Secret Service and he denied knowing Oswald or having any connection to the assassination. That weekend, he had driven to Houston and had gone ice skating in Galveston with some friends. His whereabouts were quickly verified and he was released.

There was another New Orleans connection. Dean Andrews was a short, overweight lawyer who was in the hospital that weekend being treated for pneumonia. He had a high fever and was heavily sedated. On Saturday, November 23, he claimed to have received a call from Eugene Davis, a bar owner in the French Quarter who had previously sent Andrews clients from the gay community. He supposedly told Davis, while still woozy from medication, that he could be famous if he was Oswald's defence attorney. It wasn't long before Andrews phoned his secretary and told her that he had just received a phone call to represent Oswald. When she asked him who had hired him, Andrews just said 'Bertrand.'

On Sunday, November 24, Jack Ruby shot Lee Harvey Oswald. That let Andrews off the hook with his crazy story, but it also allowed him to add more details. He started telling people that Oswald had visited his office on at least three occasions in the past seeking legal advice and that he was always accompanied by up to five homosexuals. He then told the FBI and Secret Service that Bertrand's full name was Clay Bertrand, that he was also gay, and that he might have accompanied Oswald on his visits.

FBI and Secret Service agents spent ten days looking for Bertrand with no success. Andrews then backed away from his allegations and told the FBI that the call from Bertrand was a "figment of his imagination." But he stuck to his original story about Oswald visiting his office. In July, 1964, Andrews testified before the Warren Commission and repeated all of his stories—this time with a differing physical description of Bertrand. The Warren Report spent one paragraph discussing his allegations and noted that he "was able to locate no records of any of Oswald's alleged visits" and that his secretary "had no recollection of Oswald being there."

In late 1966, Jim Garrison was on a flight with Louisiana Senator Russell Long who convinced him that the Warren Commission Report was fiction. This rekindled his interest and Garrison ordered the 26 volumes of the Warren Commission evidence. He decided to revisit the New Orleans connections and his first step was to have dinner with Dean Andrews. Unfortunately, his recollections were hazier than ever and he refused to be pinned down on the identity of Bertrand.

Garrison then went back to Jack Martin, who was only too happy to talk. During the night of the assassination, Martin had been pistol-whipped by his boss, the gumshoe Guy Banister. Now Martin was claiming that he was beaten because he had made an off-hand comment about seeing Lee Harvey Oswald, David Ferrie, and some Cubans in Banister's office in the summer of 1963.

The inclusion of David Ferrie made Garrison believe that his ice-skating trip to Galveston the weekend of the assassination was perhaps something much bigger—might Ferrie have been Oswald's get-away pilot who would fly him to safety? Once again, Ferrie was brought in for questioning and he denied everything.

It didn't take long for Garrison to figure out Clay Bertrand's identity. His Assistant District Attorney had scribbled a note on a copy of the Warren Report next to the paragraph on Dean Andrews. He asked himself: who was gay, lived in the French Quarter and had the first name Clay? Perhaps it was the New Orleans businessman Clay Shaw. Garrison saw the note and knew instantly that Shaw had to be Bertrand. After all, they were both homosexuals, both spoke Spanish and both had the same first name. Garrison believed that gay people, when using a pseudonym, always keep the same first name.

So just who was Clay Shaw? He served in World War II as *aide-de-camp* for General Charles Thrasher and was responsible for stockpiling supplies for the Normandy invasion. Shaw was a major at discharge in 1946 and received decorations from three different nations, including the Bronze Star, the Legion of Merit, and Le Croix de Guerre. After the war, he returned to New Orleans and created the Center for International Trade in 1948 and became its managing director. In 1963, he oversaw the creation of a new Trade Mart building on Canal Street. Shaw retired in 1965 and the City of New Orleans awarded him its international Order of Merit medal.

He also authored a number of published plays and one, *Submerged*, was performed across the country. Shaw also restored properties in the French Quarter, and several magazines, including *House & Garden*, featured his work. One of his most important renovations was the 1821 residence of naturalist John James Audubon. Shaw was named one of the "most important men in New Orleans" in the March 1967 issue of New Orleans' *Town and Country Magazine*.

Shaw stood out in New Orleans—he was 6'4" tall, 225 lbs, with a shock of white hair. He had been interviewed on television hundreds of times and was very well known. He was also active in the New Orleans social scene (he was friends with Tennessee Williams) but only those closest to him knew he was gay. He was called the "unlikeliest villain since Oscar Wilde."

Once Garrison figured out that Shaw was Bertrand, he invited Andrews for another dinner to corroborate his thesis but Andrews refused to play along. Garrison wouldn't let up and Andrews decided to test him. Andrews noted, "He [wanted] to shuck me like a corn, pluck me like a chicken, stew me like an oyster. I wanted to see if this cat was kosher." He invented a fictitious Cuban acquaintance of Oswald, Manuel Garcia Gonzales, and soon enough Garrison was announcing that this person was a triggerman in the JFK assassination.

The media picked up the story. *Ramparts* ran a long article on the Garrison investigation in June, 1967, which noted "A third individual expected to figure prominently in the Garrison inquiry is Manuel Garcia Gonzales. The New Orleans D.A. has come into possession of a photograph taken at Dealey Plaza just before the assassination which shows several Latin men behind the low picket fence at the top of the famed grassy knoll….and Garrison thinks Gonzales is one of the men in the photograph. Gonzales has disappeared and has probably fled the country." *Ramparts* also ran caricatures of the major players in the case, including Gonzales, but they had to admit that "his exact features are unknown."

Andrews had all the proof he needed that Jim Garrison was dangerous.

At this point, Garrison started to think that the Kennedy assassination was some sort of homosexual plot. He met journalist Hugh Aynesworth at his home in January, 1967, and told him a remarkable story:

> "Hugh," he said at last, "you're lucky you're in town today. We've just verified this guy, and believe me it's dynamite."
> Explaining no more for the moment, Garrison then called one

of his assistant DAs, ex-boxer Andrew Sciambra, known as Moo, who arrived a short while later with this slight little guy from Houston, a piano player, who proceeded to tell us how he knew that Ruby and Oswald were longtime gay lovers.

He went into great detail, naming clubs in Dallas and Houston where he said he had been performing when Ruby and Oswald dropped by. He even described one occasion when the owners of a Houston club had booted out the two of them "because," he said, "they had been groping each other all evening long."

Garrison beamed.

"You might be the most important witness we've run across yet," he told the piano player. "And you are certain they were with each other on several occasions?"

The little man vigorously nodded yes, clearly pleased that Garrison was buying his story.

Shaw was brought in for questioning and he denied knowing Oswald, Ferrie, and Bertrand.

After the initial story about Garrison's investigation broke in the New Orleans *State-Item* on February 17, Ferrie called the newspaper and said that "he was being persecuted by the DA's office" and that "he was afraid of arrest." He also told reporter David Snyder that he was physically sick. Snyder went to meet him at his apartment and noted that "his steps were feeble as we climbed the steps to the second floor" and he complained of headaches.

Ferrie said there was nothing to Garrison's allegations and "said he would like to file a suit that allow him to subpoena Garrison and expose the harassment he was going through." He also wanted to sue Jack Martin who had supplied Garrison with a list of names in connection with the assassination. Snyder asked Ferrie "if he thought the Garrison investigation was a phony," and Ferrie replied, "Why certainly, how could it be anything else?" Snyder reported that Ferrie "wanted me to arrange a lie detector test for him in case he was hauled in."

Ferrie was found dead in his apartment on February 22nd. The coroner determined he died of natural causes from a berry aneurysm which is a congenital defect. Garrison claimed that it was suicide—and that Ferrie had overdosed on Proloid, his thyroid medication. He convinced a lot of conspiracy nuts, but the coroner knew better, because there was also some scar tissue that indicated that Ferrie had suffered from an earlier bleed. The toxicology results also came back negative.

Two days after Ferrie's death, Garrison told ABC News that he had solved the case, that arrests would be made, that he knew everybody who was involved, and that the assassination had been planned in New Orleans.

Then a 25-year-old insurance trainee in Baton Rouge, Perry Russo, called a local newspaper to say that he knew Ferrie and had heard him talk about how easy it would be to assassinate a president. He also claimed that Ferrie had said "we" will get Kennedy. He did not mention a plot, nor did he mention Oswald or Shaw. Garrison sent one of his attorneys, Andrew Sciambra, to interview Russo and he hit pay dirt. Russo now claimed that Oswald had been Ferrie's roommate but that he remembered him having a beard. He also thought he had once seen Shaw with Ferrie at a service station.

Russo also remembered seeing Clay Shaw at the Nashville Street Wharf when he went to see JFK speak in May of 1962. Sciambra's memo notes that Russo "remembers this guy because he was apparently a queer. It seems that instead of looking at JFK speak, SHAW kept turning around and looking at all the young boys in the crowd. He said that SHAW eventually struck up a conversation with a young kid not too far from him. It was perfectly obvious to him that SHAW stared at his penis several times. He said that SHAW eventually left with a friend. He said that SHAW had on dark pants that day which fit very tightly and was the kind of pants that a lot of queers in the French quarter wear."

This description did not fit Clay Shaw, who was a very conservative dresser and who wasn't known for hanging out with young boys. He was way too much of a gentleman to act in an inappropriate way in public.

Russo was brought to New Orleans and administered Sodium Pentothal (a so-called truth serum) by Dr. Nicholas Cheeta. He was questioned by Assistant District Attorney Andrew Sciambra who "asked him if he could remember any of the details about CLAY BERTRAND being up in FERRIE'S apartment." A few days later, Russo was then put under hypnosis in sessions with Dr. Fatter, a New Orleans family physician. During the interview, Fatter was quite suggestive:

> Dr. Fatter: Continue looking at the television program and Clay, the white-haired man is going to come into the room. You are at Ferrie's apartment and there are many people. Who did he introduce Clay to?

******

> *Dr. Fatter: Let your mind go completely, blank, Perry—see that television screen again. It is very vivid—now notice the picture on the screen—there will be Bertrand, Ferrie and Oswald and they are going to discuss a very important matter and there is another man and girl there and they are talking about assassinating somebody. Look at it and describe it to me.*

It is Dr. Fatter and not Perry Russo who first uses the name 'Clay' and the word 'assassinating.' Surely this a textbook case of creating a memory—a party at Ferrie's apartment where Clay Bertrand (Shaw) and Lee Harvey Oswald are all discussing killing Kennedy.

Garrison was almost there. He needed Russo to identify Shaw as Bertrand. So he had Russo walk up to Shaw's house in the guise of selling insurance, and Russo was able to identify Shaw as being Clay Bertrand. Garrison now had his case and on the following day, March 1, 1967, Claw Shaw was arrested for conspiring with David Ferrie and Lee Harvey Oswald to kill JFK.

He was brought in for more questioning, and Russo looked through a one-way mirror and identified him as Bertrand. Garrison searched Shaw's home and released to the press a list of some of the contents including a black gown, hood, cape, chains and five whips. Shaw said these were Mardi Gras costumes—it would have been hard for him to admit publicly he was into S&M—but in any event, he was outed as a homosexual. *Newsweek* noted that "Garrison's decision to concentrate on homosexuals, a relatively vulnerable group, tended to produce a line-up of alleged conspirators that much of the public found difficult to take seriously."

Paul Hoch wrote in one his *Echoes of Conspiracy* newsletters that "Garrison apparently failed to weigh the likelihood of a secret but social and non-conspiratorial relationship between Shaw and Ferrie. By refusing to do so—and targeting someone who would not come out of the closet in his own defense—I think Garrison crossed over the line into objectively homophobic persecution."

A few days after Shaw's arrest, investigators visited Mrs. Lawrence Fischer, a friend of Shaw's. She told author James Kirkwood what happened:

> "Wanted to know how long I'd known him. Since he was seventeen. Wanted to know if we'd ever discuss sex." Mrs. Fischer slapped her leg. "Well, it would be pretty unusual to go for over thirty-five years with a good friend and never bring the subject up, now, wouldn't it? Of course we had. Then this young man asked, 'Has Mr. Shaw ever told you the intimate details of his sex life?' 'No,' I shot back at him, 'and furthermore I haven't told him the intimate details of my sex life either. Are you here to discuss his political leanings with reference to the Garrison farce, or are you conducting a sort of Kinsey report. Then he wanted to get into the black robe and the hood and the black hat and finally I just couldn't take it any longer and I said, 'Listen, my good young man, I don't know whether you've ever heard of it and it's called Mardi Gras! Everybody in town gets dressed up in costumes."

Garrison told Richard Billings of *Life* magazine that "I'm now convinced it was a sadist plot" and that he had read the Marquis de Sade and knew that sadists escalate from whipping to killing. In mid-March, Garrison flew to Las Vegas to meet with reporter Jim Phelan of the *Saturday*

Evening Post. They had known each other for years and Garrison wanted to spell out the specifics of the plot.

> *In an effort to get Garrison's story into focus, I asked him the motive of the Kennedy conspirators. He told me that the murder in Dallas had been a homosexual plot.*
>
> *"They had the same motive as Loeb and Leopold, when they murdered Bobbie Franks in Chicago back in the twenties," Garrison said. "It was a homosexual thrill-killing, plus the excitement of getting away with a perfect crime. John Kennedy was everything that Dave Ferrie was not—a successful, handsome, popular, wealthy, virile man. You can just picture the charge Ferrie got out of plotting his death.*
>
> *I asked how he had learned the murder was a homosexual plot.*
>
> *"Look at the people involved," Garrison said. "Dave Ferrie, homosexual, Clay Shaw, homosexual. Jack Ruby, homosexual."*
>
> *"Ruby was a homosexual?"*
>
> *"Sure, we dug that out," Garrison said. "His homosexual nickname was Pinkie. That's three. Then there was Lee Harvey Oswald."*
>
> *But Oswald was married and had two children, I pointed out.*

> "A switch-hitter who couldn't satisfy his wife," Garrison said. "That's all in the Warren Report." He named two more "key figures" whom he labeled homosexual.

> "That's six homosexuals in the plot," Garrison said. "One or maybe two, okay. But all six homosexuals? How far can you stretch the arm of coincidence?"

Garrison told *Newsweek* that he "had proof that Shaw, Ferrie and Oswald were conspirators, but was still looking for a 'gay boy' who resembled Oswald and actually fired the fatal shots." Merriman Smith, the UPI reporter who first reported that JFK had been shot, wrote to the FBI saying that Garrison claimed that some "high-status fags" had been involved in the assassination. And Robert Northshield, Executive-Producer of the Huntley-Brinkley Report on NBC, contacted the FBI and informed them that "at the preliminary hearing Shaw was to be portrayed as a "sadist" and "masochist" who made the plans for the assassination because he wanted to destroy the "world's most handsome man."

Muckraker Jack Anderson, partner of syndicated columnist Drew Pearson, also spent some time talking to Garrison. According to Pearson's March 24, 1967, diary entry, Garrison told Anderson, "The CIA definitely had a plot to assassinate Castro and had approached Clay Shaw, a reputable, wealthy homosexual businessman, as a man who could execute the plot. Shaw was part of a homosexual ring, including Ferrie and Ruby in Dallas." At this point, Garrison thought the plot was to assassinate Castro but "when Oswald was refused his visa to Cuba, the conspirators then turned around and decided to assassinate Kennedy. They used Oswald as the patsy. He was the only non-homo member of the ring. They figured he was so mentally disturbed, and so at odds with the world, that he could be used as the fall guy."

Shaw's arrest reverberated around the globe. In Rome, a small Communist Party-owned newspaper, *Paese Sera*, ran a story on March 4 claiming that Clay Shaw was involved in unsavoury activities while serving on the Board of the Centro Mondiale Commerciale (CMC). *Paese Sera* alleged that the CMC was a "creature of the CIA…set up as a cover for the transfer to Italy of CIA-FBI funds for illegal political-espionage activities." Shaw was indeed on the Board of the CMC from 1958-1962, but there was nothing evil about the organization. Its goal was to simply take advantage of the new European Common Market and make Rome an important trading hub.

The story then appeared in *Pravda* (the official newspapers of the Communist Party of the Soviet Union), *L'Unita* (the newspaper of the Italian Communist Party), *L'Humanite* (the newspaper of the French Communist Party), and then in *Le Devoir* in Canada, which ran the *Pravda* article in the March 8, 1967, edition, and then ran a larger article on March 16 written by their New York correspondent Louis Wiznitzer. He mentioned the items confiscated from Shaw's apartment and commented that he was a "Marquis de Sade." He also alluded to Shaw's homosexuality, writing, "Finally, another detail that doesn't lack for a certain spiciness: in his youth Clay Shaw published a story from which John Ford took his film, *Men without Women*."

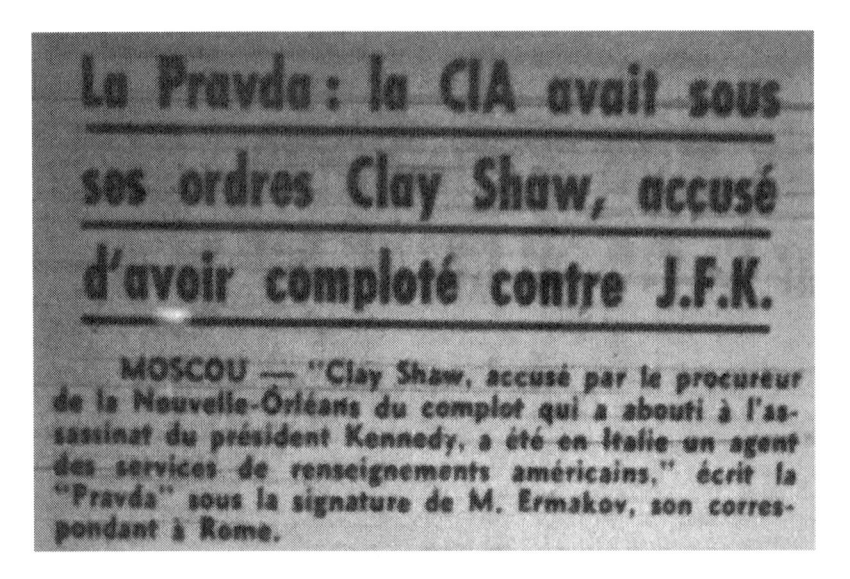

> **La Pravda : la CIA avait sous ses ordres Clay Shaw, accusé d'avoir comploté contre J.F.K.**
>
> MOSCOU — "Clay Shaw, accusé par le procureur de la Nouvelle-Orléans du complot qui a abouti à l'assassinat du président Kennedy, a été en Italie un agent des services de renseignements américains," écrit la "Pravda" sous la signature de M. Ermakov, son correspondant à Rome.

Clark Blaise's article, "Neo-Fascism and the Kennedy Assassins," in the Sept-Oct, 1967, issue of *Canadian Dimension* referenced the articles in *Le Devoir* and noted that they have a "breezy disregard for documentation." Blaise "expected to see the story spelled out that afternoon in the *Montreal Star*, or at least to see a solid article or two appear in the liberal journals. Nothing more ever appeared." He was also disappointed that the *New York Times* never mentioned any of the details about the activities of the CMC and felt "it was useless" to write the CBC and NBC.

Ramparts ran "The Garrison Commission" in the January, 1968, issue which referenced *Paese Sera* and *Le Devoir* as its sources on Clay Shaw and the CMC.

Author Max Holland wrote a number of articles suggesting that the *Paese Sera* story was planted by the KGB. *The Mitrokhin Archive* is a collection of notes made secretly by KGB archivist Vasili Mitrokhin documenting the activities of the Soviet Union around the globe. His subsequent book co-authored with Christopher Andrew claimed that "In April 1961 the KGB succeeded in planting on the pro-Soviet Italian daily *Paese Sera* a story suggesting that the CIA was involved in the failed putsch mounted by four French generals to disrupt de Gaulle's attempts to negotiate a peace with the FLN which would lead to Algerian independence." Holland also found a note in the archive that "In 1967, Department A of the First Chief Directorate conducted a series of disinformation operations…One such emplacement in New York was through *Paese Sera*." Sure enough, an article in the *National Guardian*, the same left-wing newspaper that published Mark Lane's screed back in 1963, discussed Shaw's arrest on March 19th.

This technique was corroborated by a senior KGB officer, Sergey Kondrashev, who told Tennent Bagley, Deputy Chief of the Soviet Bloc Division in CIA counterintelligence, that "the most obvious route toward the broad Western public was, of course, newspapers, and magazines—planting articles in cooperative papers (of the many Kondrashev remembers *Paese Sera* in Italy…."

By mid-March, 1967, Garrison had received copies of the article, quite possibly sent to him by Ralph Schoenman, who was Bertrand Russell's personal secretary. We know this from the diary of Richard Billings, a senior editor at *Life* magazine, who was a confidante of Garrison's. His entry for March 22 reads, "Story about Shaw and CIA appears in Humanite [sic], probably March 8…[Garrison] has copy date-lined Rome, March 7th, from la press Italien [sic]"

Jim Phelan wrote in the *Saturday Evening Post* that, after the *Paese Sera* article, Garrison's switchboard "blazed like a pinball machine gone mad." He now had a direct link from Shaw to the CIA. In addition, the plethora of left-wing conspiracy buffs who had flocked to New Orleans convinced Garrison to move away from a homosexual thrill killing and to talk about something much bigger. Over time, Garrison's conspiracy included "Minutemen, CIA agents, oil millionaires, Dallas policemen, munitions exporters, 'the Dallas Establishment,' reactionaries, White Russians, and certain elements of the invisible Nazi substructure." But the heart of Garrison's thinking was some sort of massive CIA-planned assassination plot, although even that was somewhat malleable.

For instance, Garrison called Warren Hinckle, editor of *Ramparts*, in January of 1968 and told him, "This is risky, but I have little choice. It is imperative that I get this information to you now. Important new information has surfaced. Those Texas oilmen do not appear to be involved in President Kennedy's murder in the way we first thought. It was the Military-Industrial Complex that put up the money for the assassination—but as far as we can tell, the conspiracy was limited to the aerospace wing. I've got the names of three companies and their employees who were involved in setting up the President's murder. Do you have a pencil?"

Veteran reporter James Phelan penned an apt limerick:

> Cried Big Jim, the world owes me praise.
> And I'll get it, come one of these days.
> Earl Warren, the dunce.
> Solved the killing just once.
> But I solved it seventeen ways!

One of the strangest episodes of the Garrison affair concerned an entry in Clay Shaw's address book. A researcher noticed the entry "Lee Odom, P.O. Box 19106, Dallas, Tex" and found that the '19106' matched an entry in Lee Harvey Oswald's notebook. Was this the elusive proof that Oswald and Shaw were indeed connected?

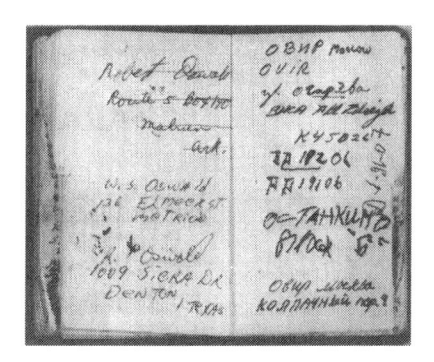

Shaw's lawyers said the entry was from 1966 and referred to a Dallas businessman with whom Shaw had discussed a business relationship. Further, the Dallas PO Box number 19106 was only assigned to Odom in 1965, well after Oswald had written his notation. And the notation in Oswald's book was preceded by two Cyrillic Ds, which is not Russian for P (ost) O (ffice).

Sylvia Meager, one of the critics, thought this was all silly. She knew that the Cyrillic Ds in Oswald's notebook did not refer to a post office box and that the notation was written when Oswald was in the Soviet Union. She sent a registered letter to Garrison spelling out her reasons why this was all nonsense. Garrison then called her in New York, and he told her he had received her letter but "that he had also decoded from other notations in the same LHO notebook the phone numbers for (1) Clay Shaw (2) the local FBI office (3) the local CIA office. The press had blacked this out, in Garrison's opinion because the CIA had put the pressure on."

Garrison went even further. He told *Playboy* magazine that "Our investigators have broken a code Oswald used and found Ruby's private unlisted telephone number, as of 1963, written in Oswald's notebook. The same coded number found in the address book of another prominent figure in this case."

Here is how Garrison linked Oswald's notation to Jack Ruby's unlisted phone number. Garrison said, "Oswald invariably uses the dial of the telephone as conversion machinery to convert letters into numbers and back again. He systematically adds the number values resulting in a sum which can later be broken down into the real exchange listing." So, the letters 'PO' become the number 13, and Garrison claimed the only telephone exchange in Dallas which the number 13 converts to is WHitehall. If you then unscramble the number in Oswald's notebook, 19106, it then becomes 16901. And if you subtract 1300 (which was a standard coding number in Oswald's notebook) from that you get 1-5601. Ruby's number was WHitehall 1-5601.

How had Garrison decoded the local CIA office? Edward Jay Epstein, who was working in Garrison's office when the entries were discovered, explained. "Using an entirely different system of decipherment—multiplying the number by 10, rearranging the digits, subtracting 1700, and remultiplying—Garrison managed to convert the number 1147, which appeared in Oswald's book, to 522-8874, the CIA phone number."

David Lifton told a similar story in a June, 1968, story in *Open City*, an L.A. underground newspaper:

> "During one of our conversations, Garrison told me that his office had established an ironclad link between Ruby and Oswald. As evidence, he cited the fact that a Ft. Worth telephone number PE8-1951, was listed in Oswald's address

book and also was found on Ruby's phone bill. Astonished, I went home and checked it out. That telephone number, as clearly indicated in Oswald's address book, is television station KTVT, Channel 11, Fort Worth Texas.

I confronted Garrison with this the next day. He became very truculent and annoyed.

"David, stop arguing the defense," he would say.

"But, what does it mean, Jim?" I demanded. "Is there someone at the TV station whom you can prove knew both men?"

"It means whatever the jury decides it means," he said, adding that "Law is not a science."

Finally, I asked: "But what do YOU think, Jim? What is the truth of the matter."

His answer is one I will never forget. He said, with considerable annoyance and contempt, "After the fact, there IS NO truth. There is ONLY what the jury decides."

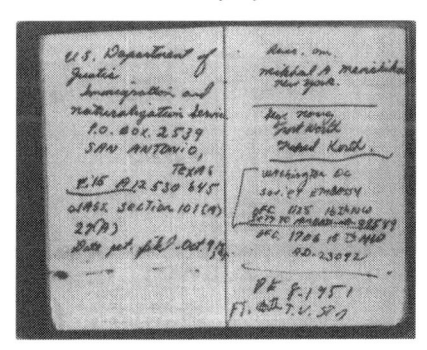

At this point, several of the 'buffs' realized that Garrison had nothing. But several remained firm in their belief that he must have 'something.' As David Lifton put it, "Rally around the plot, boys. It's not much of a plot, but it's the only plot we've got."

Garrison would never let go of this nonsense. He repeated the story of Oswald's notebook in his book, *On the Trail of the Assassins*, published in 1988, still insisting that the Cyrillic Ds were 'PO.' He ridiculed the innocent explanation of why Lee Odom's PO Box was in Shaw's address book saying, "Once again the people of this country were being asked to swallow a cannon ball, no matter how well lubricated."

The case eventually went to trial in 1969 and there were some bizarre moments. One witness, Vernon Bundy, a 29-year-old heroin addict, testified that he saw Shaw give Oswald a wad of cash at a seawall on Lake Pontchartrain while he was shooting up heroin; a postman remembered delivering mail addressed to Clay Bertrand to Clay Shaw's address but also recalled delivering mail to an assortment of fictitious names; and Charles Spiesel, an accountant, claimed he went to a party with Ferrie and overheard a conversation about killing Kennedy. Unfortunately, he was forced to admit on cross-examination that he had fingerprinted his own daughter when she went to university and once again when she came home to ensure she was the same person. He further claimed he had been hypnotized 50-60 times, against his will, by the New York City Police Department.

Garrison wrote that after hearing Spiesel's testimony he "was swept by a feeling of nausea. I realized that the clandestine operation of the opposition was so cynical, so sophisticated, and, at the same time, so subtle, that destroying an old-fashioned state jury trial was very much like shooting a fish in a barrel with a shotgun."

Dean Andrews actually testified for Clay Shaw:

Mr. Dymond: Have you ever received a telephone call from Clay Shaw?

Mr. Andrews: No.

Mr. Dymond: Have you ever known Clay Shaw?

Mr. Andrews: No.

Mr. Dymond: Have you ever been introduced to him?

Mr. Andrews: No.

Mr. Dymond: When was the first time that you ever saw Clay Shaw, Mr. Andrews?

Mr. Andrews: When I saw his picture in the paper in connection with the investigation.

And, Dean Andrews finally identified Clay Bertrand:

Mr. Alcock: Mr. Andrews, when you received this telephone call on November 23, 1963, did you have an image in your mind as to who the person was who identified himself on that occasion?

Mr. Andrews: Yes.

> Mr. Alcock: Did you know him by any other name than Clay Bertrand?

> Mr. Andrews: Gene Davis.

Andrews went further, admitting the request to represent Lee Harvey Oswald was a figment of his imagination:

> Mr. Alcock: Why is it you called Monk Zelden on Sunday then and asked if he wanted to go to Dallas?

> Mr. Andrews: No explanation. Don't forget, I am in the hospital sick. I might have believed it myself, or thought after a while I was retained there, so I called Monk. I would like to be famous too—other than as a perjurer.

> [Outburst of laughter]

> Bailiffs: Order in the court!

> Mr. Alcock: That is going to be difficult.

> Mr. Andrews: C'est la vie!

> Mr. Alcock: Are you now saying that the call, as far as it regards the representation of Lee Harvey Oswald, is a figment of your imagination?

Mr. Andrews: *I have tried to say that consistently, and nobody ever gave me a chance.*

And when Perry Russo took the stand, he was forced to admit under cross-examination that the conversations he overheard in Ferrie's apartment might have just been a "bull session." He further conceded there really wasn't much of a conspiracy:

Mr. Dymond [Shaw's attorney]: *Did Leon Oswald ever, in your presence, agree to kill the President of the United States?*

Mr. Russo: *No.*

Mr. Dymond: *Did Clem Bertrand ever agree to kill the President of the United States?*

Russo: *No.*

After the party where they supposedly discussed the assassination, Russo couldn't remember how he had gotten home.

Mr. Dymond: *"...whether or not one of the conspirators to kill the President of the United States rode you home from the conspiratorial meeting?*

Russo: *I don't call them conspirators. No, I don't know who rode me home. I may have caught a bus or hitchhiked or not.*

Mr. Dymond: *You do not call them conspirators?*

Mr. Russo: I have never used that word.

A large part of the trial had nothing to do with Shaw but with Garrison's attempt to discredit the Warren Report. The Zapruder film was shown ten times in court, one time in frame-by-frame action. One reporter wrote in his notebook, "Now playing—Criminal Court building—the Zapruder Film! Continuous showings—in glorious technicolor (Bring the kiddies)." James Kirkwood, author of *American Grotesque,* wrote that "If we thought the state's case against the Warren Report would make more sense than the case against Clay Shaw—other than a seriousness to convict—we were mistaken."

After just 54 minutes of deliberation the jury found Clay Shaw not guilty.

The next day, the New Orleans *States-Item* ran a front-page editorial calling for Garrison's resignation, and the *Times-Picayune* did the same a day later. The American Bar Association asked for an investigation into the DA's office and asked the Louisiana Bar Association to consider disciplinary action. The *New York Times* said the prosecution of Shaw was "one of the most disgraceful chapters in the history of American jurisprudence." Aaron Kohn, director of the New Orleans Metropolitan Commission, noted that there had been "22 criminal allegations…against Mr. Garrison and his staff in the course of [his] investigation" and these included "attempts to intimidate and bribe witnesses, inciting such felonies as perjury and conspiracy to commit battery…and public bribery."

Forty-eight hours later, Jim Garrison charged Shaw with two counts of perjury for his statements that he had never met Oswald or Ferrie. The charges carried a 20-year jail term. In January, 1971, Clay Shaw took Garrison to court to try and stop the perjury charges and ultimately won a permanent injunction against further prosecution. Judge Christenberry wrote that the "pending prosecution was brought in bad faith and that such bad faith constitutes irreparable injury which is great and immediate." Garrison appealed all the way to the Supreme Court and lost. Clay Shaw then filed a $5 million-dollar damage suit but the case was dropped after he died of cancer at the age of 61 in August, 1974.

In 1986, Paul Hoch noted in one of his newsletters the "vulnerability of Clay Shaw due to his apparently irrelevant CIA links and homosexuality." Jim Garrison replied that "Mr. Hoch should go straight to the bathroom and wash his mouth with soap." He added that "Throughout our trial, in everything I have ever written and in every public statement I have ever made—I never once made any reference to Clay Shaw's alleged homosexuality. What sort of human being is Mr. Hoch that he is impelled to so gratuitously make such a reference in a newsletter which he widely distributes to the public? For all his faults and virtues, Shaw is dead and unable to defend himself from that kind of off the wall canard. No matter how virtuously Hoch might couch it, a smear is still a smear."

Hoch replied, "I will let you decide if my reference was gratuitous. Out here, referring to someone's homosexuality stopped being a canard years ago; at least, it's not as serious as charging someone with conspiring to kill JFK."

Of course, Garrison was wrong. He couldn't keep his mouth shut about the supposed homosexual thrill killing before the trial. In addition, at the trial his prosecutors repeatedly asked witnesses about Clay Shaw's 'tight pants,' a clear euphemism for homosexuality.

By the end of the trial, the 'buffs' had largely deserted Garrison, with the exception of Mark Lane. Vincent Salandria never made the trip to New Orleans but remained a staunch supporter, noting that "given the ability of government to bribe, threaten, cajole or kill potential witnesses, jurors, staff members, the judge, what had to have been done would have been done to defeat Garrison. I think Jim knew that. Jim fatalistically went in and took his beating."

In May of 2005, my partner Andrew and I went to New Orleans for the Jazz & Heritage Festival. We took a walking tour of the gay sites in New Orleans and one of our first stops was Shaw's house at 1313 Dauphine Street, where there was a plaque:

> *In tribute to Clay Shaw, 1913-1974. Pioneer in the renovation of the Vieux Carre. This 1834 building, the Spanish stables, is one of nine restorations by Clay Shaw. In addition, he conceived and completed the International Trade Mart and directed the restoration of the French Market. Clay Shaw was a patron of the humanities and lived his life with the utmost grace; an invaluable citizen, he was respected, admired and loved by many.*

Three

I Was a Teenage JFK conspiracy Freak

It was Thursday, March 6th, 1975. Like millions of other people across North America, I was watching *Good Night America* with Geraldo Rivera at 11:30 pm. Geraldo was a new face, a product of the Watergate era of glamourous journalism. He was avant-garde, on the cutting edge and it sure didn't hurt that he was good-looking. *Good Night America* was the show to be watching. We were all in for a shock.

The show opened with a segment on sex-symbol Raquel Welch. Rivera then brought out author Charles Berlitz to talk about his book on the Bermuda Triangle and the unexplained disappearances of ships and planes. Perhaps that should have been a clue as to the veracity of what was to come.

Next up was the comedian and social activist Dick Gregory, veteran of the civil rights movement. The subject of conversation was the assassination of John Fitzgerald Kennedy, the 35th President of the United States. Gregory claimed that on the day Kennedy was assassinated, November 22, 1963, he started taping all the various news sources and noticed that four hours later, when the same people were again being interviewed, their stories had all changed. The common denominator was that they had all talked to the Secret Service. Gregory then alleged that the motorcade route had been changed and wondered who had the power to ensure it went right by where Lee Harvey Oswald happened to work.

Clearly some very powerful forces were at play but this was nothing compared to what happened next. Rivera brought out a certain "Robert

Groden," with little introduction, to show the Zapruder film—probably the most famous 27 seconds of film ever.

Abraham Zapruder, a Dallas dress manufacturer, managed to catch the JFK assassination on film. He made three copies of the film—one was sold to *Life* magazine for $150,000 and the other two were given to the Secret Service. As part of the deal, *Life* agreed that they would not unduly exploit the horribly graphic nature of the film.

While *Life* did publish individual frames of the film, they never sold the broadcast rights and, as such, the film had never been shown publicly. Groden had made a bootleg copy of the film while he worked for a company that produced colour slides for Life Magazine.

So, there I was, like millions of other people, watching the Zapruder film on American national TV for the first time.

The studio audience gasped at the fatal head shot. So did I.

Kennedy's head moved back, and to the left, in an unmistakeable motion. However, Lee Harvey Oswald, the supposed assassin, was in a building behind the motorcade. So why on earth did Kennedy's head go backwards?

It didn't make any sense.

The film was then replayed in slow motion and then replayed again in close-up mode and it made everybody wonder—how could anybody have believed Kennedy was shot from behind?

If he wasn't shot from behind and was shot from the front, that could only mean that there was a second gunman and hence a conspiracy and that Lee Harvey Oswald was not the lone assassin.

Rivera's next guest was writer and historian Ralph Schoenman who was introduced as someone who had investigated the assassination for over a decade.

Schoenman made several claims:

- That Watergate, the Bay of Pigs, and the Kennedy Assassination were all connected through the involvement of CIA/Counter-intelligence.
- Lee Harvey Oswald was both an FBI and a CIA agent, according to Secret Service document 767.
- There were CIA documents in the National Archives that were being withheld from investigators.
- Jack Ruby, the man who killed Lee Harvey Oswald, pleaded with the Warren Commission to take him to Washington, D.C., because he couldn't tell the truth in Dallas.
- Jack Ruby's psychiatrist reported that Ruby had told him that he was part of a plot to kill Kennedy.
- Jack Ruby's death from lung cancer in 1967 was suspicious.

Geraldo Rivera's show had national impact. The next day, the *Dallas Morning News* published a front-page article with the headline, "Shooting Gory Sight: Kennedy's Head Thrown Backward, Film Shows." The *New York Times* said the show "generated widespread response."

Ron Rosenbaum wrote in *Smithsonian* magazine that the showing of the film "resulted in a kind of collective national gasp as millions of Americans simultaneously saw something that they had previously only read about." Geraldo Rivera said that the show "created a stir" and that because of Watergate, "the American people were willing to believe that their government was capable of murder, conspiracy, and lies."

Gregory, Groden, and Schoenman went on a nation-wide tour of colleges to show the Zapruder film. After the shock of the head snap, Gregory and Schoenman gave students a dose of their left-wing politics and talk about power in America. In May, 1975, Schoenman told a University of

Cincinnati audience that "the ruling class is besieged. It cannot meet the needs of its people. That is why it resorts to official murder."

The JFK assassination industry, which Warren Hinckle of *Ramparts* said was "experiencing a recession," was back in business. Mark Lane, who had written a horrible book, *Conversations with Americans*, in 1970 about Vietnam War atrocities, would also make a comeback. Neil Sheehan, a reporter for the *New York Times*, and no fan of the war, reviewed Lane's book, and found that "Mr. Lane did not bother to cross-check any of the stories his interviewers told him with Army or Marine Corps records." As a result, "Any accusation, any innuendo, any rumor, is repeated and published as truth." Sheehan felt there should be a real investigation of atrocities like the My Lai affair, "but until the country does summon up the courage to convene a responsible inquiry, we probably deserve the Mark Lanes."

But no matter —Lane was now back on the lecture circuit and new books on the JFK assassination started popping up like crazy. The 1976 paperback, *Government by Gunplay*, a collection of essays edited by Harvey Yazijian and Sidney Blumenthal, alleged "a vast conspiracy that explains all the '60s assassinations and Watergate, these events being the visible evidence of a Manichean struggle for power fought by the appendages of an unaccountable, unseen power elite." Blumenthal went on to become a senior advisor to both Bill and Hillary Clinton, and his son Max became a rabid anti-Zionist activist.

Groden, Gregory, and Schoenman lucked out at the University of Virginia. The son of Congressman Thomas Downing was there and arranged for his father to have a private viewing of the Zapruder film. He was moved by the film and invited other congressional colleagues to see the head snap for themselves. There was already a public uproar over the Church Committee investigation into CIA assassination attempts of foreign leaders and the Rockefeller Commission investigation into illegal domestic CIA activities. Downing then sponsored a bill to reopen the investigation and Congress created —the House Select Committee on Assassinations (HSCA) in 1976 to investigate both the John Kennedy and Martin Luther King assassinations.

Of course, at the time of the showing of *Good Night America*, I didn't know that there wasn't a scintilla of truth to anything Gregory, Groden, or Schoenman had said.

Dick Gregory was absolutely wrong on the parade route. It was never changed. The descriptions of the parade route appeared in both Dallas newspapers on November 19th. The parade had to turn on to Elm Street, and hence go by the Texas School Book Depository, because it had a turnoff onto the Stemmons Freeway which took them to the Dallas Trade Mart, where Kennedy was to deliver a speech. However, on the morning of November 22, the *Dallas Morning News* published a very small map with a scale that was too small to show the turn on to Elm Street. To conspiracy mongers this was proof enough that the parade route had been changed.

Kennedy's backwards head snap intrigued me. I had to find out more. I ran down to a second-hand bookshop and found an old paperback copy of the Warren Commission Report. They certainly knew about the Zapruder film—the report published several individual frames including the head shot at frame 313. Unfortunately, there was no discussion of Kennedy's 'back and to the left' movement after the final shot.

Next step was the Dawson College library in Montreal. The only book on the assassination was Mark Lane's 1966 best-selling *Rush to Judgment* (see Chapter One). At the time I was mighty impressed by its seemingly ample documentation. I had no idea of the misrepresentations, the omissions, and the errors littered throughout his book. Nor did I know that

Lane was an ambulance chaser who was always on the lookout for the hot topic of the day.

His chapter on the medical evidence in *Rush to Judgment* claimed the autopsy X-rays and photographs would "constitute the best evidence as to the nature of the wounds." Unfortunately, they had been "confiscated" by "federal police agents" and were not in the National Archives.

That was written in 1966 and it was now 1975. Had anything happened in the nine years since Lane's book had come out? I headed back to the library and went through the subject periodical indexes where I discovered that the autopsy X-rays and photographs were in the possession of the Kennedy family. In 1972, they were examined by two doctors—John Lattimer, a urologist who had made a hobby out of JFK's assassination, and Cyril Wecht, past President of the American Academy of Forensic Science, coroner for Allegheny County, Pennsylvania, and one of the foremost forensic pathologists in the United States. I found a directory of physicians, looked up their addresses, and wrote them both letters. About three weeks later I had received packages from both of them with all of their articles.

Lattimer was firmly in the lone-gunman camp and his illustrated articles on the medical evidence were superb. He conducted experiments by firing a Mannlicher-Carcano bullet through a simulated neck and found that the bullet started to tumble after exiting. His depiction of the single-bullet theory, published in the November 1974 issue of *Medical Times*, explained how such a bullet would explain the elongated wound in the back of Connally. The bullet would also enter Connally's wrist while almost backwards, thus accounting for the recovered lead particles, the bullet's flattened base, and it's so-called 'pristine' nature. This was a far better explanation of the single-bullet theory than described in the Warren Report.

FIGURE 10—THE PATH OF BULLET 399

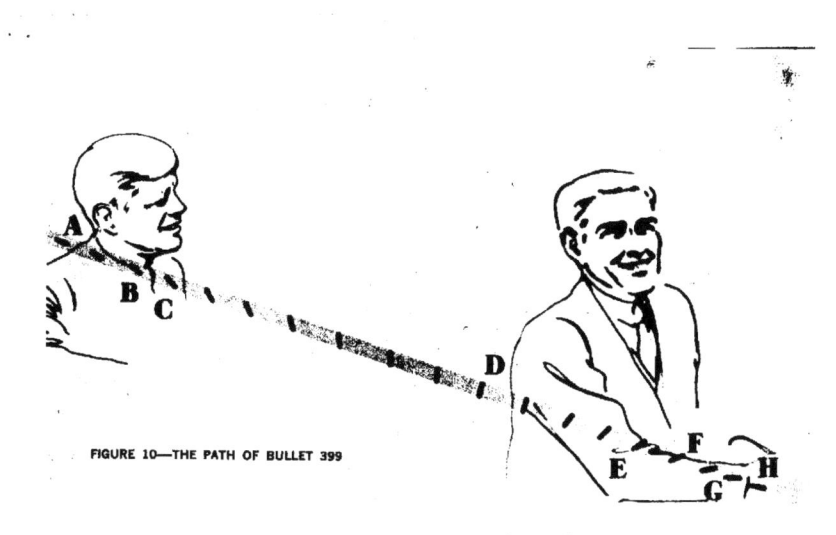

Drawing courtesy of Dr. Douglas G. Lattimer, son of Dr. John K. Lattimer, who was the first private doctor to examine the JFK autopsy X-rays and photographs. He also conducted experiments that proved a Mannlicher-Carcano bullet would tumble after exiting something like President Kennedy's neck.

I was much more interested in Wecht's articles since he was a forensics expert and was an outspoken critic of the Warren Report. But all of his articles were quite adamant—the head shot was *NOT* fired from the front. He wrote in *Forensic Science* that "The available evidence, assuming it to be valid, gives no support to theories which postulate gunmen to the front or right-front of the Presidential car. The wound in the President's head, as evidenced by the autopsy photographs and X-rays, can only have been fired from somewhere to the rear of the President."

Wecht wrote that the Zapruder Film showed that "when the President received his head wound, his head was momentarily driven forward about two inches." This was further proof that the bullet was fired from the rear—the fact that Kennedy's head moved forward before it moved back and to the left. That second movement was probably caused by a neuromuscular spasm causing involuntary muscle movement. There might also have been some minor movement due to something called the "jet effect" —the mass of material exiting from the right front of Kennedy's head may have helped push it backwards.

So if one of the best forensic pathologists in the United States believed that the shot came from behind, who am I to argue?

I experienced all this first-hand in December, 1975, at Concordia University when JFK critic Rusty Rhodes came to speak. During his presentation, he showed the Zapruder film a number of times and never mentioned anything about the autopsy X-rays and photographs. I wrote an article for the student newspaper calling Rhodes a "sensationalist."

Rusty Rhodes sensationalist

By FRED LITWIN

The *Montreal Gazette* account of his talk noted that "His $750 speaking fee will go toward completing the $12,000 he'll need to lead a team of forensic scientists into the National Archives." We're still waiting for his report.

Geraldo Rivera, Rusty Rhodes, and a host of other critics were all committing incredible errors of omission. They didn't dare mention that the autopsy materials—clearly the best medical evidence available— totally refuted a shot from the front. Rivera could have had Dr. Lattimer or Dr. Wecht on his show but that wouldn't have made for great television.

Ralph Schoenman's claims were also tendentious.

Secret Service document #767, dated December 16, 1963, does not say that Oswald was an agent of the FBI or the CIA. It contains rumours that Oswald was an FBI informant in regards to "subversive investigations." This was fully investigated by the Warren Commission and no evidence ever turned up to support the allegation.

The story was initially spread by *Houston Post* reporter Lonnie Hudkins. Assistant District Attorney William Alexander had told him that Oswald's phone directory had an entry for FBI agent James Hosty. Oswald had defected to the Soviet Union in 1959 and the FBI was trying to keep tabs on him after his return in 1962.

Hudkins called Hugh Aynesworth of the *Dallas Morning News* to see if he had also uncovered evidence that Oswald was an informant. Aynesworth had been on the ground in Dallas talking to many witnesses before they spoke to the police or the FBI. Here's a passage of Aynesworth's book, *Witness to History*:

> *Lonnie called once more and asked me, "You hear anything about this FBI link with Oswald?" Tired of him bugging me, I said to him, "You got his payroll number, don't you?"*
>
> *"Yeah, yeah," Lonnie said.*
>
> *I reached over on my desk for a telegram and read part of a Telex number to him.*
>
> *"Yeah, yeah," he said, "that's it. That the same one I've got." I knew that if Lonnie accepted the number as legitimate, he had nothing."*

Hudkins went on to publish a front-page story in the *Houston Post* titled, "Oswald Rumored as Informant for U.S." The story was completely speculative.

While Schoenman might not have known the Aynesworth story, he certainly could have just talked to Hudkins. Just five days after the airing of *Good Night America*, Hudkins told the *Dallas Morning News* that "he and two other Dallas men fabricated the FBI-Oswald story as a device to determine whether their phones were being tapped. Hudkins admitted that he had "no idea whether he worked for the FBI or not."

Schoenman was right that some documents were indeed locked in the National Archives. But there was nothing outrageous about this. It was standard policy to keep Presidential Commission records secret for 75 years. A request by Lyndon Johnson in 1965 led to the general release of Warren Commission documents, and by July, 1966, approximately 80% of records from the FBI and CIA and other agencies that the Warren Commission had placed in the National Archives had been released.

Ruby did plead to be taken back to Washington D.C. But he was a paranoid schizophrenic who believed that "through certain falsehoods that have been said about me to other people, the John Birch Society, I am as good as guilty as the accused assassin of President Kennedy." He worried that he would be "used as a scapegoat, and there is no greater weapon that you can use to create some falsehood about some of the Jewish faith, especially as the terrible heinous crime such as the killing of President Kennedy."

Thus, only by going to Washington could Ruby convince President Johnson that a new Holocaust was afoot. "I want to say this to you. The Jewish people are being exterminated at this moment. Consequently, a whole new form of government is going to take over our country, and I know I won't live to see you another time. Do I sound sort of screwy in telling you these things?" Ruby further said that "Now maybe something can be saved. It may not be too late, whatever happens, if our President, Lyndon Johnson, knew the truth from me."

And yes, while Ruby did believe that there was a larger conspiracy, he always maintained he had no direct knowledge of any plot. In 1965, while in jail, he had a series of psychological examinations conducted by Dr. Werner Tuteur, Professor of Psychiatry at Loyola University in Chicago. Ruby told him "he would make me acquainted with a conspiracy which I was to guard with the utmost secrecy." He then told Tuteur that he would obtain the book *Who Killed Kennedy?* by Thomas Buchanan, "from another inmate for me." Buchanan claimed that Kennedy was killed by oil magnates "who feared that Kennedy was about to curb their special tax interests." Ruby had no direct knowledge of any plot.

Tuteur wrote that "there were silences during the interviews, when Ruby would hold his head in his hands and would carefully listen to incidental noises, such as the squeaking of a door or the shuffling of feet by other prison inmates. He would then look at me, moving his chair somewhat, have a mournful expression and say, 'Do you hear crying?' He was convinced Jewish women and children were being slaughtered right there and then. This came to a climax when during the last interview a crew of plumbers began to dismantle a piece of equipment with heavy hammer blows, creating a great noise. Here Ruby found 'proof' of his allegation of the manslaughter of Jews on premises." An article on European antisemitism in the *Dallas Morning News* "acted upon Ruby's vast and unlimited system of fixed false beliefs like a match on a keg of dynamite. Now he was convinced that Jewish women and children were being killed in the adjoining room and all over the United States."

And finally, there was nothing suspicious about the death of Jack Ruby. After all, if somebody wanted him dead, why would they wait over three years—with many opportunities to spill the beans on any conspiracy—from when he killed Oswald? Ruby died on January 3, 1967, of a pulmonary embolism, secondary to lung cancer. The coroner of Dallas, Earl Rose, conducted an autopsy and found nothing mysterious. When his brain was sectioned after the autopsy they found lesions indicating that the cancer had spread.

All three of these men—Groden, Gregory, and Schoenman—would go on and disgrace themselves, each in their own way. But while Groden was new on to the stage, Gregory and Schoenman already had a track record which should have alerted any television producer.

Dick Gregory's lectures at college campuses around the country were just plain kooky.

Ramparts described one in 1975. "He said that unless the government began radical programs to assure the fair distribution of food to everyone, 80 percent of those now alive in America would be dead in four years…He said the government was deliberately alienating letter carriers, that the military was learning how to take over the Post Office, that the Interstate highways were built to provide landing strips for military airplanes. Fluorine and chlorine were being added to the water supply, he said, to program 'the super subconscious' to be hostile and aggressive."

After that lecture, about sixty students milled around and "He cautioned them against smoking, drinking, taking drugs, eating meat, fish or fowl. He told them that any sexual activity without procreation as its goal was degenerate and harmful. He said that maintaining an erection for more than 45 seconds led to cancer of the prostate. That an ejaculation proceeding from more than 45 seconds of intercourse shot the cancer into the womb."

After his appearance on Geraldo's show, he co-wrote a book with Mark Lane, *Code Name Zorro*, which postulated a conspiracy in the assassination of Martin Luther King. Back in 1968, Lane had been Gregory's running mate when he ran for president (he received 47,000 votes). Mark Lane would go on and represent James Earl Ray, the convicted assassin of King, before the HSCA. They weren't impressed, concluding that "the facts were often at variance with Lane's assertions. In many instances, the committee found that Lane was willing to advocate conspiracy theories publicly without having checked the factual basis for them. In other instances, Lane proclaimed conspiracy based on little more than inference and innuendo."

Gregory was interviewed on NPR in 2005 and they asked him, "what do you say to critics who say you always have a conspiracy theory?" His reply: "Well, first is I don't have to be validated by the *New York Times* or the *Washington Post*, and I tell them simply; go back and look at my books. I sit with Kathy Hughes on August 19th, the year that Princess Di was killed on August the 30th, and we did an hour-and-a-half show where I say, 'Kathy, if Princess Di owe [sic] any of you-all any money, or your friends, you better get it quick, because she'll probably be dead by the end of the month."

A 2006 article on the NBC news site encapsulated Gregory's conspiracy theories:

> "...federal agents actually shot Malcolm X and John F. Kennedy; the federal government blew up the levees in New Orleans; the D.C.-area sniper attacks were perpetrated by a White man in a white van, not by the two convicted Black simpletons; and Ron Brown, President Clinton's Commerce secretary, was killed by a bullet to the head, not in a plane crash as reported. Ghetto intelligence, he says, tells him nobody ever landed on the moon: "Those images of dust rising

and falling again when that astronaut steps on the planet could not be accurate because there's no gravity on the moon, and how could there be all those pictures with shadows when the moon is completely dark?"

Gregory spoke at the 97th annual convention of the NAACP in Washington, D.C., in 2009. He blamed pollution as the source of criminal violence in the black community. "Malt liquor is made by white beer companies but only sold in black neighborhoods, and you don't get suspicious? They put a thing called manganese, and once you get so much manganese in you, you will kill your momma, but they've got you believing that's normal for you to act that way."

He was also a 9/11 truther. He wrote an article for Global Research, a conspiracy website, started by Michel Chossudovsky, a former professor of economics at the University of Ottawa, announcing that he was starting a hunger strike in 2012 until what really happened on 9/11 is revealed. He believed that World Trade Center Towers One and Two were the victims of a controlled demolition, saying that "the official government story of those events, as well as what took place that day at the Pentagon, is just that, a story." That hunger strike got him on the Alex Jones Show, the first of three appearances, where he said that he was warned about 9/11 the night before and was told to leave New York City.

And in 2014 at a rally for a living wage bill in Washington, D.C., Gregory told a rally that "When you look at Hitler and those thugs, you can put Walmart right next to them."

Dick Gregory died in 2017 at the age of 84.

To Schoenman, the minutia about the JFK assassination was only interesting insofar as he could link it to Watergate and the Bay of Pigs via CIA counterintelligence. He submitted a 28-page report to the Rockefeller

Panel in 1975, which was investigating CIA involvement in domestic activities. The report used a "six degrees of separation" style to link disparate people together. "An examination of the life of Oswald reveals that his constant associations and involvement were with military intelligence and CIA." Nice sentence but Schoenman provided no evidence to back it up.

In a 1992 article, he wrote, "The uncovering of their murder [Robert & John Kennedy], thus, has always been in the realm of 'Who Killed Caesar' rather than the crucifixion, the latter more analogous to the fate of Martin Luther King and Malcolm X. It does not require romanticizing John and Robert Kennedy to understand the dynamics of their executions nor who rules America."

So just who was Ralph Schoenman?

In 1958, he studied at the London School of Economics and graduated with a Master's degree. He then became involved with the famous philosopher Bertrand Russell and ultimately became his personal secretary. In September, 1961, they were both arrested at a Campaign for Nuclear Disarmament (CND) demonstration and the British Home Office attempted to deport Schoenman.

Paul Johnson, in his book, *Intellectuals*, writes that "large numbers of prominent progressives signed a petition that he be allowed to stay, and the government relented. Later they bitterly regretted their intercession when Schoenman appeared to establish complete mastery over Russell's mind, as Chertkov had over Tolstoy's. It was sometimes difficult for old friends to speak to Russell on the phone: Schoenman answered the calls and merely undertook to relay the messages. He was also accused of being the real author of the many letters Russell wrote to The Times or the statements sent in his name to press agencies, commenting on world events. He claimed that 'every major political initiative that has borne the name of Bertrand Russell since 1960 has been my work in thought and deed'; it was, he said, at least 'a partial truth' that the old man had been 'taken over by a sinister young revolutionary".

In 1967, the *New York Times* published an article by UK journalist Bernard Levin, "Bertrand Russell: Prosecutor, Judge and Jury," accusing Schoenman of fanning Russell's anti-Americanism. "How has it come about that a man possessed of one of the finest, most acute minds of our time—of any time—has fallen into a state of such gullibility, lack of discrimination, twisted logic and rancorous hatred of the United States that he has turned into a full-time purveyor of political garbage indistinguishable from the routine products of the Soviet machine?"

The Harvard *Crimson* profiled Schoenman in March, 1968, and he told them that he shared Che Guevara's vision of continuing revolution. He quotes Che: "The struggle of the Cuban revolution is the struggle for the extension of the Revolution in Latin America." Schoenman pauses and then continues. "Elan is only a thing which can mobilize the people." Warren Hinckle wrote that "There is scarcely a left-wing case the doorway of which Schoenman has not darkened."

By the end of 1969, Russell had disavowed Schoenman publicly (page 3 in the December 10, 1969, edition of the *New York Times*) and dictated a 7,000-word "Private Memorandum Concerning Ralph Schoenman," posthumously published in the *New Statesman*. A large part of the document is clearly self-serving; after all, Schoenman worked for Russell for almost nine years, and he couldn't be totally oblivious to Schoenman's style. But he does capture Schoeman's essence—"his utter incapability of imparting reliable information. His reports of people's reactions and his observations were—and unfortunately, I fear, still are—very often excessively and misleadingly incorrect and his quotations must always be verified...this letter leaves me with the impression that Ralph must be well established in megalomania."

According to Warren Hinckle, "Ralph's capacity to sire dislike was greater than any person I have known; Sartre was said to gargle after speaking with him."

Did Geraldo Rivera and his staff not know any of this about Ralph Schoenman? Did they not know what a loon Gregory was? I suspect they did but just didn't care. Dick Gregory was a big draw and the three of them were a package deal—putting them all on the air was the only way to show the Zapruder film.

Schoenman continued his descent with his April 1988 book, *The Hidden History of Zionism,* where he argued that "to most people it appears anomalous that the Zionist movement, which forever invokes the horror of the Holocaust, should have collaborated actively with the most vicious enemy ever faced by the Jews. The record, however, reveals not merely common interests but a deep ideological affinity rooted in the extreme chauvinism which they share."

Schoenman took his anti-Israel animus on campus and in November, 1994, he spoke at San Francisco State University. His lecture was entitled, "Zionism is Racism!" and the flyer for the event said he would talk about "Isreali [sic] brutality and Zionist imperialism throughout Africa, Latin Amer., and Palestine…Come find out why the Zionists hide behind the term, 'anti-Semitic' when they are condemned by the masses for their evil actions against helpless people."

In the early 1990s, Schoenman became a board member of the Socialist Organizer, a Trotskyist organization based in San Francisco. In 1995, he wrote for their publication, *The Organizer,* that "the killing of John F. Kennedy in a virtual *coup d'état* permitted massive intervention in Indochina—and profits of $800 billion…The death of the Kennedy brothers, like that of Julius Caesar, flows from such combat over forms of investment and the means of their imposition. Captains of capital unite, however, in the official terror required to maintain their bloody rule."

9/11 was another opportunity for Schoenman to continue his ridiculous narrative. Once again writing for *The Organizer*, he claimed that "—The missile attacks upon the civilian population of Khartoum [President Clinton bombed a chemical factory in Sudan in response to the attacks on the American Embassies in Tanzania and Kenya] and of Afghanistan are part of a vast campaign of official state terror which includes the terrorizing of the American people with operations planned and executed by U.S. rulers. Vast military budgets—$9 trillion in 40 years—sustain the profits of the ruthless oligarchy who rules America through a network of clandestine agencies at the service of banking and corporate capital."

For several years, Schoenman was out peddling his decrepit left-wing politics on radio. His show, *Taking Aim Audio*, on WBAI-NY allowed him to continue his 9/11 truther diatribes, tout a variety of alleged false flag operations, and analyze the so-called 'terror state.' The show ended in 2010 because he claimed WBAI's "methods are those of any corporate-capitalist management." It then moved online, although as of October, 2017, the website is no longer available.

Robert Groden would go on and become a consultant to the HSCA. He charged that some of the JFK autopsy photographs had been doctored, an allegation which was totally refuted by the HSCA. In 1993, he published *The Killing of a President*, a coffee-table book which contained hundreds of photographs. Groden theorized a total of eight shots coming from five different locations. He continued his claims that the autopsy photographs were "tampered with, and forged," and insisted that there is a "shadow enemy we are fighting—and must continue to fight."

In the 1996 civil trial of O.J. Simpson, Groden testified that a picture of Simpson wearing Bruno Magli shoes (investigators had identified a bloody shoe print at the crime scene that was made by Bruno Magli shoes) was forged. He credibility was demolished when thirty other pictures by another photographer captured Simpson with the same shoes.

You can still find Robert Groden today sitting at a table in Dealey Plaza selling his DVDs and books.

Gregory and Schoenman used the JFK assassination to drive home myths about who controlled America. But if there was no conspiracy in the Kennedy assassination, there could be no connection to Watergate, the Bay of Pigs, or any other abuses of power, so they latched onto events like 9/11 to further their discourse on power in America.

This wouldn't be the last time someone used the assassination to further their political views. The next person would shake America to the core.

Four

Oliver Stone's Excellent Homosexual Adventure

Homosexuals have been portrayed as evil since the story of Sodom & Gomorrah. Easy prey who would not fight back, gays were often the targets of novelists and filmmakers. According to the 1995 documentary, *The Celluloid Closet,* gay men were originally portrayed as 'pansies' in the 1930s but moved to 'sexual perverts, sadists, psychopaths and social villains' in the 1940s. The famed author Norman Mailer wrote *The Homosexual Villain* in 1954, in which he apologized for his laziness in purposely making two of his own characters evil homosexuals. He wrote, "I have been as guilty as any contemporary novelist in attributing unpleasant, ridiculous, or sinister connotations to the homosexual (or more accurately, bisexual) characters in my novels."

The censorship code began to liberalize in the 1950s and 1960s and there were fewer and fewer wicked homosexuals. Still, some authors couldn't help themselves—in 1988, the right-wing novelist Tom Clancy was profiled in a cover story in *Newsweek*. "A devout and conservative Roman Catholic, he is an unapologetic homophobe: the leaky Congressman in *Cardinal of the Kremlin* is gay and the female KGB agent is a lesbian."

But guess who produced a hugely popular modern-day movie about an evil homosexual conspiracy? Well, that would be none other than the leftist film director Oliver Stone. His 1991 film, *JFK,* featured, yes, you guessed it—a ridiculous homosexual plot behind the assassination of U.S. President John F. Kennedy. But Stone didn't just make a film about homosexuals killing Kennedy; he made a film about Jim Garrison—yes, the real-life prosecutor who wrongfully charged a gay man of conspiring with other homosexuals to kill Kennedy. A man whose life he wrecked and who ultimately spent most of his life savings defending himself. Incredibly, Stone made Garrison the hero and his innocent gay victim, Clay Shaw, the evil villain.

JFK was nominated for eight Academy Awards (and won two), Stone was nominated for Outstanding Directing by the Directors Guild of America, and he won a Golden Globe for Best Director. More than 25 million people saw *JFK* and it grossed over $205 million worldwide. Historian Michael Kurtz wrote that "with the exception of *Uncle Tom's Cabin*, Harriet Beecher Stowe's explosive novel dramatizing the horrors of the institution of slavery, *JFK* probably had a greater impact on public opinion than any other work of art in American history."

Now that's filmmaking!

In early 1970, Jim Garrison published *A Heritage of Stone*, blaming the CIA for the JFK assassination. The name Clay Shaw didn't appear once in the book, largely because of ongoing litigation. Ralph Schoenman wrote Garrison a letter In July 1971, proposing a new strategy: "By stopping you from using the courts against Shaw, they have FREED you to put the case into a book. Now it cannot be considered sub judice or prejudicial to a trial. So, I suggest urgently that we take the offensive. Let's get out a book, hard and fast, which nails the case against Shaw that we couldn't get into the courts.... let's put THEM on the defensive by blowing the Shaw case sky high with a muck-raking book that closes in on the company even closer."

On the Trail of the Assassins: My Investigation and Prosecution of the Murder of President Kennedy was published in 1988. Fifteen major publishers turned the book down and it took Garrison four years to find a small press willing to put it out. Garrison once again laid out the same non-existent case against Shaw, except he now claimed that Oswald was a "CIA recruit—an agent provocateur—who soon became their patsy."

But one person was mightily impressed, and that was filmmaker Oliver Stone who read it three times, and then purchased the movie rights for $250,000. To Stone, "it read like a Dashiell Hammett whodunit," and he felt that Garrison was "somewhat like a Jimmy Stewart character in an old Capra movie." Stone hired Garrison's editor, Zachary Sklar, to write the screenplay. He also licensed *Crossfire: The Plot That Killed Kennedy* from Jim Marrs, a crackpot author who would go on to publish titles such as *Our Occulted History: Do The Global Elite Conceal Ancient Aliens?*; *Rule by Secrecy: The Hidden History that Connects the Trilateral Commission, the Freemasons, and the Great Pyramids*; *The Trillion-Dollar Conspiracy: How the New World Order, Man-Made Diseases, and Zombie Banks are Destroying America*; and *The Rise of the Fourth Reich: The Secret Societies that Threaten to Take Over America*.

Crossfire left no conspiracy stone unturned. As one author put it, "By purchasing the rights to *Crossfire*, he was in effect buying the rights to dozens of different conspiracy theories without buying the rights to dozens of books."

Stone believed that Garrison had tried to "force a break in the case" and that he was a man out for the truth who was willing to take on the CIA, the military-industry complex, and the national security infrastructure. It was "worth the sacrifice of one man" and so Stone kept Clay Shaw as the evil gay mastermind along with his band of conspiring homosexuals.

In the early part of his film *JFK*, Garrison has dinner with Dean Andrews who paints Lee Harvey Oswald as a homosexual:

Garrison: You tell them [the Warren Commission] *the day after the assassination, you're called on the phone by this Clay Bertrand and you're asked to fly to Dallas to be Oswald's lawyer.*

Andrews: Right.

Garrison: That's pretty important, Dean. You also told the FBI that when you met him he's 6-foot two. Didn't you tell the Commission he's 5-foot 8? How the hell does a man shrink like that, Dean?

Andrews: They put the heat on me, man, just like you doing. I gave them anything that popped in my cabeza. Truth is, I never met the dude. I don't know what that cat looks like or... furthermore, I don't know where he's at. All I know is sometimes he sends me some cases. One day he is on the phone, talks to me about going to Dallas repping Oswald.

Garrison: You ever speak to Oswald in Dallas?

Andrews: Hell no. Like, I told that Bertrand cat right off this ain't my scene, man. I deal in muni court. I'm a hack. He needs a hot dog.

Garrison: Then how did you get in the Warren Commission?

Andrews: Like I told to the Washington boys, Bertrand called that summer and asked me to help the kid upgrade his

> *Marine discharge. There was no conspiracy, Jim. If there were, why didn't Bobby Kennedy prosecute as attorney general? He was his brother, for Christ sake. How the fuck all these people can keep a secret like that, I don't know. It was Oswald, he was a fruitcake. He hated this country.*

(The scenes from *JFK* in this essay are all transcribed directly from the film, and not from the official screenplay which is far more homophobic. For instance, in the above scene the screenplay uses the word faggot instead of fruitcake.)

The main witness against Clay Shaw, Perry Russo, is transformed in *JFK* into a homosexual prostitute, Willie O'Keefe, who talks to Garrison while in prison.

> *Garrison: I want to thank you, Mr. O'Keefe for your time.*
>
> *O'Keefe: Yah, I got nothing but time, Mr. Garrison. Minutes, Hours, days, Years of it. Time just standing still here. Like a snake sunning itself.*
>
> *Bill Broussard (Garrison's Assistant): Clay Bertrand, Willie?*
>
> *O'Keefe: Clay? Met him sometime in June of '62. The Masquerade Bar. Dave Ferrie took me there for the express reason to meet him.*
>
> *Garrison: Sexual Purposes?*
>
> *O'Keefe: Well, yeah!*

Garrison: Did he pay you for this?

O'Keefe: $20 each time. Hell, ain't no secret. That's what I'm in here for.

Garrison: Anything else unusual about him, you'd be able to describe in a court of law?

O'Keefe: He had some kind of thing wrong with his leg. A limp. You know, don't get me wrong. He's not one of those limp wrists. He's a butch John. Meet him on the street, you'd never snap. You could play poker with him, go fishing, you'd never snap.

Then O'Keefe tells Garrison about a party at David Ferrie's apartment in the summer of 1963 with Ferrie, O'Keefe, Bertrand, Oswald, and two Cubans.

O'Keefe (voiceover): Dave pulled out some clippings that he'd been carrying around. He'd been obsessed with Castro and Kennedy for months. He started in again.

Ferrie: Little ass-wipe closed down the camps! Took all our C-4! Took 10,000 rounds! 3,000 pounds of gunpowder! All our fucking weapons! Shit, you want to free Cuba? You gotta whack out the fucking beard!

First Cuban: Kennedy won't let us. Our hands are empty. How can we kill him?

Bertrand: Problem is getting to him. Castro has informers on every block.

Ferrie: Bullshit. They got new stuff! I could show you dozens of fucking poisons! Just stick it in his food, he'd die in three days. No trace! Put something in his beard, make his beard fall out. He'd look ridiculous....

Second Cuban: Fucking Kennedy is doing all kinds of deals with that bastard Khrushchev. Licking his ass (in Spanish). An inspired act of God should happen here and put a Texan in the White House!

O'Keefe (voiceover): Then, the Cubans left. Dave was drunk. Now, really drunk. He started in on Kennedy again.

Ferrie: I will kill! Right in the White House! Stab him in the heart! Somebody got get rid of this fucker!

O'Keefe: C'mon Dave, ain't nobody going to get that son of a bitch!

Ferrie: It won't be long. Mark my words. That fucker will get what is coming to him. It could be blamed on Castro; the country will want to invade Cuba. All we got to do is get Kennedy out in the open.

Bertrand [who is Clay Shaw]: David, David, David. Always some harebrained scheme. [He looks down at his crotch and sees an erection.] What have we here? Let's have some more champagne, shall we?

O'Keefe: What about the Secret Service? The cops?

Ferrie: If it's planned right, no problem. Look how close they got to De Gaulle. Eisenhower was always riding in an open top. We need three mechanics in three different locations. An office building, with a high-powered rifle. Triangulation of crossfire, that's the key. That's the key. A diversionary shot gets the Secret Service looking the other way. Boom! Get the kill shot. Crucial thing is that one man has to be sacrificed. Then, in the commotion of the crowd, the job gets done. The others fly out of the country, somewhere with no extradition...

Bertrand: Why don't we drop this subject? It's one thing to engage in badinage [banter] *with these youngsters...but this sort of thing could be so easily misunderstood.*

O'Keefe (voiceover): I didn't think much about it at the time. It's just bullshit. You know everybody likes to act more important than they are. Especially in the homosexual underworld. But when they got him (merging to the present) ...man...I got scared. Real scared. That's when I got popped.

There's the conspiracy—hatched by the "homosexual underworld." Not surprisingly, the notes to *JFK: The Documented Screenplay* admits that "At times, however, we had to put words in Ferrie's mouth to write the scene."

Soon afterwards, O'Keefe goes to Clay Shaw's house for dinner. David Ferrie stops by, they change into a variety of costumes, with Ferrie's body painted in gold, consume some cocaine, and then engage in an orgy with some light S&M, all of which is a complete Oliver Stone invention:

> *We see the four men in drag, smiling for the flash camera, champagne bottles in hand. Ferrie sniffs some poppers, then shoves a popper in Shaw's face.*
>
> FERRIE: *You're mine, Mary. You're mine.*
>
> *Ferrie forces more poppers on Shaw. The camera moves to Shaw's bedroom, where Ferrie seems to have Shaw in chains.*
>
> *Ferrie grabs Shaw by his hair: The only way you get this is do what I say. Go on, big boy. You want it.*

In another scene, Garrison puts up a distraught David Ferrie in a hotel—and Stone makes up some more incredible dialogue.

> *Garrison: Who are you scared of, Dave?*
>
> *Ferrie: Me? Everybody. The Agency, mob, Cubans. That's it. Follow the Cubans. Check them out. Here. In Miami. Dallas. Check out a guy named Eladio del Valle. He was my paymaster when I flew missions into Cuba. Somewhere in Miami. You're on the right track. Hey, hey, don't be writing this down! I ain't cooperating with no one! What's going on here? There's a death warrant for me! Don't you get it? Damn!*

Wait a minute! You ain't bugged, are you? Son of a bitch, Lou! Are you?

Lou (Garrison's Assistant): Dave, I always play square. No bugs. I'd love you to go on the record, but I'm in no hurry.

Ferrie: I haven't slept since that shit article came out. Why'd you guys have to get me involved, Lou?

Lou: Did we get you involved? Or did Shaw, Dave?

Ferrie: Cocksucking faggot. He got me by the balls.

Lou: What do you mean?

Ferrie: Photographs, compromising stuff. He'll use them, too. Agency plays for keeps. I knew Oswald. He was in my Civil Air Patrol unit. I taught him everything. He was a wannabe, you know. No one really liked him. Thought he was a snitch. But I treated him good. He talked about his kid. He really wanted...to grow up with a chance. But, what's this? What's going on?

So now we have Shaw blackmailing Ferrie through the use of photographs and other compromising material. This scene clearly places Shaw as the ringleader of the homosexual cabal, although he was the slave at the orgy at Ferrie's home. But Stone has bigger fish to fry than just a bunch of homosexuals sitting around plotting to kill a president, and so he ties Clay Shaw to the CIA by repeating the slander from *Paese Sera*:

Garrison: Mr. Shaw, this Italian newspaper saying you were a board member of Centro Mondo Commercial [sic] *in Italy. That this company was a creature of the CIA for the transfer of funds in Italy for illegal political espionage activities. It says this company was expelled from Italy for these activities.*

Shaw: I'm well aware of that asinine article. I'm thinking of suing that rag.

Garrison: It also says this company is linked to the Schlumberger Tool Company, near Houma in Louisiana, which provided arms to David Ferrie and his Cubans.

Stone's *JFK: The Documented Screenplay* also tosses out the spurious charge that "Charles de Gaulle drew attention to Permindex [parent company of the CMC], publicly accusing it of raising funds for the Secret Army Organization (OAS) that tried on several occasions to assassinate him." His sources are Jim Marr's book *Crossfire*; the *Executive Intelligence Review*, a Lyndon LaRouche publication; the *Le Devoir* newspaper [the article referenced in Chapter Two]; and an insane conspiracy document known as the "Torbitt Memorandum," which posits that all sorts of fascists, including Werner von Braun, killed Kennedy, and which was published as a book, *NASA, Nazis & JFK: The Torbitt Document & the Kennedy Assassination,* in 1996. All of these sources circle back to *Paese Sera*.

Now that the film connects Shaw to the CIA, Stone introduces us to a former military man, X. Garrison meets him in Washington, D.C., and X reveals why Kennedy was killed. "The organizing principle of any society is for war," he tells Garrison and adds that Kennedy had to be killed because he was going to violate that tenet by pulling troops out of Vietnam and ending the Cold War. In addition, X claimed that the 112th Military Intelligence Group at Fort Sam Houston was ordered to "stand down" on Kennedy's protection in Dallas and that standard security procedures were violated on November 22.

All of this was delusional.

Kennedy did have plans to remove 1,000 troops by the end of 1963 because of supposed progress in training the South Vietnamese Army. National Security Memorandum #273, signed by Lyndon Johnson a few days after the assassination, said that "The objectives of the United States with respect to the withdrawal of U. S. military personnel remain as stated in the White House statement of October 2, 1963."

In September, 1963, Kennedy told CBS reporter Walter Cronkite that "I don't agree with those who say we should withdraw," and he told NBC reporter Chet Huntley that "we are not there to see a war lost." In the speech he was supposed to give in Dallas, Kennedy was going to say that Vietnam was going to be "painful, risky and costly…but we dare not weary of the task," adding that "reducing our efforts to train, equip and assist [the allied] armies can only encourage Communist penetration and require in the time the increased overseas deployment of American combat forces." Secretary of State Dean Rusk "had hundreds of talks with John F. Kennedy about Vietnam, and never once did he say anything of this sort to his own secretary of state." Robert Kennedy also confirmed in an oral history interview in April, 1964, that JFK never contemplated pulling out of Vietnam.

This is not to say that Kennedy would have sent half a million ground troops to Vietnam. We just don't know what he would have done in the same circumstances as Lyndon Johnson.

There were also no orders to stand down protection in Dallas. In fact, the 112th Military Intelligence group provided eight to twelve people to protect Kennedy, in addition to the regular Secret Service contingent. Security was lax in the early 1960s and there was no evidence that the Secret Service did not follow standard operating procedures.

It's a left-wing myth that Kennedy wanted to end the Cold War. His planned speech for Austin, Texas, bragged about his increases in the military budget. "In the past three years we have increased our defense budget by over 20 percent; increased the program for acquisition of Polaris submarines from 25 to 41; increased our Minuteman missile purchase program by more than 75 percent; doubled the number of strategic bombers and missiles on alert; doubled the number of nuclear weapons available in the strategic alert forces; increased the tactical nuclear forces deployed in western Europe by 60 percent; added 5 combat ready divisions and 5 tactical fighter wings to our Armed Forces; increased our strategic airlift capabilities by 75 percent, and increased our special counter-insurgency forces by 600 percent." Kennedy was a Cold Warrior through and through.

So where did Stone get such nonsense? His technical advisor was Colonel L. Fletcher Prouty who worked in the Pentagon's Office of Special Operations before retiring in December, 1963. Prouty had a history of crackpot relationships: he was a consultant to the cult-like Lyndon LaRouche organization; he consulted for lawyers working for the Church of Scientology; and he was a speaker at the 1990 Convention of the Liberty Lobby, a far-right organization whose founder, Willis Carto, also set up the Institute for Historical Review, an organization that denied the Holocaust. Carto believed that the Jews were "public enemy number one."

The Institute for Historical Review also republished Prouty's 1973 book, *The Secret Team: The CIA and Its Allies in Control of the United States and the World* in 1991. According to Edward Jay Epstein, a long-time JFK researcher, "when the Liberty Lobby held its annual Board of Policy convention in 1991, he [Prouty] presented a special seminar, 'Who is the Enemy?' which blamed the high price of oil on a systematic plot of a cabal to shut down oil pipelines deliberately in the Middle East. 'Why?' he asked and explained to the seminar: 'Because of the Israelis. That is their business on behalf of the oil companies. That's why they get $3 billion a year from the U.S. taxpayer.'"

None of this mattered to Oliver Stone. Robert San Anson wrote a history of the making of the film in *Esquire* magazine and he recounts that when Prouty was asked about Carto's belief that the Holocaust never happened, he replied that "I'm no authority in that area." He quotes a Stone assistant saying, "If this gets out, Oliver is going to look like the biggest dope of all time."

And guess who introduced Prouty's work to Oliver Stone? None other than Jim Garrison.

The biggest laugh is that Prouty's knowledge about the so-called "organizing principle" of society came from a study that was supposedly suppressed by the Kennedy administration. The Iron Mountain Group report wondered if the U.S. could survive "if and when a condition of permanent peace should arise?" But the report was a complete hoax—it was a spoof written by satirist Leonard Lewin in 1967. Victor Navasky, who went on to become editor of *The Nation*, persuaded the publisher to put it on the non-fiction lists. It certainly fooled a lot of people but Prouty should have known better—Lewin admitted to the hoax in the *New York Times Book Review* in 1972, where he said his intention "was simply to pose the issues of war and peace in a provocative way."

Prouty's 1992 book, *The CIA, Vietnam, and the Plot to Assassinate John F. Kennedy* (first serialized in *Freedom* magazine, a Church of Scientology publication) refers to the Iron Mountain Group Report over ten times and claims it originated with "an organization whose existence was so highly classified that there is no record, to this day, of the men in the group were or with what sectors of the government or private life they were connected."

To give you an idea of the utter craziness of Prouty's book, here's a paragraph about the "power elite:"

> The man was Thomas Malthus, who, in 1805, postulated the idea that humanity is multiplying its numbers at a geometric rate while increasing its life-supporting capability at only an arithmetic rate. As a result, it has been universally concluded by the power elite that only a relatively few humans are destined to survive successfully in generations to come. The Malthusian theory thus provides a rationalization for the necessity of somehow getting rid of large numbers of people, any people, in any way—even genocide. With the Malthusian theory as the power elite's philosophical guide, this becomes an acceptable objective, because, they believe, Earth will never be able to support the progeny of so many anyhow. From this point of view, genocide—then as now—is accepted as all but inevitable. Who cares and why be concerned?

It's one thing for Prouty to fall for this nonsense, but Oliver Stone?

In fact, Stone wrote the Introduction to Prouty's book. He said the Iron Mountain Report asked "the key question of our time," and accepts the myth that it was "commissioned by Defense Secretary Robert McNamara in August 1963 to justify the big, planned changes in defense spending contemplated by Kennedy." Stone was impressed that "Colonel Prouty points once again to the infusion of Nazi personnel, methods, and ultimately a Nazi frame of mind into the American system." Stone surmised that "If Mr. Hitler had won the Second World War, the version of events now given to us (invasion of Third World lower slave races for mineral-resource conquest and world-round economic-military power) would not be too far off the mark. But instead of Nazi jackboots, we have men in gray suits and ties with attaché cases."

Stone ended *JFK* with two additional slights of Clay Shaw. The film closed with a note: "In 1979, RICHARD HELMS, Director of Covert Operations in 1963, admitted under oath that CLAY SHAW had worked for the CIA." Shaw did have a relationship with the CIA but it was as an unpaid domestic contact who reported what he saw on various foreign trips from 1949-1956. All of his reports were on international trade. Stone also added that "CLAY SHAW died in 1974 of lung cancer. No autopsy was allowed." This makes it sound suspicious but the New Orleans police department investigated his death and found that "no evidence has been found to indicate that Mr. Shaw's death was anything but natural." He didn't need an autopsy because his attending physician had been present quite often in the week while his health deteriorated.

There was huge critical reaction to *JFK*.

David Ehrenstein, writing in the *Advocate*, a popular gay magazine, called *JFK* "the most homophobic movie ever to come out of Hollywood." Stone replied that "the characters of Shaw, Ferrie, and the composite character Willie O'Keefe were historically gay. You cannot be—at the same time, politically correct and a historical revisionist. They were gay, and they were involved in this conspiracy." It's almost like Stone had no choice in the matter.

Oliver Stone's JFK — Pinko Homos Iced the Prez?

THE ADVOCATE

JANUARY 14, 1992 • THE NATIONAL GAY AND LESBIAN NEWSMAGAZINE • ISSUE 594

Of course, the homophobic nature of the film goes beyond the script. As Ehrenstein notes, "Forget about bullet trajectories and smoke seen coming from the grassy knoll. All Stone has to do is show a sinister Jones [actor Tommy Lee Jones playing Clay Shaw] groping sleazy tootsie Bacon [O'Keefe in the film] and acting simperingly haughty toward true-blue Costner [Garrison] and you know who 'really' killed Kennedy." An opinion piece in the *New York Times* added that "Shaw's homosexuality is meant to signify nothing except the fact that he's sinister, and capable of murder. The inclusion of the orgy scene is gratuitous. Mr. Stone might as well have shown Jack Ruby bargaining with other Jews in the back row at temple."

Columnist George Will wrote that "Stone is forty-five going on eight. In his 3-hour lie, Stone falsifies so much he may be an intellectual sociopath." *Washington Post* reporter George Lardner, the last person to see David Ferrie alive, called the film, "Dallas in Wonderland." Charles Krauthammer pointed out that "In one corner, a $40 million Hollywood film, featuring the nation's number one heartthrob, endowed with a publicity budget of millions, shown in 900 theaters. In the other hand, perhaps a dozen scribblers, writing in various magazines and op-ed pages. You don't need Marshall McLuhan to figure out who's got more clout."

Stone spent most of 1991 and 1992 battling *JFK*'s critics. He wrote letters, op-eds, and was forced to dive into the minutia of the assassination.

People wanted to talk about magical bullets, the backwards head snap, and Clay Shaw, not Vietnam. And so, when 9/11 happened, Stone avoided the truthers. He was far more interested in talking about the end results of 9/11, like the Iraq war. Still, he couldn't help but say stupid things. The following discussion took place at a panel discussion, in October 2001, on "the role of filmmaking in the national debate:"

> *Stone: There's been conglomeration under six principal princes—they're kings, they're barons! And these six companies have control of the world. Michael Eisner decides, "I can't make a movie about Martin Luther King, Jr.—they'll be rioting at the gates of Disneyland!" That's bullshit! But, that's what the new world order is. They control culture, they control ideas. And I think the revolt of September 11th was about 'Fuck You! Fuck your order –"*
>
> *Christopher Hitchens: Excuse me, revolt?*
>
> *Stone: Whatever you want to call it.*
>
> *Christopher Hitchens: It was state-supported mass murder* [by Islamists], *using civilians as missiles.*

In December, 2001, Stone spoke at Brown University and said that "Bin Laden was completely protected by the oil companies in this country who told [President] Bush not to go after him because it would piss off the Saudis."

Stone has gone on to kookier and kookier projects—combining his post-modern leftism with his conspiracy groupthink. In 2003, Stone made a documentary, *Commandante*, about Cuban dictator Fidel Castro. HBO was going to show the film on TV, but Castro then threw 75 dissidents in jail and the film was pulled. He then sat down with Anne Louis Bardach of *Slate* for an interview:

> *Bardach: So, after 60 hours with Castro, what do you make of this man?*
>
> *Stone: I'm totally awed by his ability to survive and maintain a strong moral presence ... and we ignore him now at our peril if we start another war with Cuba.*
>
> *Bardach: You say we ignore him at our peril. It seems to me that we're obsessed with him.*
>
> *Stone: No, I think the focus is wrong. Fidel is not the revolution, believe me. Fidel is popular, whatever his enemies say. It's Zapata, remember that movie? He said, "A strong people don't need a strong leader."*
>
> *Bardach: So, you think that if he went off the scene the revolution would continue?*
>
> *Stone: If Mr. Bush and his people have the illusion that they're going to walk into an Iraq-type situation, and people are going to throw up their arms and welcome us, [they are] dead wrong. These people are committed. Castro has become a spiritual leader. He will always be a Mao to those people.*

Stone fell into further dementia in 2010 when he told the *Sunday Times* that Jewish control of the media was preventing an open discussion of the Holocaust and that an upcoming film of his would put Hitler and Stalin in context. To Stone, "Israel had 'f***** up American foreign policy" for years and current American policy towards Iran was "horrible." Stone apologized for his "clumsy association" about the Holocaust but told the *New York Times* that "I had to apologize because I should not have used the word 'Jewish'. That was the only thing that's frankly wrong in that statement. I was upset at the time about Israel and their control, their seeming control over American foreign policy. It's clear that Jews do not dominate the media…but certainly AIPAC [American Israel Public Affairs Committee] has an undue influence. They were very much militating for the war in Iraq. They got it."

Stone could never put Hitler and Stalin in context. In 1997, he was one of the signatories on a petition in Germany protesting the persecution of Scientologists, claiming that "the Bonn government is oppressing members of the group in the same way that the Nazi regime persecuted the Jews."

In 2012, he released *South of the Border,* which looked at the rise of left-wing leaders in Latin America with a focus on Hugo Chavez of Venezuela. *Foreign Policy* magazine said that "more troubling is how *South of the Border* masquerades as journalism…the film leaves the viewer flush with platitudes about the leader's Bolivarian revolution, but with a head full of unanswered questions about how it actually works… In the end, the film tells us less about Latin America than it does about Oliver Stone, and his career-long quest to expose Washington's supposedly implacable hegemonic designs." Ron Radosh, writing in *Pajamas Media* noted that "there are no dissenting voices in this film. Nor is there any mention of the fact Mr. Chavez has closed down television and radio stations that disagree with him and arrested dissenting political figures."

Stone went one step further in 2013 and produced *The Untold History of the United States*. The 750-page book (mostly written by Peter Kuznick) and ten-episode mini-series allowed Stone to present an 'alternate' view of American history, one that portrayed the US as the perpetual bad guy always on the wrong side. This was clearly the film he was referencing when he criticized the Jewish lobby back in 2010.

Just a short perusal of the book shows the twisted view of Stone and co-author Kuznick. In 1988, "Palestine Liberation Organization Leader Yasir Arafat, under pressure from Moscow, renounced terrorism and implicitly recognized Israel's right to exist."; Osama bin Laden was "part of the CIA netherworld, recruiting and training the foreign militants who flooded into Afghanistan to battle the Soviet infidels;" it was "U.S. obtuseness and inflexibility" that led to the Taliban not turning over bin Laden to the U.S.; that Iraq under Saddam Hussein in the early 2000s "posed no threat;" and that "among the groups lobbying Congress to support the war was the American Israel Public Relations Committee (AIPAC), an influential organization that was considerably to the right of mainstream American Jewish opinion and general in lockstep with the neocons on Middle East policy."

And then there's this delusion about Iran: "Then, after extensive informal discussion, Iran proposed a grand bargain in May 2003. In exchange for enhanced security, mutual respect, and access to peaceful nuclear technology, Iran offered recognition of Israel as part of two-state solution, "full transparency" on its nuclear program; help in stabilizing Iraq; action against terrorist groups in Iran; the halting of material support for Palestinian opposition groups, including Hamas, and pressuring them to "stop violent actions against civilians" in Israel, and a concerted effort to transform Hezbollah into a "mere political organization within Lebanon." Stone and Kuznick claim that the administration neocons "rejected the Iranian initiative and girded for war." Except that there was no such offer—the Swiss Ambassador overstepped his authority and inserted some of his own terms into a supposed offer from Iran. No one at the State Department, particularly those who were in the realist camp, believed this was a true offer from the Khomeinists.

He also quotes Zbigniew Brzezinski noting "a recent BBC poll of 28,000 people in 27 countries" that ranked Israel, Iran and the United States "as the states with 'the most negative influence on the world.' Alas, for some," he emphasized, "that is the new axis of evil."

On the 50th anniversary of the assassination, in November, 2013, Stone was busy being feted at the St. Louis film festival. He told the crowds that "Garrison knew he had a weak case, he always did…he was trying to bring the CIA into the light of day, in 1968. Imagine what it was like. Today with Snowden, WikiLeaks, and Bradley Manning and you can still see how difficult it is to talk about this stuff in the light of day. Garrison had enormous courage—I was very impressed with his integrity."

Stone went back to Venezuela to release *Mi Amigo Hugo* on the one-year anniversary of Chavez's death in 2014. Jeffrey Tayler in *Foreign Policy* magazine noted that Stone "depicts Chavez and Castro bantering chummily on the former's *Alo Presidente* talk show. Nary a word from Stone about one of the most disturbing aspects of the Chavez regime: its mass import of Cuban military officers and secret service personnel to assure Chavez (and now Maduro) remained in power."

Next stop was Moscow where Stone in 2015 interviewed Viktor Yanukovych, the former President of Ukraine who was forced into exile when 100 demonstrators were killed by his security forces in the Maidan protests. Stone wrote that "it seems clear that the so-called 'shooters' who killed 14 policemen, wounded some 85 and killed 45 protesting civilians, were outside, third-party agitators. Many witnesses, including Yanukovich [sic] and police officials, believe these foreign elements were introduced by pro-Western factions—with CIA fingerprints on it."

At the Toronto International Film Festival in 2016 to promote his film *Snowden*, Stone implied a 9/11 conspiracy: "There seems to be a reluctance on the part of the Bush Administration to really fight this thing, to really do something about it. In a sense you might think that they let it happen because it helped their agenda, which they put through with the Patriot Act and many other things, the war in Iraq."

In May, 2018, Oliver Stone traveled to Tehran to attend the Fajr International Film Festival. Part of the festival, "Broken Olive Branches" centred on showcasing "films of countries that have been involved in combating terrorists and "takfiris," a word used for groups such as the Islamic State, or a country such as Palestine that has been resisting against the "Zionist regime." Khaled Ghodomi, the Hamas' representative in Iran, attended some of the films and noted that "The Islamic Republic seeks to promote the culture of resistance in the world." Stone told the festival "We are outlaws, we're doing something that is outlawed internationally, we had no permission to invade Iraq from the U.N., we did it, and we continue to do this." He added that "national security has trumped artistic freedom," and claimed that "you cannot make a film critical of the United States' foreign policy."

It's easy to scoff at Oliver Stone's political delusions. But he's not the first, and he won't be the last filmmaker to use the JFK assassination to make a political point. In fact, there's another film producer who has also gone off the deep end and who has produced, not one, but six documentaries on the JFK conspiracy. And they've received very large audiences. But not in the United States. In Canada.

Five

A Conspiracy Too Big?

I was accused of being a CIA agent when I was 20 years old. After my discovery of Dr. Wecht and Dr. Lattimer's analysis of the JFK autopsy X-rays and photographs back in 1975, I started subscribing to a small newsletter out of Boston. *People and the PURSUIT of Truth* was an offshoot of a computer automation publication that had started running JFK assassination articles. It was mostly wacky stuff but it was the only newsletter I could find.

In July of 1976, they published a short article of mine on the back/throat wound of Kennedy. I tried to counter the conspiracy factoid that he was shot from the front, and I presented testimony from the Dallas doctors and excerpts from a report by a panel of forensic pathologists hired by Attorney General Ramsey Clark in 1968. I still believed in a conspiracy but I couldn't ignore the clear medical evidence.

People and the PURSUIT of Truth

Vol. 2, No. 2   June, 1976

CONTENTS	Title	Author	Pages
The Secret, Illegal, and Powerful Control of the United States Government When President John F. Kennedy Was Murdered . . . . And Subsequently / by Colonel L. Fletcher Prouty			2 to 5, 7
The Back/Throat Wound of President Kennedy / by Fred Litwin			6, 7
"Betrayal" – A Review / by David Williams			8, 7
The Strategy of the Opposition – Editorial / by Edmund C. Berkeley			1

Note who also had an article in this issue—none other than the crackpot L. Fletcher Prouty. It didn't take long for me to realize that his ideas were crazy. About a month after this issue came out, I received a small note from the publisher that another author had taken offense with my article and was accusing me of working for the CIA. The publisher wanted to know if I would debate this in a future issue. I replied that it was unlikely the CIA had any use for a 20-year-old Commerce student in Montreal, and, oh by the way, where the hell were my cheques?

I never heard back. I graduated in 1978 and headed off to Queen's University at Kingston for my MBA. The House Select Committee on Assassinations (HSCA) released their final report on the JFK assassination in January of 1979, and even though I read it, I was way too busy to go through their supporting volumes of evidence.

The HSCA had concluded that there was a second gunman shooting at Kennedy from the grassy knoll in front of his limousine. This gunman fired only one shot—and he missed—despite being only 30-40 yards away. The basis for this conclusion was a Dictabelt tape (an analog recording medium from the 1940s used to record Dallas police department radio channels) from a supposed stuck microphone on one of the motorcycles in the motorcade. Tests were done in Dallas and the acoustic signature of a rifle shot fired from the knoll matched what was on the tape.

But a few things bothered me. There were no eyewitnesses to a shot from the grassy knoll, and how could a gunman miss such a close shot? Why did he only take one shot? It seemed pretty thin gruel for me.

In all other areas, the HSCA came to the exact same conclusions as the Warren Report. Lee Harvey Oswald had fired three shots from the Texas School Book Depository and two had hit Kennedy. I was surprised that the HSCA even sustained the single-bullet theory which held that one bullet went through Kennedy's neck, went through John Connally's chest, passed through his wrist and lodged in his left leg.

The other surprise was that, after two years of investigation, the HSCA suspected but could not find any evidence of a conspiracy that killed Kennedy. It appeared that they were ready to conclude there was no conspiracy but the acoustics test results made them re-think everything. In fact, their draft report of December 13, 1978, said that "The committee finds that the available scientific evidence is insufficient to find that there was a conspiracy to assassinate President Kennedy."

In July, 1979, *Gallery* magazine published a 32-page booklet on the latest news on the JFK assassination, and they included a record of the Dallas police tape. A musician living in Ohio, Steve Barber, bought the issue and listened to the tape. He could not hear any gunshots. After months of listening, he discovered the voice of Sheriff Bill Decker as well as the voice of motorcycle escort B.W. Hargis. Barber believed this was crosstalk—one transmission is being picked up by a microphone tuned to another radio frequency and then rebroadcast over the other channel. Barber heard Decker saying "hold everything secure" exactly when the shots supposedly occurred. The problem was that Decker actually said this about a minute after the shots.

By this time the National Research Council, part of the National Academy of Sciences, was in the midst of their new investigation of the acoustics evidence. Barber contacted the panel and sent them his evidence.

In 1982, their report confirmed what Barber had heard—that the tape contained impulses (initially thought to be shots) that were recorded at least a minute after the assassination. In 2013, author Larry Sabato hired a new firm to analyze the tapes and they came to the same conclusion.

In 1983, I took off a year to go travelling and took the Trans-Siberian Express to China where I spent two months backpacking. I then spent three months on a kibbutz in Israel. When I returned to Canada in the fall of 1984, I quickly found a job working in New York City editing a publication on telecommunications strategy. I had no time for the Kennedy assassination, and in 1991 I moved to England to run the European operations of a small software company, LAN Systems, which was subsequently bought by Intel Corporation.

I saw *JFK* while living in Oxford. I was infuriated by Oliver Stone's portrayal of Jim Garrison as the virtuous protagonist and Clay Shaw as the evil monster. But my friends just saw it as a great movie and who could really argue with them? But my senses were overloaded—exquisite sets, great acting, impressive recreations—but overall an absolutely objectionable film from start to finish. And where would I even start explaining stuff to my friends? They really didn't have the time or inclination to listen to a Fred Litwin rant. I'm sure their eyes would have glazed over—hardly a good way to keep friends, so I just sucked it all up inside. There was one positive about the film—Kevin Bacon was delicious as a gay hustler.

In July of 1993, I was visiting my friend Peggy in The Hague in Holland. We went to the North Sea Jazz Festival and I finally saw one of my idols, Etta James perform live. While shopping one afternoon with Peggy, we stopped into a discount bookseller and I saw a new book on the JFK assassination. Harrison Livingstone's *High Treason II* was on sale and I snagged a copy.

This was his second book on the assassination but he was new to me. The book was rushed into production to take advantage of the film *JFK* and had spent nine weeks on the *New York Times* bestseller list.

I was quite excited about reading his book since it focused on the medical evidence, which was a favourite topic of mine. The book was a slog to get through—it was poorly written, poorly organized and contained many small errors. The gist of the book was that the recollections of the doctors who treated Kennedy in Dallas were different from the conclusions of the autopsy report. Livingstone found witnesses from Parkland Hospital who remembered a huge wound in the back of Kennedy's head which is indicative of an exit wound. But the autopsy X-rays and photographs only showed a small wound in the back of Kennedy's head—evidence of an entry wound. Livingstone concluded that the autopsy evidence had all been forged.

In addition, the Zapruder film shows the back of Kennedy's head to be intact after the fatal shot and you can see a visible exit wound in the right front. This is all consistent with the findings of the autopsy. But to Livingstone, this meant that the Zapruder film must have also been faked. Rather than conclude that 30-year-old memories are mistaken, Livingstone posited a massive fraud. And his witnesses all disagreed with each other. This was all too fantastic for me. It would be one thing if he actually had witnesses and evidence of people who had been part of the forgery, but he had nothing of the sort.

Even Livingstone recognized the problems of decades-old memory. He writes that "During periods of great stress, in a crisis or emergency when events are unfolding with great rapidity—such as the events of November 22, 1963—the mind plays tricks and does not register each detail." He also says that "In the stress and pressure of events during those terrible hours, people make all sorts of mistakes, and their memories are not always perfect." And Livingstone goes on to say that "I am inclined to think that the conflicts in the evidence stem more from semantics and normal misperceptions under great stress, rather than actual differences in fact." Even one of Livingstone's own witnesses, Petty Officer Paul O'Connor, who attended the autopsy, said that "it has been so many years and so much has happened, I kind of doubt my own ability to remember fine details."

High Treason II also had the typical stuff about Kennedy ending the Cold War and Livingstone outlined a massive conspiracy that was "to some extent hatched and operated out of Dallas/Ft. Worth. The plotters controlled the police and the city government there. Numerous of their relatives and connections were in the military and in the CIA and the DIA in Washington. Some of them, like General Charles Cabell of Dallas, had been fired by Kennedy." Vietnam was key and "high officials remaining in the government after Kennedy died" were the "handmaidens of the conspiracy that killed him. It is not unreasonable to suppose that some of them had foreknowledge of the murder, and that some even participated in the plot."

My head was spinning from this book, which was using 30-year-old memories to override hard physical evidence like the autopsy X-rays and photographs. And evidence once thought to prove conspiracy, like the Zapruder film, was now also fake, largely because of its consistency with the autopsy material.

High Treason II might have been a terrible book but it rekindled my interest in the JFK assassination. The notes from the book referenced a JFK journal, *The Third Decade*, and I started a subscription. In January, 1994, I noticed an article, "Eyewitness to the Kennedy and Tippit Murders" by Ian Griggs, an ex-detective. Attached to the article was a note about a UK group, Dallas '63, that met monthly in Liverpool. There was also a phone number listed for John Rudd, the secretary of the group. I called John and found that the next day they would be meeting with another JFK group in Coventry, which wasn't that far from Oxford.

I drove up to Coventry and spent an afternoon with John, Ian, and many other people interested in the life of JFK. Most were believers in a conspiracy and it was great fun arguing the night away in the pub. The more I talked with Ian, the more I wanted to lean against conspiracy. I've always liked to take a contrary position, but Ian rejected reasonable arguments about the evidence—it seemed he was stuck in the mid-1960s before a lot of stuff was debunked.

Ian then started a UK group called "Dealey Plaza UK" which met once a month in a pub on the outskirts of London. At one meeting, John Rudd from Liverpool brought me a stack of newsletters written over the years by conspiracy author Paul Hoch. I spent an entire evening going over them—Hoch had basically written a blog as a physical newsletter (although he might say that people who write blogs are writing cyber newsletters). Each issue went over new developments with his commentary on what was going on. But Hoch was not your run-of-the-mill conspiracy freak—he actually wanted to follow the facts, no matter where they led.

In the November, 1993, issue Hoch wrote about his two talks at The Second Annual Midwest Symposium on Assassination Politics held in Chicago in April, 1993. On the physical evidence, Hoch wrote that "the specific items of Dealey Plaza conspiracy evidence have tended to get weaker over the years. This has been a surprise, naturally underappreciated—especially by newer buffs and non-technical buffs." Hoch pointed to the HSCA who "took a stab at the tests the critics wanted—not completely, and not perfectly, but we expected that <u>any one</u> of the tests would demolish the WC [Warren Commission] reconstruction—neutron activation analysis, trajectory analysis. And they didn't."

Further, "the single bullet theory is not a joke. Despite its well-known flaws, the Warren Commission/House Committee reconstruction may be in better shape than any other single detailed reconstruction. At least, it has to be taken seriously."

The real kicker of his newsletter was his take on conspiracy: "My model is that there were many coverups, probably many independent ones…One possibility—ironically—is that Oswald did it alone but so many people had things to cover up that the reaction of the government made it look like the assassination resulted from a conspiracy." Indeed, the CIA covered-up its joint efforts to kill Castro with the mob and anti-Castro Cubans. The FBI covered-up by destroying a note from Oswald to FBI agent James Hosty warning him to stay away from questioning his wife. Hoch elaborated that "some of the withholding of information resulted from conventional concerns about apparently unrelated intelligence matters. (For example, the secrecy of intercepts of Oswald's mail, or Soviet Embassy mail, would have been enough reason to keep that information from the [Warren] Commission.)"

Hoch was on to something.

I remembered my pledge to investigate the HSCA documentation further and now decided to have a look at all the scientific tests that were performed during its investigation. But I doubted many libraries had their 12 volumes of evidence. Fortunately, computer technology came to my rescue. Someone had put the HSCA hearings and exhibits on a CD-ROM, and that had the added benefit of making everything searchable.

Reading the actual evidence was a revelation. The HSCA had conducted a lot of scientific tests—ballistic, photographic, forensic—and had hired top experts in many different areas. Not only was Hoch right about the tests, you'd be hard-pressed to find any acknowledgment, positive or negative, of what the HSCA was able to accomplish in any conspiracy book.

Here's a summary of their tests:

Authentication of Autopsy X-rays and photos: The HSCA retained experts in anthropology, forensic dentistry, photographic interpretation, forensic pathology, and radiology to conduct new tests on the autopsy materials. Anthropologists compared the autopsy X-rays with premortem X-rays obtained from the Kennedy Library. They found a number of unique anatomical characteristics that confirmed that all the X-rays were of the same person and that the person in question was indeed John F.

Kennedy. They consulted with a forensic odontologist to look at dental comparisons in the X-rays and who concurred with the conclusions. A radiologist looked for differences in density, discontinuities of bone structure, and any abnormal patterns and found no evidence of alteration.

In addition, the radiologist who took the X-rays at the autopsy verified that the X-rays in the National Archives are the same X-rays he took that night. He said that "none are missing, none have been added, and none have been altered."

The skull and torso X-rays taken at the autopsy match the antemortem X-rays of Kennedy "in such a wealth of intricate morphological detail that there can be no reasonable doubt that they are in fact X-rays of John F. Kennedy and no other person."

Photographic experts determined that the emulsion numbers on the film matched batches produced in 1963. They also looked at several stereo pairs of pictures which enables one to see the scene in three-dimensions. This was an important test since "to avoid detection of picture alteration requires that each picture of a pair be altered identically, which is essentially impossible." There were several stereo pairs and there was no indication of alteration.

Forensic Pathology Panel: This panel consisted of two separate teams—a team of forensic pathologists who had previously examined the autopsy materials and a team who was new to the materials. Both teams agreed that Kennedy was hit by two bullets from behind. They also agreed that the autopsy material is authentic. The bullet that hit Governor Connally must have yawed or tumbled prior to hitting him which is indicative of its striking an intervening object—such as Kennedy. The majority of the panel believed that the medical evidence is consistent with the single-bullet theory. And other non-medical evidence (like the position of the two men, the ballistic studies of the ammunition, and neutron activation analysis of the bullet fragments) "strongly indicates that a single bullet injured both men."

Photographic Panel: The HSCA consulted with the American Society of Photographic Scientists and Engineers and picked a panel of 22 experts with expertise in photographic image enhancement, photogrammetry, photointerpretation, and forensic photography. The panel concluded that Kennedy and Connally's alignment in the limousine was consistent with the single-bullet theory. Trajectory Analysis indicated that the single-bullet shot intersects in the plane of the Texas School Book Depository (see Chapter Six for the trajectory diagrams). The panel also determined that the rifle in the backyard photographs is the same rifle found in the Texas School Book Depository after the shooting. The panel also found "no evidence of fakery in any of the backyard picture materials." As to another gunman, the panel concluded that "there is no definitive visible evidence of any gunman in the streets, sidewalks, or areas adjacent to Dealey Plaza. Nor was any evidence discerned of a flash of light or puff of smoke."

Earwitness Analysis: Bolt, Beranek, and Newman conducted an analysis of earwitness reports relating to the assassination. They concluded that "it is hard to believe a rifle was fired from the knoll. Such a shot would be extremely loud, even if silenced, and it would be hard to imagine anyone in the vicinity of the knoll missing such an event." Dr. David Green, Professor of Psychophysics and Chairman of the Department of Psychology and Social Relations at Harvard University told the HSCA that "If you go over the statistical survey of the 178 observers who gave reports, there are exactly 4 that mentioned dual locations, that is, that say the locus of the shots came from two places. I find that a strikingly low number given the hypothesis that the weapon was actually fired from two places."

I Was a Teenage JFK Conspiracy Freak 153

One of three pictures of Lee Harvey Oswald in his backyard taken by his wife

Handwriting and Fingerprint Panel: The HSCA picked a team of three people recommended by the American Society of Questioned Document Examiners, and they also hired Vincent Scalice, former-detective first grade with the New York City Police Department, for finger and palm print analysis. More than fifty documents signed by Lee Harvey Oswald were examined and they concluded that the signatures and handwriting was that of one person. The alias used by Oswald on his 1963 Fair Play for Cuba card, A. J. Hidell; the U.S. postal money order used to purchase the rifle; and the notation on one of the backyard photographs, "To my friend George from Lee;" all were written by Oswald. The finger and palm prints on three ID cards; a palm print lifted from the underside of the rifle; and a fingerprint from the paper bag used to transport the gun; all were Oswald's.

Mannlicher-Carcano Firing Test: The HSCA hired Sgt Cecil Kirk and other members of the D.C. Police Department to test-fire a Mannlicher-Carcano rifle. They concluded that "there was ample time for Oswald to have fired 3 shots, hitting with two of them, within 8.31 seconds. All series of 3 shots were fired in less than 8 seconds, two were fired in less than 7 seconds, two in less than 6, and two in less than 5."

Firearms Panel: A team of five people were chosen by the Association of Firearm and Tool Mark Examiners, the Forensic Science Foundation, and the American Academy of Forensic Sciences. They concluded that the windshield of the limousine could only have been fractured from the inside; the three cartridge cases found in the sniper's nest in the Texas School Book Depository had been fired from Oswald's Mannlicher-Carcano; the bullet nose fragment and the bullet-base fragment, found in the front seat of the limousine, were fired from the same rifle; and the four cartridge cases recovered from the scene of the Tippit murder were fired from Oswald's revolver.

Neutron Activation Analysis: This nuclear-based test analyzed bullet fragments to determine the elements present in them. All of the fragments came from only two bullets and the bullets were Mannlicher-Carcano ammunition. A fragment from Connally's wrist matched the bullet found on a stretcher at Parkland Hospital. It is highly likely that the bullet used in the attempted assassination of General Walker was a Mannlicher-Carcano bullet. There was no evidence of a third bullet.[1]

The HSCA had hired a lot of experts and they conducted a lot of tests. They sustained the conclusion of the Warren Commission that Lee Harvey Oswald fired three shots and killed Kennedy. But few books reference *any* of this material. It's almost like it all never happened.

The HSCA volumes and the Paul Hoch newsletters all started to coalesce in my mind and I knew I had to write an article. I was then invited by the Dallas '63 group to give a lecture in Liverpool. I put together a presentation and drove up to Liverpool to meet with John Rudd. He took me around to see the sights, including a stop at the Cavern Club where the Beatles started playing in the early 1960s.

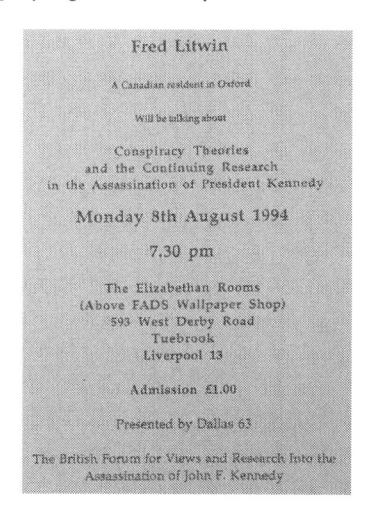

> Fred Litwin
>
> A Canadian resident in Oxford
>
> Will be talking about
>
> Conspiracy Theories
> and the Continuing Research
> in the Assassination of President Kennedy
>
> Monday 8th August 1994
>
> 7.30 pm
>
> The Elizabethan Rooms
> (Above FADS Wallpaper Shop)
> 593 West Derby Road
> Tuebrook
> Liverpool 13
>
> Admission £1.00
>
> Presented by Dallas 63
>
> The British Forum for Views and Research Into the Assassination of John F. Kennedy

---

1 Neutron Activation Analysis is no longer used by the FBI as it was found to be unreliable. In 2002, the FBI asked the National Academy of Sciences to "evaluate the scientific basis of comparative bullet lead analysis." Their report "expressed concerns, however, relating to the interpretation of the results of bullet lead examinations," and the FBI stopped their examinations of bullet lead. What I find probative is that the test did not *disprove* the single-bullet theory, even though we now know it did not *prove* the theory.

This was my first public speaking appearance on the JFK assassination, and I was amazed that about 60 people came out to see me talk. I presented a quick overview of the assassination literature and spent a large amount of time on the HSCA and their tests. I noted that every forensic pathologist who had viewed the autopsy evidence had concluded that Kennedy was shot from behind. I posted a list of all the many suspects in Kennedy's murder and I asked for hands to see who believed what. As researcher Wallace Milam had said, "we have identified twelve of the three gunmen." In the room of sixty people there was only one other person who believed that Lee Harvey Oswald acted alone. After my presentation, I spent over two hours answering questions until we were kicked out of the building. I don't think I changed one mind – in subsequent meetings, I was always the only person who didn't believe in a conspiracy.

I turned my presentation into a paper entitled "A Conspiracy Too Big? Intellectual Dishonesty in the JFK Assassination." I wondered what kind of conspiracy killed Kennedy. "Are we talking about one assassin with an accomplice or are we talking about something larger? If one were to believe the current literature, we are faced with not just 'something larger' but a monster conspiracy that consists of several assassins, several accomplices, and the destruction and forgery of vital evidence. The critics have constructed a conspiracy so massive that it ultimately falls of its own weight."

I was concerned about the state of the critical literature. "If the autopsy X-rays and photos show evidence of a single head-shot from the rear, well, they must be fakes. If the wounds on Kennedy's body are consistent with a single-gunman, well, the body must have been altered. If neutron activation analysis shows the single-bullet theory to be correct, well, the evidence has been tampered with. And if you do not like the conclusions of a professional panel, well, they must have ties to the government. One could go on and on. This is extremely dangerous."

Just look at the conspiracy the critics have constructed. From forgery to evidence-tampering to the murder of witnesses and the planting of evidence, to police complicity to evidence destruction to impersonation and body alteration, let alone multiple assassins, the conspiracy just keeps on getting bigger and bigger and just becomes impossible.

My article referenced several examples where the critics ignored the HSCA test results. For instance, as mentioned above, the HSCA photographic panel went to great lengths to authenticate the backyard pictures of Lee Harvey Oswald. Yet the critics continued with exactly the same criticisms as before the HSCA. Robert Groden, who first showed the Zapruder Film on Geraldo Rivera's show in 1975 (see Chapter Three) spends three pages in *The Killing of a President* analyzing the backyard photos but just briefly mentions the conclusions of the photographic panel—with no explanation. Jim Marrs, in his book *Crossfire,* the basis of Oliver Stone's film *JFK*, spends four and a half pages on the photos. While he mentions the HSCA conclusions, his text makes it clear that their analysis was on very narrow grounds—the examination of the edges of the negatives—and he neglects to tell readers about all the other tests done by the panel. He then brings up many of the same concerns that had already been answered. He quotes Major John Pickard of the Canadian Department of National Defense saying, "the photos have the earmarks of being faked." Yet, as you will see in Chapter Six on the Canadian Broadcasting Corporation, Pickard told the Photographic Panel that he had performed no scientific tests on the pictures. Marrs conveniently left that detail out.

Oliver Stone, who should have known better, has a scene in *JFK* where intelligence operatives are cutting out pictures of Lee Harvey Oswald and pasting them on backgrounds of his backyard.

The single-bullet theory is another issue that the critics can't wrap their heads around. Robert Groden, in *The Killing of a President*, says that "the single bullet theory, when depicted in pictures or diagrams, can seem plausible, the effect of angle or trajectory can be easily manipulated or obscured." Yet Groden goes on to show not one but three separate mutually-exclusive diagrams of the single-bullet theory. And guess who else used Groden's faulty diagrams? None other than Oliver Stone in his film *JFK*, who hired him as a consultant for his film. He also wrote the foreword to *The Killing of a President* where he said that Groden was "highly instrumental in ensuring the resulting accuracy of key scenes in Dealey Plaza, the Parkland Hospital trauma room, the Bethesda Hospital autopsy room, and the 'single bullet theory' demonstration in the courtroom at the Shaw trial."

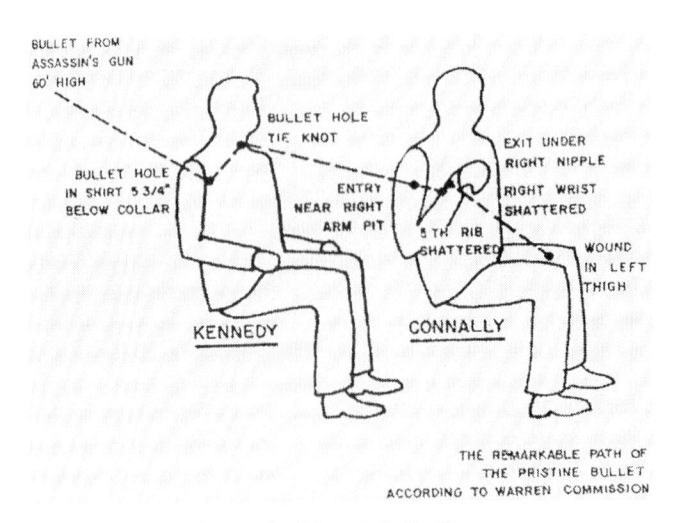

This is the standard "magic-bullet" diagram you will see in just about every conspiracy book

I Was a Teenage JFK Conspiracy Freak 159

The above diagram also appears in Jim Marrs' *Crossfire*, and Dr. Cyril Wecht's *Cause of Death*. The good doctor should have known better since he was a member of the HSCA forensic pathology panel which positioned Kennedy's neck wound well above what is shown in the diagram.

When Robert Groden testified before the HSCA, he showed the committee this faulty diagram.

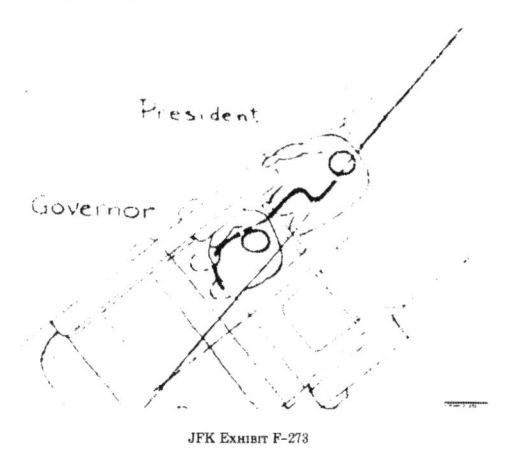

JFK Exhibit F-273

Here are two diagrams showing how Kennedy and Connally were actually positioned in the limousine. They were perfectly aligned and the wounds point back to the sixth-floor window of the Texas School Book Depository—the location of the sniper's nest.

Drawing courtesy of Frank Warner

160   *A Conspiracy Too Big?*

Here's what Kennedy and Connally looked like from the sixth-floor window of the Texas School Book Depository. They were in perfect alignment for a shot to hit both men. Animation still courtesy of Emmy award-winning animator Dale K. Myers. © 1995-2018 Dale K. Myers. All Rights Reserved.

Another area that bothered me was the continued insistence that witnesses were dying under suspicious circumstances. Groden's *The Killing of a President* and Marrs' *Crossfire* continue the stupidity. *Crossfire* has a complete chapter called "Convenient Deaths." Groden includes 43 sidebars in his book on suspicious deaths. Marrs lists all the mysterious deaths in chronological order, saying that "the possibility of convenient deaths leads one into a well of paranoia, yet this long list cannot be summarily dismissed." Like Penn Jones (see Chapter One), his list includes Earlene Roberts, the housekeeper at Oswald's rooming house, despite the fact the HSCA investigated her death. Jacqueline Hess testified that "there is no indication in the records relating to her death…as to what exactly was mysterious about a 60-year-old woman with large calcium deposits and a case of pneumonia, dying of acute heart failure."

Groden's 2013 book, *JFK Absolute Proof*, continued with the mysterious deaths. "There have been literally hundreds of these convenient deaths. We may never be aware of all of them, and the deaths have kept us from learning a great deal of evidence in the investigation of the assassination." Groden adds ominously, "For every one death, one must ask how many dozens more had decided to keep quiet out of fear for their personal safety and the safety of their loved ones." But not one conspiracy author has been killed in over fifty years. Groden claimed that "I too kept quiet about what I knew of the murder of the President for a very long time out of fear."

Over the years, the critics have tried repeatedly to find assassins lurking in the backgrounds of various photographs. Raymond Marcus was fascinated by a Polaroid photograph taken by Mary Moorman. She was located right across from Abraham Zapruder and her picture was snapped at the moment of the fatal head shot. The grassy knoll is in the background.

Back in May, 1965, David Lifton bought a JFK commemorative magazine and was fascinated by the Moorman photograph. The more he looked, the more he believed he saw a puff of smoke and the figure of a gunman in the background.

The Polaroid photograph taken by Mary Moorman just a fraction of a second after the fatal head shot

Lifton obtained the best negative of the photograph he could find, and in the subsequent print he found four additional figures. He did admit that "an act of photo interpretation was needed to 'see' my first discovery," but that that the last figure was "visible from the waist up, and he was holding something in his hands in a horizontal position." Lifton showed Marcus and they numbered the men from one to five.

The five supposed locations in the Moorman photograph that might be gunmen

One of the early critics, Maggie Field, felt that Lifton had "truly made a monumental discovery." When Sylvia Meagher received copies of the photographs, she was in such "a state of shock" that she "very nearly fainted" because "here at last was physical evidence to confirm what one was convinced had really happened."

However, as the photograph started making the rounds, some people "had to study them for a while" before they saw anything. It took Field twenty minutes to find them. Leo Sauvage, another early critic, wasn't impressed. Sylvia Meagher wrote that "He sees no weapon and regards the claims about the photos as symptomatic of 'desperate and dishonest' people." On the other hand, some critics were eyeing new discoveries. Vincent Salandria saw a man he believed was wearing headphones who was clearly part of the radio-controlled assassination.

Marcus found corroboration that man #5 was a human from a frame from the Orville Nix film. Unfortunately, others still couldn't see it. Sylvia Meagher "said she thought she could see the figure but wasn't sure." A CBS News producer, Leslie Midgley, "said he could not see anything resembling a man in any of the pictures."

James Kirkwood, in his book *American Grotesque*, interviews Bill Gurvich, one of Jim Garrison's chief investigators. Gurvich defected when he realized the entire prosecution was a sham. His story of Raymond Marcus coming into Garrison's office with his pictures is a classic.

> "So, these photographs had been enlarged so many times that they looked like a checkerboard—they were black and white squares… You couldn't distinguish anything. I joked with them when they showed it to me, and I said it looked like a Purina checkerboard sign. So Garrison called me over and said, "Look!" He had a pencil and a magnifying glass. He says, "Look at this, Bill. You can see a man." So I looked in the glass, he was holding the glass. I looked over his shoulder. I saw nothing. I said, "Jim, I don't see—what-maybe I-." Then he had to come and back and focus his eye on it again and he said, "Well, its right here!" But then he couldn't find it."

Marcus told them the reason they couldn't see anything was that they were too close to the photograph. He took the photo across the room and sat it on a sofa some 15 feet from Garrison. They both still couldn't see anything, so Marcus left the building and went across the street.

Gurvich continues. "And lo and behold, standing across the street, at about 5 in the late afternoon, during the peak hour of traffic, is Raymond Marcus. On the opposite side of the Avenue, holding up this Purina sign!...And I could read his lips: "Can you see it now?" And it was worse than ever."

Despite this, Jim Garrison brought Raymond Marcus before his grand jury. Here is what he told them:

> "He [David Lifton] came over to the house and he pointed out some images that he thought he saw there, and I didn't see them at first, they are very, very tiny. Then we had blow-ups made of the images and I want to show you what emerged.... After a number of people, interested people, had studied the images of David Lifton, believe it or not, there appeared to be five men. Maybe some of them are valid, maybe some are not. I said appeared to be. When I ask you to see the images I am not asking you to draw a conclusion that these are men. I am only saying do you see images?"

Marcus then showed them blown-up images, which ended up being just a bunch of dots. "I have to show you this photograph at considerable distance and I am going to ask you and go to the back of the room as you should see this at a distance where you no longer can see the dots. I want you to lose the dots. If you can see the dots you are too close. You can't see the picture if you see the dots."

In the *Ramparts* magazine office, Lifton became known as "Blowup" because "his specialty was enlarging photographs of Dealey Plaza taken the morning of the assassination and finding figures lurking in the background." Hinckle wrote that he was insistent that staffers "pick out the figure of a man among a forest of black and white dots in a twenty-times enlargement" of the Moorman photo. One colleague "swore that if you looked at the blow-up long enough you could make out the figure of a man wearing a Prussian helmet."

The reason for this is because the Moorman photograph is tiny. The actual image measures 2.125 x 2.875 inches, so when you blow it up, you are getting far more noise than signal. It then becomes a Rorschach test—you can see whatever you want to see in it.

Might this be a gunman firing at Kennedy?

That wasn't the end of the story. Several years later, numerous researchers claimed there is an image of a policeman firing a gun, known as the "Badgeman" in the photo. The HSCA sent a high-quality negative copy to the Rochester Institute of Technology, which made a series of photo enlargements and enhancements. Unfortunately, the Moorman photograph "was so underexposed in the region of the retaining wall that the alterations in contrast produced no significant increase in detail. The Panel could find no evidence of a person in a position on the retaining wall." They couldn't carry out any enhancement work in the area of the fence on the grassy knoll because that part of the picture was of even lesser quality.

To get people to see these other assassins, critics have resorted to painting on the pictures. On page 200 of Groden's book, *The Death of a President*, there is a colour picture of the "badgeman" with the caption, "An extreme enlargement of a portion of Mary Ann Moorman's photograph shows a distinct image of a man in uniform, especially when the shadowy images are colored in as in the illustration above."

It should be noted that *The Death of a President* was published in 1993, almost fifteen years after the HSCA report.

"A Conspiracy Too Big" was published by Dallas '63 in their January, 1995, newsletter. Several angry letters to the editor appeared in the next issue with one person writing that "Opinions like Mr. Litwin's do not constitute healthy arguments and debate. They are, instead, like arguments by the flat Earth proponents and Holocaust deniers. Such views are either mistaken due to ignorance of the facts, or they are deliberate attempts to express absurdity or political extremism."

The June, 1995, issue had a four-page rebuttal from Harrison Livingstone himself. He said that my article "shows how effective the mind control apparatus among the Warren Commission critical community in America influences foreign opinion." He objected to my line of reasoning that a massive conspiracy would fall under its own weight. "To assume that it would collapse merely because there are too many people is a fractured method of thought when such a conspiracy succeeds in its goal and takes power. Once in power, it may not matter if it is exposed, because those who won can prevent their own overthrow until a more powerful force removes them."

One small victory. In my article, I wrote that "Livingstone's erratic writing style makes it extremely difficult to follow his arguments." And he agreed, writing that "It's true under the pressure of researching and writing three such massive works in four years, my writing may have suffered at times."

In November of 1994, I relocated to Singapore to manage Intel Corporation's networking division in Asia. I kept in touch with John Rudd in Liverpool and he told me that he was going to organize a conference in the UK on the assassination. I told him I wanted to give a talk but he was hesitant. The people he was working within the United States were conspiracy theorists and they wouldn't be keen on having somebody like me at their conference. I told him not to press the issue and to just forget it.

The "Who Killed Kennedy" conference went on in Liverpool in July, 1996, and a host of American conspiracy buffs made the trip. John Rudd was supposed to give a talk but found he was way too busy with organization to do enough research. In the November, 1996, issue of

Dallas '63's newsletter, he wrote an article on the conference and said. "the last part of my talk would have been similar to Fred Litwin's article, 'A Conspiracy Too Big.'"

My article now resides on John McAdam's JFK assassination website, which is arguably the best debunking site out there. In December, 2017, I received an email from David Lifton which said, "I keep forgetting who you are, but…aren't you the guy that wrote that silly article claiming that the plot (that is, any serious JFK plot) was 'too big,' simply because you couldn't wrap your mind around its complexities? So, your text reads like a catalogue of excuses for why various indications of conspiracy simply cannot be true? Whether its body alteration, or parade route planning, or…you name it. You just can't deal with it. Or so it seemed that way to me."

Six

Did the CBC Solve the JFK Assassination?

A Canadian Broadcasting Corporation (CBC) memo from 1983 attached a "strange message" from a Ouija board session that communicated with U.S. President John F. Kennedy. Associate Producer Maxine Sidran sent Producer Brian McKenna the transcript from a 1976 session where they asked Kennedy "who killed you?" The answer to her question was Karsland. And when asked to repeat the answer, Kennedy again responded "Karsland." When asked "Who is Karsland?" Kennedy answered, "Secret Service."

The memo claimed that "the people who used to take part in these sessions often had better than average results."

There was more—Kennedy told the participants that the truth about the assassination would soon come out via an informant and that he had been killed because of "secret plans to take over the country." The text of the session was attached with "no editing" because that is what you do if you are a "good researcher."

The best news of all? Kennedy was asked, "How are you feeling?" and the answer was "a [sic] peace."

Welcome to the world of *The Fifth Estate,* the CBC's premier investigative documentary series. In the fall of 1983, they were busy working on an upcoming episode, "Who Killed JFK?" Unfortunately, even though Kennedy told the Ouija board participants that "soon everybody will know" the truth via an informant, it wasn't in time to make it into the documentary.

Who Killed JFK? would be Producer Brian McKenna's fourth documentary on the JFK assassination for *The Fifth Estate*. It would be the most-watched *Fifth Estate* episode ever, with more than two million viewers. He went on to produce two more and also write articles on the assassination for the *Montreal Gazette*, opinion pieces for online publications like *Rabble.ca*, and JFK book reviews for Amazon. An associate producer at the CBC told me he was "obsessed" with Kennedy largely because they were both Irish-Catholic.

Brian McKenna isn't just any CBC producer. In 2007, he received the Pierre Berton Award for "distinguished achievement in popularizing Canadian History." At that point, McKenna had been with the CBC for 37 years and had won Geminis for the memoirs of Pierre Trudeau and for the controversial series, *The Valour and the Horror*. That three-part series, about the bombing of German cities in World War II, aired in January of 1992 and was attacked by veterans' groups for presenting a biased negative portrayal of Canadian military actions. The CBC ombudsman found that the documentary was "flawed and fails to measure up to CBC's demanding policies and standards."

McKenna's next big achievement was the Pioneer Award from JFK Lancer, a Texas-based organization predicated on the fervent belief that the U.S. government has conspired for over half a century to hide the truth from the world regarding the JFK assassination. McKenna was honoured in 2010 for his "lifetime of searching for the truth" about who killed JFK.

In his acceptance speech in Dallas, McKenna laid out the conspiracy to kill Kennedy. It was a "sophisticated coup plotted by the U.S. military and CIA with support from Hoover's FBI and Kennedy's bodyguards, the Secret Service." In addition, "the Mafia were co-conspirators as well as the world's richest man, the right-wing billionaire H.L. Hunt." And

Vice-President Lyndon Johnson "supported the coup which made him President."

Such a large conspiracy was necessary because McKenna had to give significant meaning to JFK's death. He was killed because he "tried to change the world" and "over and over he chose not to go to war, over Laos, over Berlin, and twice over Cuba." Kennedy was "going to be pulling out of Vietnam" beginning "with a 1963 order to start withdrawing troops." McKenna claims, "This was the last straw for his generals and the CIA. They accused him of treason."

All of this was just nonsense. As indicated in Chapter Four, Kennedy only wanted to remove troops because of supposed progress in training the South Vietnamese Army. He never contemplated pulling out of Vietnam. Kennedy was a Cold Warrior, period.

None of these facts mattered to McKenna. He was a man on a mission and that mission was to find proof of the massive conspiracy. And it didn't take him long. The CBC press release for McKenna's first documentary, *Dallas and After*, which aired in November, 1977, heralded "New evidence showing that Lee Harvey Oswald may have been the victim of a faked photograph which was an important piece of evidence in the John. F. Kennedy assassination." The Canadian press picked this up and sent out a wire story with the headline "CBC show asks if Oswald victim of fake photo."

The backyard photos of Lee Harvey Oswald have long been a staple of conspiracy theorists ever since he told Dallas police that his head was "pasted" onto somebody else's body—despite the fact that his wife Marina admitted taking the pictures. Now McKenna had Canadian military officials confirming that conspiracy buffs had been right all along. It also raised the question—if these incriminating photos were faked, wouldn't that mean that Oswald was framed?

It was all too good to be true.

172   *Did the CBC Solve the JFK Conspiracy?*

The press release for *Fifth Estate* documentary said they consulted "phototechnologists at the Department of National Defense in Ottawa. They told us that this photo and another shot at the same time bear the earmarks of having been faked. They noted that the shadows fall in conflicting directions. The shadow of his nose falls in one direction and that of his body in another."

The House Select Committee on Assassinations (HSCA), which was already in the middle of their investigation when the *Dallas and After* aired, contacted Major J.M. Pickard of the Canadian Forces, a Commanding Officer of the Canadian Forces Photographic Unit. Pickard wrote the Committee a letter (see below) stating that he performed "No scientific analysis of the transparencies" that he was given and that they were "very poor copies." He did "perfunctory measurements" and then offered an opinion. He said his "total involvement with the CBC was less than one hour."

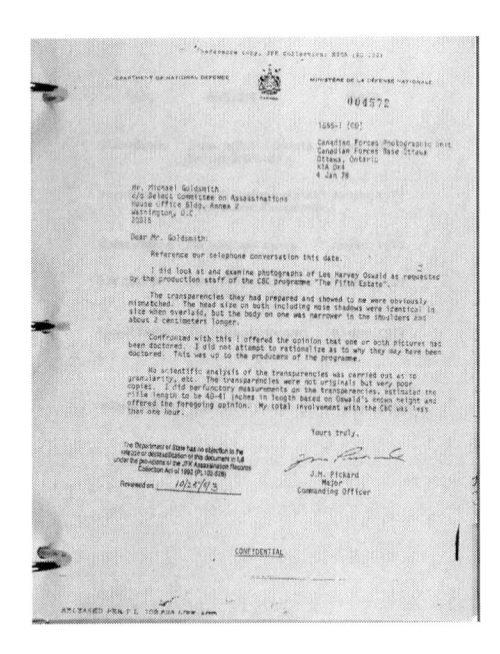

The HSCA photographic panel ultimately concluded there was no forgery and that the photos were legitimate (one of the backyard pictures is in Chapter Five).

Dallas and After was even wrong about the basic facts of the assassination.

The documentary featured Dr. Cyril Wecht, the coroner of Allegheny County in Pennsylvania, and one of the foremost forensic pathologists in the United States. He was a critic of the Warren Commission's single-bullet theory which postulated that one bullet hit both President Kennedy and Governor John Connally of Texas. While Wecht was on-air, the documentary showed a diagram of the supposed path of the bullet, making it readily apparent that the trajectory was just plain impossible (see below).

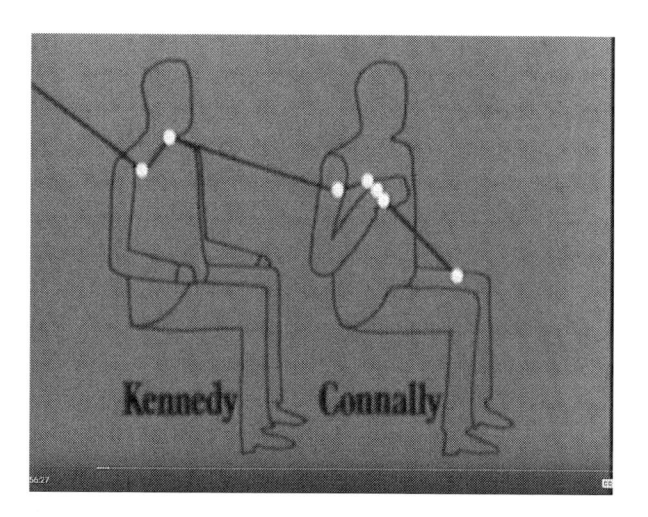

The Fifth Estate replayed the video of Wecht and his diagram of the supposed path of the bullet in their 1983, 2013, and 2017 documentaries. What they didn't show the Canadian public was the trajectory analysis performed by Thomas Canning, staff engineer for the Space Projects Division of the NASA Ames Research Center for the HSCA in 1979. His

174   *Did the CBC Solve the JFK Conspiracy?*

survey proved that both men line up perfectly in both the vertical and horizontal planes.

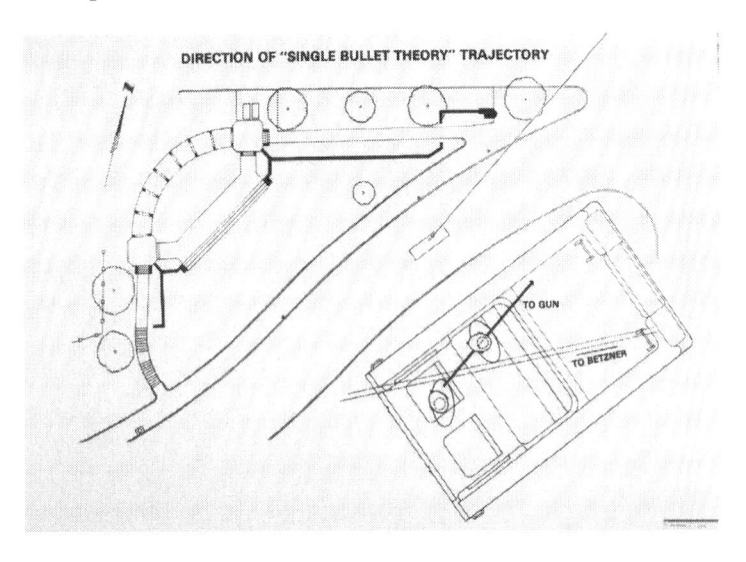

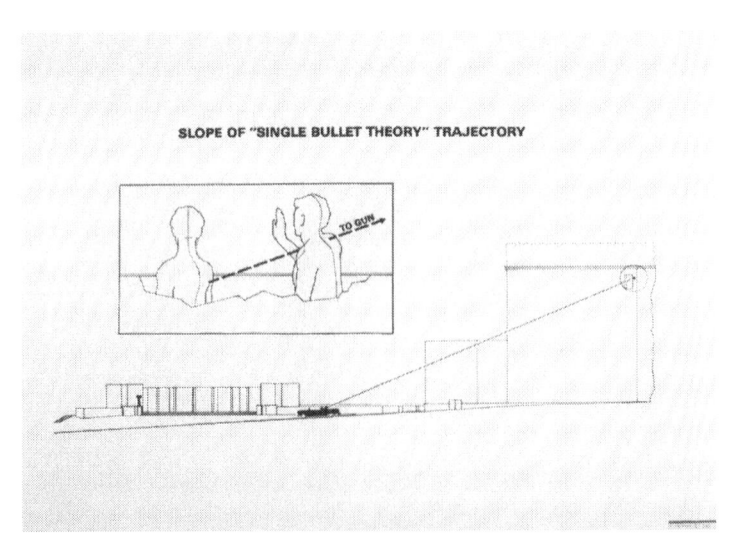

Dallas and After also claimed that Lee Harvey Oswald was a poor marksman; that there were only 5.6 seconds between the three shots; that no single gunman could achieve such a feat; that most witnesses felt the shots were fired from the front; and that the fatal head shot came from the grassy knoll in the right-front of Kennedy. These claims the CBC also repeated in 1983, 2013, and 2017.

None of these claims were true, then or now.

In fact, Oswald qualified as a sharpshooter in the U.S. Marines. Sgt. James A. Zahm, who was an NCO in charge of the Marksmanship Training Unit Armory at the Weapons Training Battalion Marine Corps School in Quantico, Virginia, testified before the Warren Commission that Oswald "in the Marine Corps" was a "good shot, slightly above average," and "an excellent shot" compared with the general population. He noted that "With the equipment he had and with his ability," the shots were "very easy." A page from Oswald's U.S Marines score book is below.

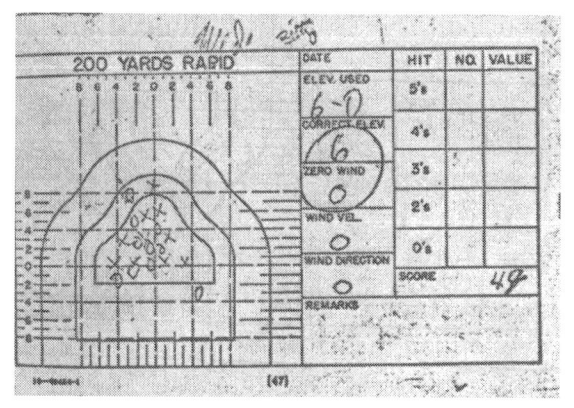

Oswald's Marine Corps rifle score book shows that on this day he scored 49 out of 50 points. This was rapid fire, in a sitting position, and with no telescopic scope. Note that this test was at 200 yards; the shot that killed Kennedy was only a distance of some 90 yards.

The 5.6 seconds used by The *Fifth Estate* for the timing of the shots came from the initial FBI report on the assassination. They believed the first shot hit Kennedy, the second shot hit Connally, and the third killed the president. That worked out to 5.6 seconds for the three shots. But their hasty conclusions were wrong—one shot hit both Kennedy and Connally. So if the first shot missed—and there were numerous witnesses who heard a shot before Kennedy was hit in the neck—Oswald would have had at least eight seconds, and perhaps longer, to fire his three shots, which was well within his capability.

Did the shots come from the front? As indicated in Chapter One, Dealey Plaza was a bit of an echo chamber. The HSCA analysis (see below) found that about 40 percent of witnesses were unable to distinguish the direction of the shots. While *The Fifth Estate* claimed that 64 witnesses "said the shots came from the grassy knoll," the HSCA could only find 20 such witnesses. This compares to the 46 witnesses who thought the shots came from the Texas School Book Depository behind the motorcade. Only four witnesses believed the shots came from more than one direction—a very good indicator that there was only one gunman.

Number of Shots Reported

	2	2 or 3	3	4	DON'T KNOW	TOTAL
TSBD	3 (4.6)	2 (1.9)	38 (35.5)	2 (1.6)	1 (2.4)	46
KNOLL	5 (2.0)	2 (0.8)	11 (15.4)	0 (0.7)	2 (1.1)	20
OTHER	2 (2.9)	1 (1.2)	22 (22.4)	3 (1.0)	1 (1.5)	29
DON'T KNOW	7 (7.5)	2 (3.1)	61 (58.6)	1 (2.7)	5 (4.0)	76
TOTAL	17	7	132	6	9	171*

The first entry is the obtained data. The number in parenthesis is the expected number of such judgements if the source and number of shots are independent judgements.

*7 other witnesses report 1, 4-5, 5, 6 or 8 shots.

JFK Exhibit F-360

A staple of *The Fifth Estate* JFK documentaries was the Zapruder film, the best complete film of the assassination. Bob McKeown, the host of 2017 *The Fifth Estate* documentary, narrated. "For the first time, the world could see John Kennedy put hands to his throat as the first bullet rips through him, from back to front. But watch as another bullet strikes; the President's head snaps backwards, convincing many of a second gunman in front of the car."

But the infamous head snap (back and to the left) is somewhat misleading—a computer analysis of the Zapruder film by Itek Corporation in 1976 showed that his head actually goes forward just over two inches between frame 312 and frame 313—indicating the shot pushed his head slightly forward before a neuromuscular spasm pushed him backwards.

The medical evidence is definitive that the fatal head shot could not have been fired from the grassy knoll in front of Kennedy. As indicated in Chapter Three, the autopsy X-rays and photographs are crystal clear—they show a small entrance wound in the back of Kennedy's head, which is indicative of an entry wound. Every forensic pathologist who has ever examined the autopsy materials agrees that he could only have been shot from behind.

The Fifth Estate also spread a lot of misinformation about Jack Ruby, the nightclub owner who shot Oswald two days after the assassination. The narrator in *Dallas and After* tells us that "When the Warren Commission came to Dallas, Jack Ruby pleaded to be moved from the Dallas jail to Washington. Do that he said and I think I can put it all together for you. Until his death from cancer in 1967 Ruby maintained he was part of a larger conspiracy." This is same accusation Ralph Schoenman made on Geraldo Rivera's show and that Mark Lane made in his book *Rush to Judgment*.

Extreme right-wing groups like the John Birch Society claimed that Ruby was part of a conspiracy to kill JFK. Ruby was paranoid and felt that, because he was Jewish, people might believe that the Jews were responsible. He believed that a second Holocaust was about to happen.

And while *The Fifth Estate* cast Ruby as a typical Mafia hitman, it didn't tell you the reason he phoned Mafia-related characters in the weeks before the assassination. Ruby needed help dealing with the American Guild of Variety Artists (AGVA). He owned two strip clubs and his competitors were using unpaid amateurs. He made frantic calls trying to get the AGVA to enforce its own rules against the employment of strippers who weren't being paid. Nobody was willing to help him.

In addition to getting the basic facts wrong about the assassination, *Dallas and After* enlisted the aid of Peter Dale Scott, a former Canadian diplomat and Professor of English at University of California, Berkeley, and an erudite scholar whose conclusions were, nonetheless, ill-founded. He went on to write several books on the 'deep state' which showcased his use of the 'six degrees of separation' theory. He paraded out an endless array of corrupt people with ominous connections—but with no actual proof of anything. He helped the CBC find a bunch of crackpots and cranks.

As an example, he wrote a letter to the editor of the *New York Review of Books* in 1975 about Oswald's mysterious intelligence connections. In September of 1963, Oswald wanted to travel to Mexico City, which required an entry permit from the Mexican consulate in New Orleans. Scott writes that "One notes moreover that Oswald's Mexican travel permit followed in numerical sequence that of editor William C. Gaudet, who later volunteered information to the FBI about Jack Ruby in New Orleans, and later still identified himself as a former 'employee of CIA.'"

Sounds suspicious, no? Gaudet just happened to get his permit to travel to Mexico right before Oswald got his in New Orleans. But he told investigators that he didn't see Oswald, and his denial is plausible given the fact that few people were applying for visas. Further, Gaudet didn't travel to Mexico with Oswald; he travelled a week before Oswald, and his ultimate destination was somewhere in Central America.

And while he did in fact contact the FBI, it was only to "advise that he had heard Jack Ruby from Dallas, Texas, had purchased paintings from one Lorenzo Borenstein who has an art gallery somewhere in the 500 block of Royal Street." Borenstein then told the FBI that Ruby did buy paintings from him in 1959. As for being an employee of the CIA, Gaudet was never an agent—he just volunteered information to the CIA as part of its Domestic Contacts Service about his travels to Latin America from 1948-1955. Conspiracy buffs have long maintained that the CIA helped fund his newsletter but the HSCA reviewed his CIA file and found that he "tried unsuccessfully to obtain financial loans from the Agency, through DCD [Domestic Contacts Division], to support his publication."

Despite Gaudet's complete non-involvement in anything relating to JFK assassination, he "was tracked down" by Scott and interviewed in *The Fifth Estate* documentary. He was introduced first as a "CIA agent" and then as a "CIA contract man." You might have thought that *The Fifth Estate* would ask him what he actually did for the CIA. They didn't, or if they did, they didn't put in their documentary.

Scott mentions ominously that the Warren Commission removed all mention of his receiving his tourist card right before Oswald's. He neglects to mention that Gaudet was left out of some documents because they were only focusing on people whose final destination was Mexico. And despite the fact that Gaudet never even met Oswald, he tells *The Fifth Estate* that "I think Oswald was nothing more or less than just a patsy in my book. That's my opinion of Oswald. I think he was used." Gaudet goes further and claims that "Apparently there were many persons involved in a conspiracy for Kennedy. You had many persons who wanted him dead."

Another talking head that McKenna used in two of his documentaries was Colonel L. Fletcher Prouty, the Mr. X in Oliver Stone's film *JFK*. He charged that there was a 'sheep-dipping operation' to hide Oswald's CIA activities; that witnesses were dying unnatural deaths; that there was a huge change in American foreign policy after the assassination; and that there was a huge coverup. He helped conclude the 1977 documentary by claiming that "Today the biggest crime is the crime of the coverup. Think of how carefully the coverup has been put on from the beginning….and here we are now 13 years later and there is still a coverup of the death of President Kennedy. That takes power."

All nonsense, of course. Oswald had no connection whatsoever to the CIA. The HSCA investigated every possible angle and concluded that there was "no evidence of any relationship between Oswald and the CIA."

And witnesses were not dying unnaturally. In fact, the HSCA asked the Congressional Research Service arm of the Library of Congress to investigate the circumstances of deaths of 21 people connected in some way to the assassination. They did not find anything mysterious at all. Researcher Jacqueline Hess testified that "Our final conclusion on the issue is that the available evidence does not establish anything about the nature of these deaths which would indicate that the deaths were in some manner, either direct or peripheral, caused by the assassination of President Kennedy or by any aspect of the subsequent investigation."

As pointed out earlier, U.S. foreign policy did not change in the aftermath of the assassination.

McKenna should have had some idea that Prouty was a crank. In 1975, Prouty wrote "The Guns of Dallas," in *Gallery*, a Penthouse-type magazine which billed him as its "National Affairs Editor." Prouty claimed the Watergate burglars were "working for somebody much higher up. They were all pawns, just like Nixon was. This is a game for the biggest stake of all—absolute control of the government of the United States of America; and, with control of this government, control of the world." The JFK assassination was the "crime of the century" and "if we the people of the United States do not demand its resolution this year, it will stand in the way of a free election in 1976." There was a "massive conspiracy" that "hired at least four expert 'mechanics' (assassins). This group wielded control over elements of the Dallas police, the Sheriff's office, the FBI, the Secret Service, and the CIA. This great cabal had control high enough in government…to be able to influence the travel plans of the President, the Vice-President, and a Presidential candidate (Nixon) and all members of the Kennedy cabinet. They were powerful enough to have orders issued to the Army, and they were able to mount a massive campaign to control the media during and after the assassination."

The most sensational part of *Dallas and After* is when Adrienne Clarkson talks to Gerry Patrick Hemming, an ex-Marine soldier of fortune who was involved in the fight to overthrow Castro. He told *The Fifth Estate* a wonderful story indicative of a healthy imagination. Here's the complete discussion:

> Hemming: I'd been to the White House earlier that year [1963] in March. I was in the east wing of the White House having an interview with the military aide to the President, General Clifton. I'd been to the Pentagon, the State department, what have you earlier in 1963. I'd done quite a bit of travelling. Had new contacts, dealt with very prominent people and in travelling I heard constant comments as to a

solution to the Kennedy problem. It got very serious as to why uh waste time in Cuba. Why risk lives. The whole problem is in the White House. That should be taken care of."

Adrienne Clarkson: Did someone walk in with a case of money and ask you to kill John Kennedy?"

Hemming: Well only one time was there money on the table. All other times we got out of the conversation and out of the meeting gracefully enough to avoid discussing any figures. Obviously these people had uh they'd been recommended to us and we'd been recommended to them and now suddenly we were discovering why these recommendations had been made and why these introductions had been made.

Clarkson: What kinds of techniques were discussed?

Hemming: Just proper standard techniques.

Clarkson: Such as?

Hemming: Sniper's techniques, explosive techniques. Remote control explosive devices. Shooters.

Clarkson: Do you think number of different groups were putting out a contract on Kennedy's Life?

Hemming: That was the feeling we had before Dealey Plaza. My name was thrown into the mill and into the Warren Com-

mission right off the bat. I was prime shooter. My crew was the only capable team in the whole United States of America. This was from day one this was pushed. And it upset me to a great degree and I've made it a point to find out who did what who didn't do what in the last 14 years. I've answered a lot of questions myself.

Clarkson: Answer me one. Who did it. Who did the job?

Hemming: I know personally of more than one group of individual that collected money and they ripped them off. They didn't do the job. They took credit for it. Well they only, they'd taken money beforehand. Stroke of luck for them.

Does any of this make any sense? Tantalizing clues about absolutely nothing.

Less than six months later, Hemming testified before the HSCA. His first-hand story morphed into "offhand remarks" at a meeting in Dallas sometime in 1962 which Hemming characterized as "loose conversation." It took up less than a page in a deposition of 200 pages, and Hemming wasn't even mentioned in the HSCA Final Report.

Over the years, Hemming's spiel has included more and more characters from the assassination saga (Oswald, Ruby and others), he was willing to tell stories to any researcher and any JFK conspiracy group with the time to listen. The 1996 JFK Lancer conference convened a panel discussion with him, and researcher John Kelin wrote that "as far I could tell, [he] provided little more than a measure of comic relief." He elaborated that "we were not, however, treated to many serious answers during the hour or so the panel lasted. In fact, many of his answers were couched in sarcasm, and somewhat condescending irony." Hemming went on to charge that Oswald was following him around at an anti-Castro training camp near Lake Pontchartrain, north of New Orleans. The moderator asked Hemming, "What would you perceive to be the purpose, or function of Oswald being on your tail?" He answered, "They [the anti-Castro Cubans] pegged him as a Soviet agent. Who knows what's in these peoples' heads, what they had him doing. I want you to penetrate these exile groups, kid, and I'll give you an extra Snickers bar."

Hemming also hung out on JFK assassination bulletin boards on the Internet. He was asked about his interview in *Dallas and After* in 2006 and he disputed the accuracy of the transcript. He wrote that "The CBC lady who was doing the interviewing...she didn't know sxxx-from-Shinola, and I quickly became aggravated that she hadn't a clue about the subject matter." Hemming died in 2008 and will forever remain a small footnote in the JFK assassination.

In *Who Killed JFK?*, the 1983 documentary, the CBC issued a memo to their regional publicists bragging that "we are the only network and program to devote a full hour exclusively to the assassination 20 years after Kennedy's death." Another memo from Ron Haggart, Senior Producer of *The Fifth Estate*, to Brian McKenna noted "our mastery of responsible sensationalism."

Unfortunately, their sensationalism was anything but responsible.

Brian McKenna was also taken with a conspiracy book, *Best Evidence*, published in 1981 by long-time researcher David Lifton who claimed to have uncovered explosive new evidence proving conspiracy. Lifton had noticed a strange sentence in an old FBI report written about JFK's autopsy. The two FBI agents, James Sibert and Francis O'Neil, noted that at the start of the autopsy, the pathologists mentioned that "a tracheotomy had been performed, as well as surgery of the head area, namely in the top of the skull." Lifton saw this and wondered what it all meant.

His book figured out the puzzle.

He noticed that there was a discrepancy between the wounds the doctors in Dallas remembered (a large one in the back of Kennedy's head) and the description of the those by the autopsy pathologists (a small entrance wound in the back of Kennedy's head). Lifton theorized that the "surgery" altered Kennedy's wounds to make it look like he had been shot by a lone gunman from behind.

A wave of criticism hit Lifton's book. Harrison Salisbury wrote in *The New York Times* that "no one before Lifton has constructed a theory so complicated, so quirky, in such violation of every law of common sense and reason." Thomas Powers wrote in *New York* magazine that *Best Evidence* "is a shocking mishmash. I challenge anybody connected with it—always excepting the author—to stand up in public and say he believes things happened this way."

Brian McKenna felt that this was a story worthy of national airtime. He called Lifton's research "riveting" and featured him in four of his six documentaries. In *Who Killed JFK?*, Lifton explained what happened. "Between the Dallas shooting and the Bethesda autopsy six hours later, President Kennedy's body was secretly removed from the casket. It was then surgically changed. Wounds were altered. Bullets were removed. The body was returned in time for the autopsy—returned as a medical forgery which told a false story of the shooting."

The Fifth Estate did not air a JFK assassination documentary in the 1990s. But there was something in the works. A Montreal researcher, Ulric Shannon, who is now the Canadian Consul General in Ankara, was contacted in the beginning of 1994 about serving as a consultant for a new documentary. In an article for a research conference in 1996,

Shannon wrote that the producers weren't excited about his proposals because "the areas I found most interesting conspiracy-wise would be like Chinese to anyone outside this room. I think the producers expected me to start telling them about the magic bullet or the Zapruder film head snap; but when instead I began talking about Oswald's possible relationship to the Dodd subcommittee [Senator Thomas Dodd was the chair of a Senate subcommittee looking into the Fair Play for Cuba Committee of which Oswald started a chapter in New Orleans], and the vagaries of the acoustical evidence, and the disinformation campaign of the Mexico City CIA station, all I got back was a blank state: What the hell is this guy talking about? None of that stuff was in *JFK*!"

McKenna brought David Lifton back for his 2013 documentary, *The Conspiracy Files: JFK and 9/11*. Lifton tells viewers that "I'm going to use the word I don't like to use, but basically we had a coup. That's what this is all about, not about a second assassin or whether there's somebody hiding behind a fence or a bush. Is the story that Oswald shot the President a true story or fictional story? If it's a true story, Johnson became President by a quirk of fate. If it's a fictional story, he became President by design. Now I say it's a fictional story because the evidence is fraudulent."

Of course, Lifton's theory is absolutely ridiculous. Wounds created after the heart stops pumping blood have a lighter colour and would be easily recognizable by autopsy surgeons. Even Dr. Cyril Wecht, McKenna's resident forensic pathologist, told author Gerald Posner that "Lifton gets away with crap and no one challenges him. I could assemble a whole team of the best surgeons in the country and still not be able to accomplish in a day what Lifton says was done in a few hours. I have never bought this stuff. It can't be done." And McKenna conveniently left out of his documentary any mention of his conversation in September, 1983, with Dr. Michael Baden, Chair of the HSCA Forensic Pathology Panel. Baden told McKenna that there was "no merit" to Lifton's hypothesis and that there was "absolutely no evidence of surgery before the autopsy." *Fifth Estate* viewers never heard what Baden had to say.

And *The Fifth Estate* also didn't mention that fact that four of the Dallas doctors involved in treating Kennedy went to the National Archives in Washington, D.C., in 1988 to view the autopsy X-Rays and photographs. They all went on the record to confirm the authenticity of the autopsy materials. There was no discrepancy between what they saw in Dallas and the body at the autopsy in Bethesda. The evidence is irrefutable: Kennedy's body was not altered to hide evidence of anything.

In November, 2017, McKenna and *The Fifth Estate* were back with a new documentary, *The JFK Files: The Murder of a President*. This time, the focus was on newly-released documents which included tidbits about CIA schemes to kill Fidel Castro and the FBI's dim view of Martin Luther King but nothing particularly revelatory about the Kennedy assassination. Some documents were withheld by the Trump administration in the name of national security. That was enough to inspire McKenna to recycle some hoary old myths about the "truth" and the "cover-up."

But, once again McKenna had some big news—a document dated two days after the assassination in which FBI Director J. Edgar Hoover is quoted as saying: "The thing I am concerned about is having something issued so that we can convince the public that Oswald is the real assassin." This was presented as new evidence confirming the belief held by "many" that "Lee Harvey Oswald was the U.S. government's patsy in JFK's death."

But the document is not "new" at all. It was written by Walter Jenkins, an aide to President Lyndon Johnson, and it was published 38 years ago by the HSCA. All it confirms is Hoover's concern that "the public needed to be settled down" as FBI inspector James Malley, in charge of the investigation in Dallas, explained to the House Committee.

There was much concern about public reaction in the wake of the murder. Gossip about an international conspiracy was rampant because Oswald was a communist who had defected to the Soviet Union in 1959. Hoover and Kennedy's successor in the White House wanted to stop the rumours from escalating into a full-blown Cold War panic.

A major segment of *The JFK Files* concerns the theories of Jefferson Morley, a former reporter for the *Washington Post* and author of *The Ghost: The Secret Life of CIA Spymaster James Jesus Angleton*. Morley claims that the CIA "were paying attention to Oswald from November 1959 to November 1963" and that they had the "capabilities to monitor and manipulate Oswald." He asks whether the CIA could "have been manipulating him for other purposes, like to gather intelligence or you know to lure the KGB into something. Or they could have been manipulating him for something that was going to happen on November 22nd?"

VIDEO

New JFK documents suggest CIA had 'very intensive' interest in Oswald before assassination: Fifth Estate

Author says files show Central Intelligence Agency gave 'cover story' on surveillance

CBC News · Posted: Nov 17, 2017 5:00 PM ET | Last Updated: November 17, 2017

Intriguing headline masks an article with very little substance

According to Thomas Powers, "That's a question more than a little like standing up in church to ask the minister if he is sexually abusing his daughter. A man must earn the right to pose such a question. There can be no excuse for putting it casually, and none for failing to follow it with an adequate answer. If the answer is 'yes' it demands a true bill of supporting evidence. Morley offers none. If the answer is 'no' it demands a frank admission that the answer is 'no', but Morley cannot bring himself to say it. With this silence he forfeits all claim to be taken seriously as a historian."

Journalist and author Max Holland, who has written extensively on the JFK assassination, believes that "Morley desperately tries to peddle abroad (in Canada, Mexico, and elsewhere) what he can't sell at home. Ignorance is his necessary companion."

The plain fact of the matter is that the CIA noticed Lee Harvey Oswald's defection in 1959. They actively intercepted his mail for a while and then stopped in 1962 when he returned to the United States. When Oswald visited the Soviet and Cuban embassies in Mexico City in 1963, they picked up his activity—not because they were specifically targeting him but because they were watching the missions.

McKenna foreshadows his next *Fifth Estate* Kennedy expose by suggesting the JFK files that were held back contain the "crown jewels—there's something explosive there." But don't hold your breath. In *Reclaiming History*, Vincent Bugliosi's exhaustively-researched 2007 account of the assassination, Judge John Tunheim, Chairman of the Assassinations Record and Review Board (ARRB), said he had examined all of the redacted material and found "nothing in any of the documents that was central to the assassination. There's no smoking gun, and no *substantive* information was protected and not released by way of redactions." He further told Bugliosi that the only materials still protected were the names of intelligence agents "who proved to us that there could be some harm to them by the release of their name" and methods of intelligence gathering and issues related to presidential security.

Fortunately, McKenna had a source none of the other investigations had—Cuban dictator Fidel Castro. He got a chance to quiz Castro on the Kennedy story when he visited Cuba in 1992 for his miniseries

Pierre Trudeau: Memoirs. Castro told McKenna that Oswald was a CIA agent hooked up with anti-Castro Cubans. McKenna bought the story and reported it to his national CBC audience on November 17 as gospel: "They [the CIA] were running him, they were controlling him."

As of March 2018, thousands more documents have been released and no crown jewels have emerged.

And, while *The Fifth Estate* is upset that Trump is still withholding some documents, they sure don't mind keeping their own documents secret. I filed several Access to Information requests about McKenna's various documentaries, and the CBC either claimed an exemption to the Act or said they could find no files. In one filing, I just asked for a list of documentaries on the JFK assassination produced by Brian McKenna for *The Fifth Estate,* and the CBC replied that "no records were found to respond to your request." All of the cases are under appeal and it's been almost a year without an answer.

I did manage to find a transcript of the 1977 documentary, *Dallas and After*, from the Harold Weisberg Archive on the web. McKenna had corresponded with Weisberg about the JFK assassination and had sent him a transcript. I even have a copy of the CBC envelope used to send the document. So, a private researcher in the United States can get a transcript but a Canadian citizen can't?

And what has the CBC done with all the interviews it has conducted with witnesses for its documentaries? In a letter to Harold Weisberg from April 20, 1978, Mckenna wrote that "As far as transcripts of our interviews are concerned, we sent all the tapes to Mary Farrel [sic] and I understand she was going to transcribe them all, and make copies available to anyone who requested them." E-mails sent between members of the ARRB indicate that 25 audio cassettes were indeed sent to the Mary

Ferrell Foundation. They have yet to be transcribed. It's too bad Canadians cannot get them from the CBC.

In the absence of any "crown jewels," what comes next for Brian McKenna and *The Fifth Estate*? There are clues in his 2010 speech to JFK Lancer in Dallas and in a book review on Amazon. There are two more crackpot theories just waiting for the Canadian viewing audience, and McKenna calls them "game changers."

First, McKenna has bought into the theories of an analyst who worked for the ARRB, Doug Horne, who wrote a series of books extending David Lifton's body alteration theories. McKenna told Amazon's readers that Horne's research is "unparalleled, the writing crisp and honest, it's a courageous cri-de-coeur, ranking with *J'accuse*, Emile Zola's eloquent charge that Dreyfus had been railroaded by the French ruling class. In this case, the innocent man is Oswald, the culprit America's national security state. Horne does not shirk from naming names, in the secret service, the CIA, the military, and finally, LBJ himself."

Horne believes the Zapruder film is fraudulent and so now McKenna thinks it is "radioactive" and thus its "authenticity splits assassination researchers—the old guard arguing it's an unsurpassed assassination record, the new guard arguing the CIA corrupted it the night of the murder." Yup, McKenna thinks the Zapruder film was faked and that this has been confirmed by "Hollywood special effects experts." To McKenna, this is a story "worthy of Jason Bourne."

Second, McKenna is taken with the book, *JFK and the Unspeakable: Why He Died and Why It Matters*, by James Douglass. This book accepts the wacky theories of researcher John Armstrong who believes that there were two Oswalds—one being the real Lee Harvey Oswald who was a patsy, and the other an imposter who leaves a trail of incriminating evidence tying him to the crime. Douglass even claims that Oswald was "an FBI informant trying to stop the CIA plot to kill the President." McKenna told the JFK Lancer audience that he recommended *JFK and the Unspeakable* because it "made the second Oswald story so credible." He wasn't the only one to find the book credible. Yoko Ono, the widow of John Lennon, wrote "I cried all night reading it, and didn't sleep a wink."

The 60th anniversary of Kennedy's murder is coming up in November, 2023. Set your clocks. My bet is that Brian McKenna and *The Fifth Estate* will be back with yet more "responsible sensationalism."

Seven

The Quest for the Holy Document

When Jim Garrison addressed the jury in his closing remarks in the Clay Shaw trial, he told them that "We're forced either to leave this country or to accept the authoritarianism that has developed—the authoritarianism which tells us that in the year 2039 we can see the evidence about what happened to John Kennedy."

Jim Marrs wrote in *Crossfire* that there was an "effort on the part of federal authorities to lock assassination evidence away from the public" and that "President Johnson ordered evidence locked up until the year 2039."

Actually, Earl Warren helped fuel this belief when he told the press after his report was released that there were things that would not be revealed in our lifetime. Warren was taken out of context. He actually commented when Marina Oswald was testifying (she was the first witness before the Commission) that some security matters might come up because Lee Harvey Oswald had defected to the USSR and had been visiting the Cuban and Soviet embassies in Mexico City. Warren said that "we don't know yet what that will involve." He added that "Yes, there will come a time—but it might not be in your lifetime. I am not referring to anything especially—but there may be some thing that would involve security. That would be preserved but not made public."

Over the years, more and more documents and records have been released but no major revelation on the assassination has emerged. Even so, the belief in the holy grail persists. You saw that in the last chapter, when CBC producer Brian McKenna clung to the mantra that very soon, it's just a matter time, any day now, perhaps tomorrow, we are indeed getting closer to the crown jewels. He'll go to his grave waiting for that glorious day.

Of course, there has always been a reluctance of governments to release documents. For instance, John McAdams lists on his JFK website several US government documents that have recently been declassified. These include "Monthly Statistical Bulletins and Current Fishery Statistics for the Ports of Boston and Gloucester, MA, 1901-1944 and Portland, Maine, 1915-1944," and "Bird Migration Schedules and Waterfowl Reports 1888-1924."

Here's a document from General Dwight D. Eisenhower to the Chiefs of Staffs regarding the end of World War II that was only declassified in 2012:

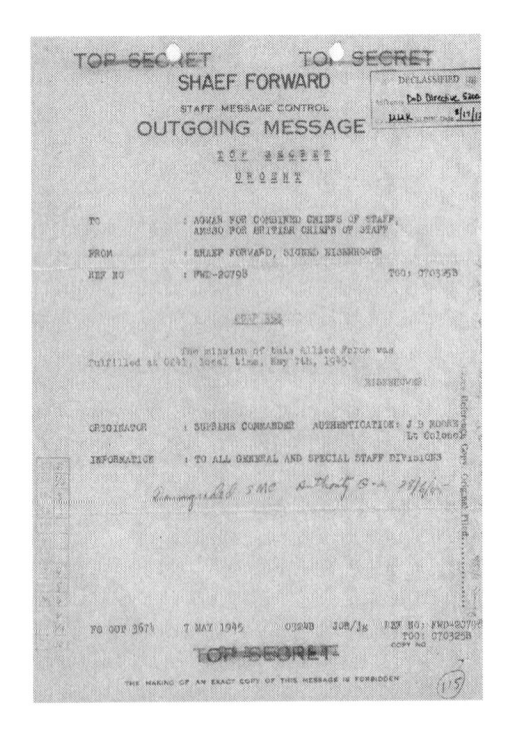

I Was a Teenage JFK Conspiracy Freak

In 2010, a *Washington Post* article discussed a lawsuit to force the government to release documents on "Secret Inks," "Detection of Secret Ink," and "German Secret Ink Formula" that date back to World War I. The CIA was reluctant to release these documents, claiming that they could compromise national security. Lawyer Mark Zaid ultimately did receive a 1945 report entitled "Secret Ink Technical Manual" but only with redactions.

A 1972 document detailing the exchange of gifts between China and the United States from 1972 was not declassified until 1997. The Americans gave the Chinese musk oxen in exchange for two pandas.

It's not just the United States that likes to keep documents secret. Canada too. Historian Dennis Molinaro was told that the Privy Council Office (PCO) holds more than 1.5 million pages from the Cold War era and that the Communications Security Establishment (CSE) is holding records dating back six decades. The PCO confirmed to the CBC that they have 1,430 cubic feet of unreleased records dating back several decades.

The UK's Foreign and Commonwealth Office (FCO) are holding documents dating back to the final years of the British Empire. The secret archive contains 200 boxes of files, and the UK government pledged in 2013 to go through the documents. Even so, many documents are still being withheld under a variety of legal exemptions.

The critics of the Warren Report always assume horrible reasons why documents are kept secret and are redacted. Warren Commission Exhibit 917 is an interesting case study in how the critics misled the public. The document (reproduced below) is a cablegram from the Naval Attaché in the American Embassy in Moscow to the Department of the Navy. Researcher Paul Hoch attended one of Mark Lane's standard presentation in August, 1966, which included a discussion of this document. The redaction seemingly describes Oswald as a "former Marine and [redaction starts]" and Lane would say, "And what? Star of stage, screen and radio?" Hoch noted that "this was one of his reliable laugh lines. The implication was that the redaction was hiding an Oswald intelligence connection."

Hoch eventually found a document with a shorter redaction:

LEE HARVEY OSWALD FORMER MARINE AND [REDACTED] FORMER NAVY.

To Hoch, this made it clear that the redaction was about another person, and not an indication of Oswald's intelligence connection. He gave Lane a copy of the document and said, "I probably said something like, great work, Mr. Lane, but I have an explanation for one point." A few days later, Lane was on the radio repeating his allegations about CD 917. In an e-mail to me, Hoch gives Lane the benefit of the doubt, saying he might have been "too busy to absorb the new information."

However, in Lane's 1968 book, *A Citizen's Dissent*, he repeats the story in a chapter on Albert Jenner, one of the Warren Commission's lawyers. Lane recounts a discussion he had with Jenner on the Jerry Williams radio program in Chicago to discuss the JFK assassination. He asked Jenner about the redaction and Jenner told him that he did not know what was removed from the document. Lane replied that the commission should have known. Fair point, but by the time *A Citizen's Dissent* was published, Lane knew that the redaction was not about Oswald, and he neglected to mention it in his book.

And, in fact, Warren Commission Document 1114 contains the complete wording of the document.

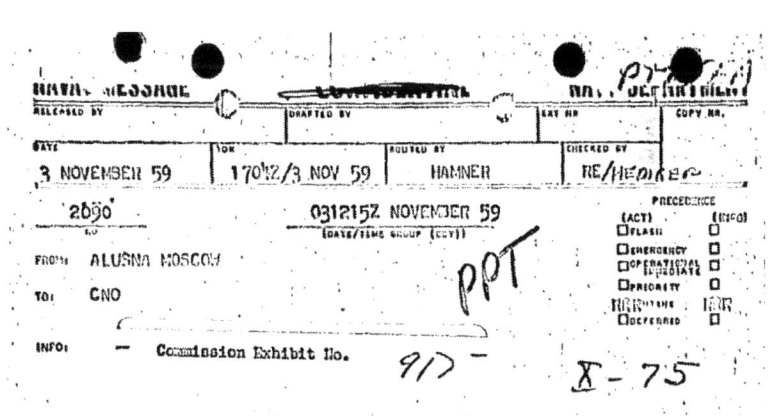

The redaction was about Robert Webster, a former navy man who had defected to the Soviet Union. This Warren Commission document also proves that investigators had actually seen the full text. I'm not sure when Lane stopped using CE 917 as part of his shtick.

So, it's not surprising that other long-sought documents ended up being just as innocuous. Jim Garrison wrote in his book, *On the Trail of the Assassins*, that Oswald's "possible intelligence role" could possibly be confirmed by two Warren Commission documents: CD 931, "Oswald's access to information about the U-2," and CD 692, "Reproduction of CIA official dossier on Oswald."

Garrison assumed that CD 931 would confirm that "Lee Harvey Oswald, who we're assured had no ties to any Government agency, had access to information about the nation's most secret high-altitude reconnaissance plane."

Unfortunately, both of these documents were still classified and Garrison could not see them.

He also put together a list of other seemingly important documents that were "unavailable."

CD 321: Chronology of Oswald in the USSR

CD 347: Activity of Oswald in Mexico City

CD 384: Activity of Oswald in Mexico City

CD 528: re: Allegation Oswald Interviewed by VIA in Mexico City

CD 631: re: CIA dissemination of information on Oswald

CD 674: Info given to the Secret Service but not yet to the Warren Commission

CD 692: Reproduction of CIA official dossier on Oswald

CD 698: Reports of travel and activities of Oswald and Marina

CD 871: Photos of Oswald in Russia

CD 931: Oswald's access to information about the U-2

CD 1216: Memo from Helms entitled "Lee Harvey Oswald"

CD 1222: Statements by George de Mohrenschildt re: Assassination

CD 1273: Memo from Helms re: apparent inconsistencies in info provided by CIA

Garrison wrote that "This provocative listing made it more apparent to me than ever that something was fishy." He told *Playboy* that he was "already training my eight-year-old son to keep himself physically fit so that on one glorious September morn in 2038 he can walk into the National Archives in Washington to find out what the CIA knew about Lee Harvey Oswald."

All of the above documents are now public and they are all online, in their entirety, on the Mary Ferrell website. And guess what? There is absolutely nothing suspicious in any of them. CD 931 actually said that Oswald had no access to information on the U-2 while stationed at Atsugi Air Base in the Marines, and CD 692, the CIA's dossier on Oswald, also contained nothing to sustain Garrison's allegations.

If you read the above documents, you may begin to wonder just why they were kept secret for so many years. The answer reflects more on the CIA's inherent desire for secrecy rather than protecting conspiratorial information on the assassination.

In any event, Jim Garrison would have to thank Oliver Stone for his son's dashed hopes.

Stone ended his film with the following screenshot:

200   *The Quest for the Holy Document*

> A Congressional Investigation from 1976-1979 found a "probable conspiracy" in the assassination of John F. Kennedy and recommended the Justice Department investigate further. As of 1991, the Justice Department has done nothing. The files of the House Select Committee on Assassinations are locked away until the year 2029.
>
> **WHAT IS PAST IS PROLOGUE**

It's interesting that Stone referenced the House Select Committee on Assassinations (HSCA) because he totally ignored all of their scientific tests confirming that Lee Harvey Oswald shot JFK. But one good thing that did emerge from Stone's film was The President John F. Kennedy Assassination Records Collection Act of 1992 mandating the public disclosure of assassination-related documents.

By the time Stone made his film, most JFK assassination documents were already public. In fact, one critic, Harold Weisberg, wrote actor Kevin Costner a letter detailing why he was being deceived when he told the press that "all those documents which the government sealed until 2029 should be opened now so that we can know what happened." Weisberg had been quite successfully using the Freedom of Information Act to pry information from the FBI and the CIA.

So, what is the truth about JFK assassination documents?

When the Warren Commission wrapped up shop in 1964, it sent all of its materials to the National Archives. This consisted of 302 cubic feet of records and 58 cubic feet of physical exhibits. The National Archives had a rule that all records from federal agencies and commissions be kept secret for 75 years. This was the automatic procedure then in place, and it had nothing to do with the Warren Commission. Seventy-five years was thought to be the life-span of individuals and would thus protect the privacy of people who might be involved with any investigation or commission.

In 1965, the mayor of Cedar Rapids wrote President Lyndon Johnson a letter complaining about the rule and its applicability to the Warren Commission records. The Johnson administration asked for a background memo on the subject and Earl Warren sent a letter to the Attorney General stating he wanted the "fullest public disclosure."

In April, 1965, the White House approved new guidelines to disclose Warren Commission documents, and by July, 1966, approximately 80% of the documents it placed in the National Archives from various agencies had been released. The guidelines were then superseded by the Freedom of Information Act of 1966, which came into effect in July, 1967. It allowed individuals to ask for FBI, CIA, and other related records. By 1992, approximately 98% of Warren Commission records had been released. By the time the JFK Act passed, only 3,000 pages of Warren Commission material remained to be released. The FBI had already released some 220,000 pages through the Freedom of Information Act.

Because it was a congressional committee, when the HSCA finished its work, its records were sealed under the standard 50-year period for Congress, until 2029. Legislation was tabled to release those documents, but the House never got to vote. Of course, any underlying FBI or CIA materials would be subject to the Freedom of Information Act. But the HSCA itself had generated over 400,000 pages of records and they needed to be released.

Jim Lesar, a lawyer who has battled for the release of documents over the years, told Vincent Bugliosi why agencies are so reluctant to let go. "What underlies their resistance to releasing documents is that they want to control the information that gets out about them, and their conduct. In many cases, they don't know for certain whether information in a document is harmful, but they consider there's always a possibility it might be in some way they don't even know about. They view requesters as subversives, a class of people who are looking for information to hurt them."

The JFK Act commissioned the Assassinations Record Review Board (ARRB) to gather and release all possible records related to the JFK assassination. One of the first tasks of the ARRB was to define an assassination record. Hearings were actually held on this topic, and in 1995, the final definition was published. They decided to use a wide net and they determined that any records that were "reasonably related" to the assassination would be a defined record. They also decided that they would "request additional records and information when necessary for identifying, evaluating, or interpreting assassination records, including assassination records that agencies that may not have initially located or identified."

So they needed the CIA to provide actual names when pseudonyms were used in records. Similarly, FBI documents sometimes used a number in place of an informant's name. The ARRB had the power to ask the FBI to reveal informant names and, in the end, the FBI had to review, process, and transfer more than 795,000 pages to the National Archives.

The ARRB reviewed over 27,000 previously redacted documents; obtained another 33,000 records from various agencies; bought the Zapruder film so that it belonged to the American people; secured records relating to Jim Garrison's prosecution of Clay Shaw; digitized all the autopsy X-rays and photographs; released thousands of pages about the Bay of Pigs and anti-Castro activities; released a broad cross-section of surveillance files of organized crime, including that of Carlos Marcello, the mob head of New Orleans, and other people like Johnny Roselli, Sam Giancana and Santos Trafficante; and they made public all FBI and CIA documents from previous investigations.

Even the National Security Agency (NSA) was forced to release files. Their files showed that intercepts from Cuba indicated that Castro was not involved in the assassination.

At the end of its life in 1998, the ARRB had released more than five million pages in over 300,000 records. This represented a cumulative total of 99.9% of all assassination-related documents. Approximately one percent of non-assassination records were withheld in full. The Chairman of the ARRB, Judge John Tunheim told Vincent Bugliosi that there was "nothing in any of the documents that was central to the assassination. There's no smoking gun, and no substantive information that was protected and not released by way of redaction."

The only material left to be released were the documents with redactions and a few thousand documents that were withheld for national security reasons or in cases of personal privacy. They were all non-assassination related.

There was a feeding frenzy when new JFK documents were released in 2017 and 2018. As indicated in Chapter Six on the CBC, some documents weren't exactly new and, as a result, the press reported a lot of sensational stories. Dale Myers, one of the best researchers on the assassination, collected a series of these so-called stories on his blog.

One CIA memo, written the day after the assassination, reported that the *Cambridge News* in the UK had received an anonymous phone call 25 minutes before the assassination saying that they should call the American Embassy for some big news. Here's the headline in *Newsweek*:

U.S.

JFK FILES: UK PAPER RECEIVED CURIOUS TIP ABOUT HALF AN HOUR BEFORE THE KENNEDY ASSASSINATION

BY MELINA DELKIC ON 10/27/17 AT 1:35 PM

Had they Googled *Cambridge News* and JFK they would have found that Michael Eddowes wrote about this in his 1977 book, *The Oswald File.* They also failed to call the Cambridge News where this had been a source of discussion for years. Senior reporter Jock Gillespie said this: "There is no way in hell that would have happened without being talked about. There are three or four of us that still get together, 'the old farts', and there's no way that wouldn't have been talked about—that would have never ever got past us. People I knew at that time wouldn't have shut up about that—it would have been published as well. That's been a windup—are you sure it isn't Cambridge Massachusetts they are talking about?" Other senior reporters, who are still alive, also disputed the story and wondered why on earth somebody would call the *Cambridge Times*, of all newspapers, with such a story. As Dale Myers puts it, "the assassination files are filled with examples of unsubstantiated clairvoyance relating to every aspect of the assassination story."

One of the so-called new documents was a deposition of former CIA Director Richard Helms before the Rockefeller Commission in 1975. They were investigating the domestic activities of the CIA and he was asked about Lee Harvey Oswald.

> *Mr. Belin: Well, now, the final area of my interrogation relates to charges that the CIA was in some way conspiratorially involved with the assassination of President Kennedy. During the time of the Warren Commission, you were Deputy Director of Plans, is that correct?*
>
> *Mr. Helms: I believe so.*

> *Mr. Belin: Is there any information involved with the assassination of President Kennedy which is any way shows that Lee Harvey Oswald was in some way a CIA agent or an age[nt]...*

The file was truncated right when Helms was about to answer. This led to an incredible headline in the Sun newspaper in the UK:

> **COVER-UP? JFK files CUT OUT CIA director's reply to whether Lee Harvey Oswald was a secret agent... so will we ever know the truth?**
>
> Bombshell revelation contained in top secret transcript shows former agency chief Richard Helms was asked about theory that JFK's assassin was a CIA agent - but the answer has been cut off
>
> By Neal Baker
> 27th October 2017, 10:16 am | Updated: 27th October 2017, 11:32 am

The story was covered by the *Washington Post* and the *Huffington Post*, and even the *New York Times* said it "may add to the questions" about conspiracy. But the truth is that Helm's testimony was declassified in 1994 along with his full answer.

> *Mr. Belin: Is there any information involved with the assassination of President Kennedy which in any way shows that Lee Harvey Oswald was in some way a CIA agent or an agent of the FBI or any other Government agency?*
>
> *Mr. Helms: Mr. Belin, this question, and I think you may recall this, was raised at the time and the Agency was never able to find any evidence whatsoever, and we really searched that it had any contact with Lee Harvey Oswald. As far as*

the FBI was concerned, my recollection is not all that precise. I believe that Mr. Hoover testified that he had not been an agent of theirs either. He was certainly not an agent of the CIA. He was certainly never used by the CIA. Whether any CIA officer ever talked to him any place or not I don't know but I certainly felt quite comfortable——I believe Mr. [John] McCone [a previous CIA director] was asked to testify before the Commission on this point. I believe he was asked to testify. It was a hot item anyway at the time. And my recollection is that I informed Mr. McCone that we could find no evidence that Oswald had any connection with the CIA.

And the height of ridiculousness was captured in this *Daily Mail* headline from October, 2017.

> **Daily Mail** News
>
> **FBI informant claimed Dallas police officer J.D Tippit was the REAL JFK assassin - not Lee Harvey Oswald, secret files reveal**
>
> - The patrolman was killed by Lee Harvey Oswald 45 minutes after he shot JFK
> - An informant claimed to the FBI that Tippit actually carried out the assassination
> - It was claimed officer met with Oswald and Jack Ruby a week before JFK's killing
> - Oswald shot J.D Tippit through head at point blank range after assassination
>
> By TARIQ TAHIR FOR MAILONLINE
> PUBLISHED: 04:16 EDT, 27 October 2017 | UPDATED: 12:09 EDT, 27 October 2017

The FBI informant heard this from Vincent Theodore Lee, who was head of the Fair Play for Cuba Committee (FPCC) in New York City. Lee Harvey Oswald had started a one-man FPCC chapter in New Orleans. What is clear from the documents is that Lee read the accounts of Mark Lane's allegations of a meeting between Bernard Weissman, Jack Ruby, and police officer J.D. Tippit (see Chapter One) and just repeated them to an FBI informant. Another FBI memo noted the similarity of the allegations.

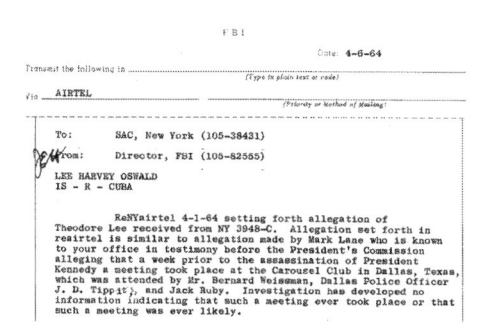

```
                                    FBI
                                             Date: 4-6-64
Transmit the following in _____
                              (Type in plain text or code)
Via   AIRTEL
                              (Priority or Method of Mailing)

    To:       SAC, New York (105-38431)
    From:     Director, FBI (105-82555)
    LEE HARVEY OSWALD
    IS - R - CUBA

         ReNYairtel 4-1-64 setting forth allegation of
    Theodore Lee received from NY 3948-C. Allegation set forth in
    reairtel is similar to allegation made by Mark Lane who is known
    to your office in testimony before the President's Commission
    alleging that a week prior to the assassination of President
    Kennedy a meeting took place at the Carousel Club in Dallas, Texas,
    which was attended by Mr. Bernard Weissman, Dallas Police Officer
    J. D. Tippit, and Jack Ruby. Investigation has developed no
    information indicating that such a meeting ever took place or that
    such a meeting was ever likely.
```

The only really important files that are waiting to be released are the files in Cuba, Russia, Mexico, and Belarus. The ARRB said that efforts to get these records "proved frustrating and fruitless owing to political and diplomatic constraints." Belarus is home to a five-foot-stack of documents that were part of the KGB surveillance of the Oswalds when they lived in Minsk. Every time the ARRB got close to getting these documents, tensions flared with Belarus. The Chairman of the ARRB, Judge Tunheim, told the press that the files "cover every damn thing that Oswald did over this three or so years in the Soviet Union."

Files held in Moscow would also include other surveillance records of the Oswalds as well as the Soviet investigation into the JFK assassination. The ARRB did not get permission to review the larger sets of files in Moscow. There are also records in Cuba although the ARRB noted that "record keeping in Cuba was spotty in the years following Castro's rise to power." The Mexican files might have some important material on Oswald's trip to Mexico City in 1963.

Another area that Russian documents might shed some light is on KGB actions to spread propaganda about the CIA and other American agencies regarding the assassination. One document that turned up in the April, 2018, release shed some light on the KGB. The CIA document was found in the FBI's Mark Lane file and it details information obtained from an unnamed foreign government.

According to the information, the KGB funnelled $1,500 through a "trusted contact" to Lane for his "work on a book" and $500 for a trip to Europe. The document says that "LANE was not told who was financing his work, but he might have been able to guess." The document says that LANE in 1964 "wanted to visit Moscow and acquaint the authorities there with the revealing materials he had regarding the KENNEDY murder." But the Soviets did "not wish to enter into difficulties with the US" and the trip was postponed. From then, "trusted contacts among Soviet journalists met with Lane" and he had regular contact with Borovik. Lane then wanted to visit again in 1969 to show them his film [*Rush to Judgment*] but "he was delicately told that the time was not right for such a trip, since the American government might begin a slander campaign against him in connection with his involvement in the anti-war movement." Further, "American communists who were in Moscow in 1971 expressed the opinion that, although LANE was engaged in activity that was advantageous to the Communists, he was doing this not without profit to himself, and sought to achieve personal popularity and become a national figure."

The memo also indicates that "other investigators and Kennedy assassination buffs were supplied by the KGB not only with money, but also with circumstantial evidence that made the affair appear to be a well-concealed political conspiracy."

Perhaps the release of Russian documents could tell who else was financed.

The document does detail one operation. In 1975, copies of a note from Lee Harvey Oswald were sent to three JFK buffs from Mexico. The letter, dated November 8, 1963, was addressed to a Mr. Hunt and said, "I would like information regarding my position" and "am suggesting that we discuss the matter fully before any steps are taken by me or anyone else."

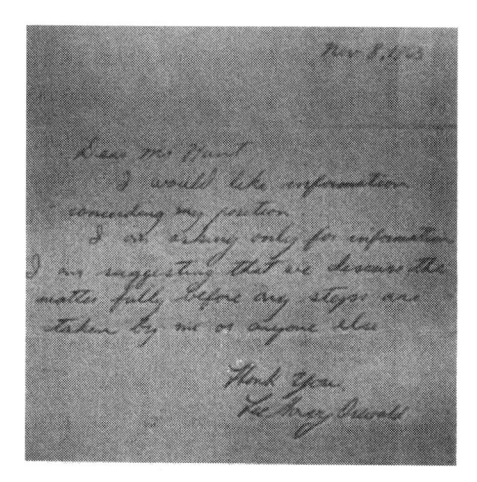

This was all part of Operation Arlington and was based "on the use of an assassination theory that was widespread in the US, according to which theory Howard HUNT, a former CIA employee, who was convicted in 1974 in connection with the Watergate affair, participated in 1963 in organizing a plot, the victim of which was President KENNEDY."

The KGB wrote the note using "individual phrases and expressions taken from letters written by Oswald during his stay in the USSR" and was written on "a scrap of writing paper that OSWALD used in Texas." Further, "the note was on two occasions subjected to graphological and chronological examination "for authenticity" by the Third Section of the KGB's OUT (Operational-Technical Directorate)."

The note was sent to JFK buffs Harold Weisberg, Penn Jones, and Howard Roffman. It was accompanied by another note saying that the document had been sent to FBI director Kelly and that he "has to date not done anything with this document." The goal was to have the researchers ask the FBI to "produce the original note" and when he would deny he had received it, "this would encourage the investigator even more to obtain the desired document." The operation was "carried out in such a way as to fuel (the flames of suspicion) with fresh news and to expose the participation of the American special services in the liquidation of KENNEDY."

The problem for the KGB was that the buffs tended to write that the Oswald letter was intended for H.L. Hunt, the Texas oil billionaire, rather than for E. Howard Hunt. The first references to the document appeared in 1977, and the *New York Times* noted its possible authenticity.

F.B.I. Studying Report Of Oswald Letter to Hunt

SPECIAL TO THE NEW YORK TIMES   MARCH 3, 1977

DALLAS, March 2 (AP) — The Federal Bureau of Investigation is investigating letter reportedly written by Lee Harvey Oswald to the late Dallas billionaire H. L. Hunt asking about Oswald's "position" on Nov. 8, 1963, two weeks before President Kennedy was assassinated.

A spokesman for the F.B.I. in Dallas said that the letter was in its hands and was under investigation.

But the CIA document notes that "the FCD's disinformation service believed that OSWALD's connection with HUNT the millionaire, rather than with HUNT, the CIA officer, was purposely played up in the American press in order to divert public attention from OSWALD's contacts with the special services."

The Oswald letter was investigated by the HSCA and it felt the letter was "much more precisely and much more carefully written" than other writings of Lee Harvey Oswald. They were puzzled that Oswald's middle name Harvey was misspelled—something he was not known to do. They were thus uncertain as to whether it was an authentic document.

Opening the Russian files could be useful in determining what else they did to influence American public opinion. The document notes that "the KGB informed the Central Committee of the CPSU that it would take additional measures to promote theories regarding the participation of the American special services in a political conspiracy directed against President Kennedy." The document also notes that other "KENNEDY assassination buffs were supplied by the KGB not only with money..."

The material in this document corroborated the exact same story found in the Mitrokhin Archive published in 1999.

Another area that might be of interest some time in the future are the documents stored in the Kennedy Library in Boston. While the ARRB did not find assassination records there, they did note that there were a lot of documents on Cuba, which were considered 'relevant'. Thirty boxes of Cuba files were released to the JFK collection of documents. However, additional papers were found in the JFK Library's closed papers of Robert F. Kennedy (then *attorney general*). In 2012, the library released seven boxes out of its 62 boxes of material. The final release of these documents, not yet obtained from the Kennedy family, might shed more light on the anti-Cuba activities of the Kennedy administration.

In April, 2018, about 19,000 more documents were released, but President Trump once again delayed the release of sensitive material until 2021. Of course, there's no reason to believe that there's anything of real significance in those files—just the odd protected name of an intelligence source or the odd piece of information that might embarrass a foreign government.

However, thanks to ex-Congressperson Cynthia McKinney, a long-time crank who believes that George W. Bush had advance knowledge of 9/11, we now know the real reason why material is still being withheld. Mordechai Vanunu, who publicly revealed details of Israel's nuclear program in 1986, told an Arab newspaper in 2004 that Kennedy was assassinated because of "pressure exerted on then head of government David Ben-Gurion, to shed light on Dimona's nuclear reactor." Yes, Israel determined that the only way to relieve that pressure—was to kill the President of the United States.

> **Cynthia McKinney PhD**
> @cynthiamckinney
>
> Ooops, he wouldn't protect GHW Bush, but he WOULD protect Israel! Is that why we the people can't see ALL of the JFK documents? I heard Mordecai Vanunu on this matter!
>
> **Donald Trump says he can't declassify JFK assassination files**
> President Donald Trump boasted last fall that he would open all remaining John F. Kennedy assassination records. So far, Trump hasn't made good on the
> washingtontimes.com
>
> 6:19 PM - 26 Apr 2018

There you have it—why Kennedy was killed, and why the documents must remain locked up. To protect Israel. Thank you, Cynthia McKinney for finally solving the mystery.

Postscript

When I first visited Dealey Plaza in Dallas in March of 2018, I was shocked. When I got out of the taxi across the street from what once was the Texas School Book Depository, I thought that perhaps I was in Legoland. As you look down Elm Street, one cannot help but wonder at just how small the entire area is. I could hardly believe my eyes. Photographs just don't do it justice. Lee Harvey Oswald's first shot only had to travel about 55 yards. The area is so small that it's impossible to believe that multiple assassins could have been shooting without being seen.

There were two tables with people out there selling their wares. At the first stand, a person immediately started in on his spiel about the head shot. When I pointed out that the picture on his board showed the back of Kennedy's head to be intact, he replied, "Ok, I have a true believer here" and shut down—realizing that he wasn't going to make a sale.

At the other table, above the pergola on the grassy knoll, two guys were selling DVDs and magazines. One was very aggressive, and when I started to argue, he just called me an ignorant fool. Well, actually he yelled. I don't think he wanted me to jeopardize business. When I told him that he was too loud and that there was no need to scream, he continued and I left.

I returned a few days later with my partner Andrew and made the same tour around the area. As we went behind the picket fence up on the grassy knoll, we were approached by an older guy with a bunch of booklets. He told us that this was where David Ferrie shot from. I told him that that was impossible because David Ferrie was in a courtroom in New Orleans when JFK was shot. Even though he had blown his credibility, he wasn't fazed at all—he just went on about the three tramps arrested after the assassination and how one of them was Howard Hunt.

As we headed to the Sixth Floor Museum, I started talking to one of their security guards stationed outside. Boy, I said, lots of people selling stuff. He replied, well, they have to make a living. I said, yes, it's just that they are all hawking crazy conspiracy stuff—you never see people saying there was just a lone gunman. "Well," he said, "that would be insulting."

If you ever go to Dallas, be sure to stop at the museum. They've done a good job telling the story of the assassination, and you can see the sniper's nest in the corner window. Unfortunately, it's all blocked off and so you can only look down on Elm Street from an adjacent window. So close. Such easy shots. And then it's off to the museum shop and café, and it's interesting to listen in on people's conversations. I heard one family arguing about Kennedy's head snap. I wanted to butt in but I kept my mouth shut. They'd have to figure it out on their own.

Most people still think there was a conspiracy. But there's been a sea change in the last 20 years—the percentage of people who think that more than one person was involved has been steadily declining. In 2000, only 13 percent of people believed that only one man was involved in the assassination; by 2013 that had risen to 30 percent.

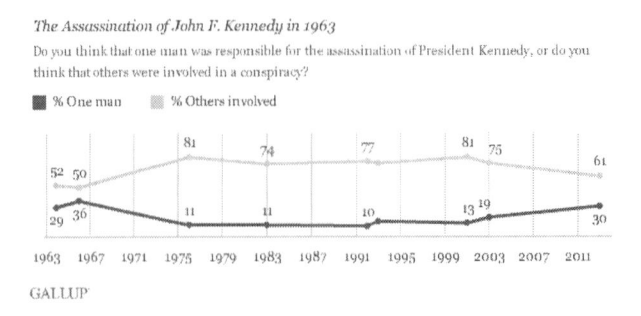

The Assassination of John F. Kennedy in 1963
Do you think that one man was responsible for the assassination of President Kennedy, or do you think that others were involved in a conspiracy?

■ % One man   ■ % Others involved

Year	% One man	% Others involved
1963	29	52
1967	36	50
1975	11	81
1979	11	74
1983	11	74
1987	10	77
1995	10	77
2003	13	81
2007	19	75
2011	30	61

GALLUP

I believe there are two reasons for this.

First, there are now many good books that support a lone gunman. I remember that, when I first went to the college library in 1975, I could only take out conspiracy books (with the exception of the Warren Report). People who now become interested in the assassination will find a much healthier mix of books in their local libraries. Mark Lane's *Rush to Judgment* will have less of an effect when you also read Gerald Posner's *Case Closed*.

Secondly, the rise of the Internet has also helped. There are several JFK debunking sites where you can "detox" after an allotment of conspiracy theory. John McAdams not only runs the best JFK web page out there, he also runs an excellent bulletin board. And on Facebook, there are many good JFK group pages (like Fair Play for JFK) that are reasonable. But what's important here is that 'lone-nutters' can argue their case and can thus expose a lot of people to the truth. It's no longer a one-way conversation—crackpot theories can be immediately rebutted.

Still, the drumbeat of conspiracy bangs on. A new wave of books continues the trend of rejecting evidence, making the plot even more bizarre. James DiEugenio's book, *The JFK Assassination* rejects just about every piece of physical evidence in the case. He's examined the chain of custody for the various bullet fragments and the bullet found in Parkland Hospital (CE 399) and believes he has found enough discrepancies to throw everything out. He then goes one step further and claims that all of that evidence was planted.

Think of what it would take to plant everything. Someone would have to decide what would have to be left somewhere and get someone to do it. And how could you be sure you wouldn't end up with too much evidence, like an extra bullet? DiEugenio can find no witnesses, no paperwork, no anything to back up such a fantastic claim.

Of course he is dead wrong on the chain of custody. For example, the chain of possession of CE 399 can be traced from the time it was found to the time it ended up in the FBI laboratory. Even so, as JFK expert John McAdams noted, even if it was inadmissible in a trial, it would still be "absolutely dispositive where *historical* judgments are concerned."

Still, all of this is exciting news for Oliver Stone. He wrote the forward to *The JFK Assassination*, and looks back, with some regret, that he spent so much time defending his film. "The truth of this matter is actually larger than I even thought at the time. I could've pulled out DiEugenio's book and pointed to the astonishing fact that *there is no conclusive evidence whatsoever* that Oswald even fired the three shots—and that was so from Day One."

It's all ridiculous hokum. But then Oliver Stone now believes that the Zapruder Film was tampered with.

INFOWARS

RADIO SHOW   NEWS   VIDEOS   STORE   TOP STORIES   BREAKING NEWS   CONTACT

OLIVER STONE: ZAPRUDER FILM WAS ALTERED

NOVEMBER 6, 2013   0 Comments

JFK 50th Anniversary: Director amazed that anyone still believes Oswald acted alone

Paul Joseph Watson
Infowars.com
November 6, 2013

With the 50th anniversary of the assassination of JFK approaching later this month, three-time Academy Award-winning director Oliver Stone says that the Zapruder film was tampered with.

He seems to be unaware that in 1996, the Assassinations Records Review Board (ARRB) hired Roland Zavada, an engineer at Eastman-Kodak, to authenticate the Zapruder film. Kodak picked Zavada even though he was retired because he was one of the world's leading experts on 8mm Kodachrome II film. He determined exactly when the film was manufactured and he actually talked to the people who developed it in Dallas. His 150-page report, published in 1998, was quite clear—the Zapruder film at the National Archives is the original film and it has not been modified.

I look at all this with some bemusement. Oliver Stone is locked in for life his with conspiracy theories—there's nothing that could ever change his mind. So is Brian McKenna. But the only way they can sustain their beliefs is to invent wilder and wilder theories, and as they continue, more and more people will see through their empty rhetoric.

The truth matters. I don't know when we'll get over our current postmodernist hangover and re-discover the beauty of objective truth. But the JFK case gives me some hope that people can come back from the abyss.

Acknowledgements

Andrew Yip has had to endure over a year and a half of discussion on the JFK assassination. That is certainly service above and beyond the call of duty. Thank you, my dear partner. I want to thank the extended Yip and Levy families for their support.

It has been a joy to work with Michael Totten whose editing prowess has made this a much better book. Thanks, Michael, and thanks for being such a terrific host & guide in Oregon.

I want to thank John McAdams and Paul Hoch who both corrected a lot of the errors in my manuscript and who were always helpful in making this a better book. Hugh Aynesworth and Peter Dale Scott also helped answering questions. Max Holland assisted with the Paese Sera articles that surfaced in Italy during the ridiculous prosecution of Clay Shaw by Jim Garrison.

It was great finally getting to Dallas in March of 2018. Zac Harmon was a very gracious host and he gave us a private tour of the Old Red Museum of Dallas County History and Culture, which he manages. He's also an amazing blues musician, and a loving human being. Thank you, Zac. I also want to thank Marj Atkinson and Krishna Shenoy who were incredibly helpful at the Sixth Floor Museum. If you are in Dallas, please visit both places.

I want to thank Dale Myers for the permission to use a still from his amazing animated reconstruction of the JFK assassination. I also want to thank Dr. Douglas G. Lattimer for permission to use a diagram from an article he co-wrote with his father and brother on the medical evidence in the JFK assassination. His father, Dr. John K. Lattimer, conducted real-life experiments while other researchers just talked. His articles have stood the test of time.

Frank Warner was kind enough to allow me use his diagram of the Presidential limousine.

The Mary Ferrell Foundation has an indispensable web site and I strongly urge anybody interested in the assassination to join. Rex Bradford, who runs the Foundations, was always helpful.

Other people to thank include Mark Collins for going through all my rough drafts; Shelley Crowley for those terrific lunches where we laugh and cry; Terry Glavin for always urging me on to write; Roy Eappen, a fellow conspirator in the Fabulous Blue Tent; Ron Radosh, who is the top historian on the Rosenberg case; Chris Champion who was kind enough to publish a version of the CBC chapter in the June 2018 issue of the Dorchester Review; and Sol Stern, a kindred sole who has also moved from left to right and then to who-knows-where.

I also want to thank many of the people who have assisted me in researching the JFK assassination over the years. Ian Griggs was very helpful in London and was very generous with his materials; John Rudd provided me with a lot of material; and Chris Mills who is one of the better minds working on the case; and many other people in the UK.

Concordia University was very helpful in opening the Brian McKenna Archives on a snowy day in January. Ellen Gressling was a gracious host at the Library at Loyola Campus.

My first articles on the JFK assassination were carried by The Georgian, the student newspaper of the Sir George Williams Campus of Concordia University. There were a lot of friends who worked on The Georgian who were hugely influential in my career and they include Raymond Masleck, John Mathewson, Kevin Quinn, John MacKinnon, and Rick Gill.

I also have to thank my blues buddies, Steve Simon and John Hahn, for all of our great adventures driving through Mississippi.

Other people who have inspired me along the way include David Roytenberg, Fred Maroun, Jamie Ellerton, Elanor Brodie, Tamara and Anthony Fulmes, Harry Weldon, Edgar Simpson, Keith Fountain, Don Cummer, Daniel Wiener and Tingwen Wang, Michael Sona, Ricky Stevens, Salma Siddiqui, Barbara Kay, Joel Diener, Scott Simon and D-Kai Ma, Tony Hahn, Jenny Roberge, David Kilgour.

Any error or mistake is mine and mine alone.

For Further Information

There's no shortage of material on the JFK assassination on the Internet, but a lot of it is not worth your time or effort. Here is an annotated list of books, videos, and websites that you would be well-advised to check out.

Official Reports

The Warren Report: The Official Report on the Assassination of President John F. Kennedy, 1964. The report has been demonized but you might be surprised at how good it is. The report is available for free online at many sites.

Final Report of the Select Committee on Assassinations, 1979, also known as the HSCA. The HSCA report sustains most of the major conclusions of the Warren Report—namely that Lee Harvey Oswald fired the shots that killed JFK. Available online for free.

Final Report of the Assassinations Records Review Board, 1998. A very good history of the documents of the JFK assassination and the process to declassify them. Available online for free.

Books

Hugh Aynesworth, *Witness to History*, (Brown Books Publishing, 2013). A memoir from a reporter who was on the ground in Dallas interviewing witnesses before anybody else.

Mel Ayton & David Von Pein, *Beyond Reasonable Doubt: The Warren Report and Lee Harvey Oswald's Guilt and Motive 50 Years On*, (Strategic

Media Books, 2014). A very good overview of the assassination and the major controversies from a lone-gunman perspective.

Milton Brener, *The Garrison case: A study in the abuse of power*, (C.N. Potter, 1969). Brener worked in the district attorney's office in New Orleans and had a first-hand look at how Jim Garrison misused the power of his office.

Vincent Bugliosi, *Reclaiming History: The Assassination of President John F. Kennedy*, (W.W. Norton & Company, 2007). While this book is very important, few people will want to wade through its 1,600 oversized pages. But if you are looking for the ultimate debunking tome, this is it. Bugliosi demolishes every conspiracy theory systematically. The book also comes with a CD-ROM with an extra 1,000 pages of material.

Jean Davison, *Oswald's Game*, (W.W. Norton & Company, 1983). If you want to learn more about the motivations of Lee Harvey Oswald, this is an excellent place to start. Davison knows her material and she provides non-conspiratorial explanations for several incidents in Lee Harvey Oswald's life. This book is out of print but you can buy it on Kindle.

Robert Groden, *The Killing of a President: The Complete Photographic Record of the JFK Assassination*, (Studio, 1993). The text is atrocious, but the book has hundreds of important photographs.

James Kirkwood, *American Grotesque*, (Simon & Schuster, 1970). This is the best account of the trial of Clay Shaw. Kirkwood was a playwright (*A Chorus Line*) and was sent to New Orleans to cover the trial. Excellent writing and lots of stories that will make you wonder how Oliver Stone could have believed in Jim Garrison.

Patricia Lambert, *False Witness: The Real Story of Jim Garrison's Investigation and Oliver Stone's Film JFK* (M. Evans & Company, 1998). Lambert has written the best account of the Garrison scandal. She has also uncovered new evidence on witnesses who claimed to have seen Oswald, Ferrie, and Shaw together. Essential reading.

David Lifton, *Best Evidence: Disguise and Deception in the Assassination of John F. Kennedy*, (MacMillan Publishing Company, 1981). I don't agree with Lifton's body alteration theory but there's a pretty good history of the JFK critics in the 1960s in this volume.

Jim Marrs, *Crossfire: The Plot that Killed Kennedy* (Revised and Updated, Basic Books, 2013). The complete compendium of conspiracy theories all in one book. But be very careful with this book—there's a lot of stuff here that just isn't true.

John McAdams, *JFK Assassination Logic: How to Think About Claims of Conspiracy*, (Potomac Books, 2011). McAdams uses the JFK assassination as a handy primer on how to think about evidence. He shows how conspiracy theorists have a very poor understanding of logic and he teaches people how to think about eyewitness testimony and evaluate documents.

Dale Myers, *With Malice: Lee Harvey Oswald and the Murder of Officer J.D. Tippit*, (Oak Cliff Press, 2013). This is the definitive account of the Tippit murder. The book also contains a lot of useful information on the assassination as well.

Gerald Posner, *Cased Closed: Lee Harvey Oswald and the Assassination of JFK*, (Random House, 1993). This is an excellent book that convinced me there was no conspiracy. If you are looking for one good overview, this is it.

Gus Russo, *Live by the Sword: The Secret War Against Castro and the Death of JFK*, (Bancroft Press, 1998). Russo is a terrific researcher, and there's a lot of excellent information in this book on the Kennedy's war against Castro and the JFK assassination.

Oliver Stone & Zachary Sklar, *JFK: The Documented Screenplay*, (Applause Books, 1992). This book contains an annotated screenplay along with reactions and commentaries on the film.

Larry Sneed, *No More Silence: An Oral History of the Assassination of President Kennedy*, (University of North Texas Press, 1998). In-depth interviews with the Dallas police, witnesses, and various investigators make his volume an important contribution to understanding what happened on November 22, 1963.

Larry Sturdivan, *The JFK Myths: A Scientific Investigation of the Kennedy Assassination*, (Paragon House, 2005). Sturdivan provides the best analysis of the scientific (ballistics, firearms, and medical) evidence in the case. Well-documented and important.

Anthony Summers, *Not in Your Lifetime: The Defining Book on the J.F.K. Assassination*, (Open Road Media, 2013). If you have to buy one conspiracy book, this is probably the best. Summers has been writing about the assassination for decades and has, over time, removed the craziest stuff from his book.

Richard Trask, *Pictures of the Pain: Photography and the Assassination of President Kennedy*, (Yeoman Press, 1994). A very good history of the photographs of the assassination.

Richard Trask, *National Nightmare on six feet of film*, (Yeoman Press, 2005). A terrific history of the Zapruder film.

Alexandra Zapruder, *Twenty-Six Seconds: A Personal History of the Zapruder Film* (Twelve, 2016). A first-hand history of the Zapruder film as told by his granddaughter.

Websites

National Archives and Records Administration
https://www.archives.gov/research/jfk
You can access all the new JFK documents at this page.

The Kennedy Assassination, John McAdams
http://mcadams.posc.mu.edu/home.htm
The best JFK assassination web page. Thoroughly debunks everything and explains every aspect of the case. Indispensable.

JFK Assassination Resources Online, David Reitzes
http://www.jfk-online.com/home.html
Reitzes also debunks a lot of nonsense. There are some very good original articles on this site—particularly on the Garrison case.

David Perry's JFK Assassination Pages, David Perry
http://dperry1943.com/
Perry is a debunker who goes out into the field and actually investigates conspiracy claims.

Mary Ferrell Foundation
https://www.maryferrell.org/pages/Main_Page.html
Mary Ferrell collected files on the assassination, and her material has become the best repository of JFK documents out there. If you want to look at the evidence first-hand, this site is for you. If you join the foundation, you can get PDFs of lots of major reports and exhibits.

JFKFacts, Jefferson Morley

http://jfkfacts.org/

Morley's is a conspiracy site, but it sometimes has some useful information.

Secrets of a Homicide, Dale Myers

http://www.jfkfiles.com/

Myers has written the best book on the Tippit murder, and his website has some very important articles on the photographic evidence, the acoustics, and a reconstruction of the assassination.

The JFK Assassination Research Page, Chad Zimmerman

http://mcadams.posc.mu.edu/zimmerman/frontmenu_000037.htm

Zimmerman is a chiropractor who deals with the medical and ballistics issues.

The Assassination of President John F. Kennedy, a Lone-Gunman Viewpoint, David Von Pein

http://davidvonpein.blogspot.com/

Von Pein has created a number of blogs that deal with various parts of the case.

Washington Decoded, Max Holland

http://www.washingtondecoded.com/

A collection of excellent articles and book reviews on the assassination and other areas of politics.

Bulletin Boards

https://groups.google.com/forum/#!forum/alt.assassination.jfk

The best discussion board on the assassination. Moderated by John McAdams so that abusive messages never reach the board.

Facebook

Fair Play for JFK, Jim Hess

https://www.facebook.com/groups/1666412776906917/

A very spirited Facebook group that has a no-nonsense approach to abuse.

Videos

Frontline: Who Was Lee Harvey Oswald? 1993. An honest biography of Lee Harvey Oswald.

Nova: Cold Case JFK, 2013. A scientific look at the assassination with new ballistics and medical tests.

On Trial: Lee Harvey Oswald, 1986. Vincent Bugliosi prosecuted Lee Harvey Oswald in this trial in London with a lot of real witnesses. A must-watch video, although Gerry Spence proved not to be the best defense lawyer.

ABC News Presents the Kennedy Assassination—Beyond Conspiracy, 2004. Completely debunks the major conspiracy theories and showcases Dale Myers' computer animation of the assassination.

Unsolved History: JFK—Beyond the Magic Bullet, 2003. Discovery Channel duplicated the single bullet theory with amazing accuracy.

Image of an Assassination: A New Look at the Zapruder Film, 1998. A terrific documentary on creating a state-of-the-art digital replication of the Zapruder film.

American Experience: Oswald's Ghost, 2008. A look at the cultural side of the assassination.

Notes and Sources

For updates, reviews and pictures about this book, please visit www.conspiracyfreak.com

The 26 volumes are referred to as Warren Commission Volume x, and House Select Committee on Assassination volumes are referred to as HSCA Volume x.

Introduction

Walter Duranty and the New York Times: Stalin's Spin Doctors: The American Press and Stalin—1932-1941 https://windowstoworldhistory.weebly.com/stalins-spin-doctors.html; Accuracy in Media Report: Lying at the Times https://www.aim.org/aim-report/aim-report-lying-times-at-the-times/; Arnold Beichman, "Pulitzer-Winning Lies," The Weekly Standard," June 12, 2003; "Stalin's Spin Doctors: The American Press and Stalin, 1932-1941," https://windowstoworldhistory.weebly.com/stalins-spin-doctors.html; "AIM Report: Lying at the Times," https://www.aim.org/aim-report/aim-report-lying-times-at-the-times/

Malcolm Muggeridge in Ukraine: See Arnold Beichman above.

Orwell put Duranty's name on a list: Timothy Garton Ash, "Orwell's List," *New York Review of Books*, September 25, 2003.

George Orwell, "Looking Back on the Spanish War," First published: *New Road*.——GB, London.——1943.

Norman Mailer and factoids: Paul Dickson, "The Origins of Writerly Words," *Time* magazine, April 30, 2014.

233

George Galloway attempting to enter Canada: Bernie Farber & Terry Glavin, "Canadians Don't Buy What Galloway is Selling," *Ottawa Citizen*, November 26, 2010.

Junket of MPs to China: Joanna Smith, "Candice Bergen: China denied my travel visa, Liberals were no help," http://www.cbc.ca/news/politics/china-travel-visa-bergen-1.4314000, September 29, 2017.

Noam Chomsky and Cambodia: Oz Katerji, "The West's Leftist Male 'Intellectuals' Who Traffic in Genocide Denial, From Srebrenica to Syria," *Haaretz*, November 24, 2017; See also Stephen J. Morris, "Whitewashing Dictatorship in Communist Vietnam and Cambodia," contained in *The Anti-Chomsky Reader*, Peter Collier & David Horowitz, Encounter Books, 2004.

WMD in Iraq: The Commission on the Intelligence Capabilities of the United States Regarding Weapons of Mass Destruction, Report to the President of the United States, March 31, 2005, page 11.

VIPS letter to President Obama on Syria: Muhammad Idrees Ahmad, "The New Truthers: Americans Who Deny Syria Used Chemical Weapons," *The New Republic*, September 11, 2013.

Information on Mint Press News: Brian Lambert, "The Mystery of MintPress News," https://www.minnpost.com/media/2015/11/mystery-mintpress-news, November 11, 2015; Rosie Gary, "The Inside Story of One Website's Defense of Assad," https://www.buzzfeed.com/rosiegray/the-inside-story-of-one-websites-defense-of-assad?utm_term=.svnlyw3RD#.ry49Q2XEn, October 1, 2013; See also https://www.mintpressnews.com/

More on Anthony Hall: Lauren Krugel, "Canadian University Professor who Questioned Holocaust Suspended," The Canadian Press, October 6, 2016.

VIPS letter on Russian hack of DNC: Patrick Lawrence, "A New Report Raises Big Questions About Last Year's DNC Hack," *The Nation*, August 9, 2017.

Supposed Afghan support for the Taliban: Doug Saunders, "Was Our Afghan Saga Useless, or Worse?" *The Globe & Mail*, January 11, 2014; Terry Glavin, "The Truth about Afghanistan," the *Ottawa Citizen*, January 15, 2014.

Quote from Warren Hinckle: If You Have a Lemon, Make Lemonade (W.W. Norton & Company, 1973), page 204.

Alex Jones and Judyth Vary Baker: https://www.youtube.com/watch?v=exT6H9Hsvh0

For a thorough debunking of Judyth's story: http://mcadams.posc.mu.edu/judyth.htm

Judyth Vary Baker and the Toronto Women's Bookshelf: Katie Daubs, "Lee Harvey Oswald's Lover Tries to Clear His Name," the *Toronto Star*, October 17, 2011; Sonia Verma, "Oswald spied on group to save JFK, alleged lover says," *The Globe & Mail*, October 17, 2011.

Conspiracy Culture shop: Peter Biesterfeld, "Conspiracy Comfort Zone," *Now Toronto*, November 7, 2014.

Sydney White account of lunch with Judyth: http://www.rense.com/general95/leeandme.htm

Judyth's response to Sydney White: http://quixoticjoust.blogspot.com/2011/10/sydney-white-meets-judyth-vary-baker.html

Sydney White on CKUW: Ryan Thorpe, "U of W radio station suspends program over anti-Semitic content, Winnipeg Free Press, November 26, 2017.

Ted Cruz's father and Lee Harvey Oswald: Philip Bump, "The 50-year-old mystery behind that photo of Lee Harvey Oswald," Washington Post, July 22, 2016; Tim Brennan, "In Search of the Third Man," *Washington*

Decoded, http://www.washingtondecoded.com/site/2016/06/cruz.html, June 11, 2016.

Barack Obama's statement on foreign policy & JFK: Patrick Lawrence, "Are We Witnessing a Coup Operation Against the Trump White House?" *The Nation*, February 22, 2017.

Ken Livingstone and JFK: "Ken Livingstone interview: 'The idea that America and Britain are good and the Russians are bad? I'm sorry—no,'" *The Independent*, March 21, 2018.

Netflix series on RFK: *Bobby Kennedy for President*, https://www.netflix.com/ca/title/80174282

Oliver Stone and the Putin Interviews: Masha Gessen, "How Putin Seduced Oliver Stone—and Trump," *The New York Times*, June 25, 2017.

Michael Weiss post on Facebook: https://www.facebook.com/search/top/?q=Michael%20D.%20Weiss%20%22News%20that%20Russia%20has%20told%22

Stone on Russian non-interference in the 2016 American election: Kristopher Tapley, "Oliver Stone and Kevin Costner Look Back at the Legacy of 'JFK,' 25 Years Later," *Variety*, December 20, 2016.

Tweets from actor T.J. Miller: https://twitter.com/mousterpiece/status/874405689065697280

Roger Stone, *The Man Who Killed Kennedy: The Case Against LBJ*, (Skyhorse Publishing, 2013).

Review of Stone's book: Hugh Aynesworth, Book Review, *Washington Times*, February 25, 2014.

Patrick Howley, "Roger Stone: LBJ Had Kennedy Killed," *Daily Caller*, May 10, 2013.

Deep State covering their asses: Daniel Chaitlin, "Roger Stone: Deep State tried to 'bluff' Trump to keep some JFK files secret," *Washington Examiner*, October 27, 2017.

Oliver Stone agreeing with Roger Stone: "Oliver Stone on Release of JFK Assassination Files: 'Trump Got Rolled' by 'Deep State,'" *The Wrap*, November 15, 2017.

Chapter One: The People of the Books

Norman Mailer quote on the Warren Report and the 26 volumes: Kathryn S. Olmsted, "Real Enemies: Conspiracy Theories and American Democracy," Oxford University Press, 2009, page 135.

Josiah Thompson quote on the assassination as a religious event: Calvin Trillin, "The Buffs," *The New Yorker*, June 1967.

Warren Hinckle quote on the buffs: *If You Have a Lemon, Make Lemonade*, op. cit., page 214.

Quotes regarding Vincent Salandria: John Kelin, *Praise from a Future Generation: The Assassination of John F. Kennedy and the First Generation Critics of the Warren Report* (Wings Press, 2007), see pages 31-32.

Quotes regarding Harold Weisberg: Kelin op. cit. page 50-51.

Sylvia Meagher quote on guilt of LHO: Kelin op. cit. page 145.

Sylvia Meagher quote on JFK as political crime: Sylvia Meagher, *Accessories After The Fact: The Warren Commission, The Authorities & The Report* (Bobbs-Merrill, 1967), page xxiv.

Maggie Field quotes on conspiracy: Kelin op. cit. page 125; and Trillin op cit.

Shirley Martin quotes on innocence of Oswald: Kelin, op. cit. page 69; Kathryn S. Olmsted, *Real Enemies: Conspiracy Theories and American Democracy, World War I to 9/11* (Oxford University Press, 2009), page 133—134.

Raymond Marcus quote on the official story: Kelin, op. cit., page 128.

Penn Jones quote on mounting list of deaths: Kelin, op. cit., page 99.

Mark Lane, "Oswald Innocent? —A Lawyer's Brief," *National Guardian*, December 19, 1963.

Shirley Martin quote on Richard Coeur de Lion: Kelin, op. cit., page 17.

Bob Schieffer quote on Marguerite Oswald: "Bob Schieffer recalls driving with Lee Harvey Oswald's mother to police station after JFK assassination," CBS News, October 26, 2017.

New York Telegram story on Mark Lane: Kelin, op. cit., page 160.

Marguerite Oswald speaks at Lane event: Kelin, op. cit., page 22.

Marguerite Oswald quote on LHO being an agent: Kelin, op. cit., page 73.

Marguerite Oswald quote on Kennedy being a dying man: Kelin, op. cit., page 74.

Harold Feldman quote on Marguerite Oswald: Kelin, op. cit., page 75.

Salandria quote on Marguerite Oswald: Kelin, op. cit., page 77.

Feldman quote on Marina Oswald cooperating: Kelin, op. cit., page 78.

Salandria and Feldman discussion on killing of Oswald: Kelin, op. cit., page 34.

Salandria on Oswald's left-wing bona fides: Kelin, op. cit., page 33.

Feldman & Salandria on Oswald's spelling: Kelin, op. cit., page 37.

Ruth Paine on Shirley Martin: Kelin, op. cit., page 71.

Shirley Martin had her daughter hide a tape recorder: Kelin, op. cit., page 94.

Buffs bothering Billy Lovelady: Kelin, op. cit., page 227-228.

Joachim Joesten, *Oswald: Assassin or Fall Guy* (Marzani & Munsell, 1964).

Marzani receiving money from the Soviet Union: Christopher Andrew and Vasili Mitrokhin, *The Sword and the Shield: The Mitrokhin Archive and the Secret History of the KGB*, (Penguin Books, 1999), pages 225-230.

Aynesworth review of Marzani book: Kelin, op. cit., page 172-173.

Thomas Buchanan, *Who Killed Kennedy?* (Secker & Warburg, 1964).

Arnoni quote on JFK ending the Cold War: Kelin, op. cit., page 155.

Bertrand Russell, "16 Questions on the Assassination," The Minority of One, September, 1964.

Salandria, Weisberg, and Jones quotes on release of the Warren Report: Kelin, op. cit., page 130.

Raymond Marcus quote on Warren Report: David Talbot, *Brothers: The Hidden History of the Kennedy Years* (Free Press, 2008).

I.F. Stone, "The Left and the Warren Commission Report," *I.F. Stone's Weekly*, October 6, 1964.

Raymond Marcus Letter to I.F. Stone: http://www.kenrahn.com/JFK/The_critics/Marcus/Marcus_on_Stone.html

Todd Gitlin on the JFK assassination: Todd Gitlin, *The Sixties: Years of Hope, Days of Rage* (Bantam, 1993), page 311.

Raymond Marcus quote on fraud in the Warren Report: Trillin, op. cit.

Number of sets of the Twenty-six volumes sold: Kelin, op. cit., page 139.

Paragraph on the buffs buying the Twenty-six volumes: Kelin, op. cit., page 126; page 141; page 149; page 150.

Raymond Marcus quote on the contradictions of the Report: Kelin, op. cit., page 186.

Vincent Salandria quote on the easy pickings: Kelin, op. cit., page 200.

Calvin Trillin quote on the book "Inquest": Trillin, op. cit.

Quote on Rampart's research: Ramparts magazine, November 1966.

Warren Hinckle quote on Oswald's pubic hair: Hinckle, op. cit., page 209.

David Welsh quote on the critics doing the job of the police: David Welsh, "The Legacy of Penn Jones, Jr." *Ramparts*, November 1966.

Oswald leaving his wedding ring and $170 on the bedroom dresser: Warren Report, page 15.

Evidence against Oswald: You can find all this in the Warren Report. Vincent Bugliosi has a long list of the incriminating evidence against Oswald in his book *Reclaiming History: The Assassination of President John F. Kennedy (W.W. Norton & Company, 2007)*, page 951.

Mark Lane chapter: Mark Lane, *Rush to Judgment: A critique of the Warren Commission's inquiry into the murders of President John F. Kennedy, Officer J.D. Tippit and Lee Harvey Oswald* (Holt, Rhinehart & Winston, 1966) page 36.

Mark Lane quote on Bowers: Lane, op. cit., page 32.

Lee Bowers testimony before the Warren Commission: Volume VI, page 284-289.

Mark Lane on Abraham Zapruder and source of shots: Lane, op. cit., page 41.

Abraham Zapruder testimony before the Warren Commission: Volume VII, page 569—576.

Lane admitting shots fired from School Book Depository: Lane, op. cit., page 44.

Testimony of Bob Jackson before the Warren Commission: Volume II, page 155—165.

Mark Lane on Dallas doctors examining Kennedy's head: Lane, op. cit., Page 57.

Lane on the Tippit murder witnesses: Lane, op. cit., Page 176.

Virginia and Barbara Davis identification of Oswald: Warren Report, page 168.

The story of Carroll Jarnagin: Volume XXVI, page 254.

Penn Jones on Carroll Jarnagin: Editorials from the Midlothian Mirror, republished in *Ramparts*, November, 1966.

Hugh Aynesworth on Carroll Jarnagin: Hugh Aynesworth, *Witness to History* (Brown Books Publishing Group, 2013), page 178, 185, 189.

Oswald's whereabouts on October 4th, 1963: Warren Report, page 736—737.

Mark Lane's version of Jarnagin story: Lane, op. cit., page 248.

Weissman confrontation of Mark Lane: Volume XI, page 428.

2008 story of conversation of Oswald and Ruby: The Guardian, February 18, 2008; https://www.theguardian.com/world/2008/feb/18/usa

Linking the story back to Carroll Jarnagin: From Dale Myers' blog. http://jfkfiles.blogspot.com/2008/02/wading-through-muck.html

Ramparts circulation in 1968: Dwight Garner, "Back When Ramparts Did the Storming," *New York Times*, October 6, 2009.

David Welsh quote on Penn Jones: David Welsh, "The Legacy of Penn Jones, Jr." *Ramparts*, November, 1966.

Jones' story on the meeting in Ruby's apartment: Penn Jones, Jr., "Editorials from the Midlothian Mirror," *Ramparts*, November, 1966.

For the truth about what happened in Ruby's apartment: Richard Warren Lewis, *The Scavengers and Critics of the Warren Report* (Dell Books, 1967); Dave Reitzes, "The Men Who Gathered in Ruby's Apartment," http://mcadams.posc.mu.edu/death11.htm; Gary Mack, "What Conspiracy Books Won't Tell You," http://mcadams.posc.mu.edu/death11.htm

Mark Lane quote on the meeting in Ruby's apartment: Lane, op. cit., page 284.

Mark Lane quote on powerful influences: Lane, op. cit., page 275.

Mark Lane quote on murders: Lane, op. cit., page 276.

Warren Hinckle quote on Mark Lane: Hinckle, op. cit., page 210.

Jones on death of Earlene Roberts: David Welsh, "The Legacy of Penn Jones, Jr., *Ramparts*, November 1966.

Earlene Roberts death certificate: https://www.findagrave.com/memorial/28123630/earlene-doke-roberts

Hinckle on the overnight sensation of the mysterious deaths: Hinckle, op. cit., page 216—226.

Sunday Times article on the mysterious deaths: Testimony of Jacqueline Hess, HSCA Volume IV, page 454. Her testimony contains the article and the letter from the *Times* to the HSCA.

Sylvia Meagher quote on Penn Jones: Meagher, op. cit., page 302.

Review of "Time of Assassins": *Ramparts*, November, 1966.

Reaction to review of "Time of Assassins": Hinckle, op. cit., page 227—230.

Reaction of the critics to review of "Time of Assassins": *Ramparts*, January, 1967.

Warren Hinckle apology for review of "Time of Assassins": *Ramparts*, January, 1967.

Boston Globe article quoting "Time of Assassins": James Doyle and Stephen Zorn, "The Truth about That Day in Dallas," *Boston Globe*, November 20, 1966.

Josiah Thompson, *Six Seconds in Dallas: a micro-study of the Kennedy assassination proving that three gunmen murdered the President* (Bernard Geis Associates, 1967).

Minutia in Sylvia Meagher's book: The rifle sling, page 111; ammunition clip, page 116; rifle's serial number, page 104; pictures of Oswald, page 209, two Oswald's, page 359; speed of the limousine, page 3.

Time magazine saying Lane was the third most popular speaker on campuses: Tom Shales, "When Good Assassinationists Get Together… They Seldom Get Together," *Oui* magazine, February, 1976.

Mort Sahl and Mark Lane: Gerald Nachman, *Seriously Funny: The Rebel Comedians of the 1950s and 1960s* (Pantheon, 2003); James Curtis,

Last Man Standing: Mort Sahl and the Birth of Modern Comedy (University Press of Mississippi, 2017).

Rosemary James story: Rosemary James, "DA Here Launches Full JFK Death Plot Probe," New Orleans *States-Item*, February 17, 1967.

Garrison quotes on investigation: Jack Wardlaw & Rosemary James, *Plot or Politics?: The Garrison Case and its Cast* (Pelican Publishing, House, 1967) page 39, 47; Jim Phelan, "Rush to Judgment in New Orleans," *Saturday Evening Post*, May 6, 1967.

Mort Sahl going to New Orleans: Kelin, op. cit., page 384.

Mark Lane calling into Mort Sahl's radio show: Ibid for a partial quote; complete quote from Lane retrieved from a document on Harold Weisberg's archive.

Chapter Two: Jim Garrison's Excellent Homosexual Adventure

Oswald's life in New Orleans: Warren Report, page 375.

Election of Jim Garrison: The best account of the rise of Jim Garrison is Milton Bremer in his book *The Garrison Case: A Study in the Abuse of Power* (Clarkson N. Potter, Inc., 1969).

Tip from Jack Martin: Patricia Lambert, *False Witness: The Real Story of Jim Garrison's Investigation and Oliver Stone's Film JFK* (M. Evans & Co., 1998), page 23.

Dean Andrews connection: Lambert, op. cit., page 31.

Jim Garrison figuring out the identity of Clay Bertrand: Lambert, op. cit., page 47.

Biography of Clay Shaw: The best account of the life of Clay Shaw is by Donald Carpenter, *Man of a Million Fragments: The True Story of Clay Shaw* (Donald H. Carpenter, 2014).

Andrews quote ("shuck me like a corn") on Jim Garrison: Lambert, op. cit., page 50.

Andrews invention of Manuel Garcia Gonzales: Ibid.

Ramparts story with a picture of Manuel Garcia Gonzales: William W. Turner, "The Inquest," *Ramparts* magazine, June, 1967.

Hugh Aynesworth story about Ruby and Oswald being gay lovers: Aynesworth, op. cit., page 193.

David Ferrie's discussions with David Snyder: Memo from David Snyder dated February 24, 1967, found in FBI files.

Autopsy of David Ferrie: James Phelan, *Scandals, Scamps and Scoundrels: The Casebook of an Investigative Reporter* (Random House, 1982), page 141—142.

Full text of Sciambra memo: http://mcadams.posc.mu.edu/russo2.txt

Perry Russo questioned while under influence of sodium pentothal: http://mcadams.posc.mu.edu/hypnosis.htm

Transcript of Perry Russo interview while under hypnosis: http://mcadams.posc.mu.edu/session1x.htm

Arrest of Clay Shaw: Carpenter, op. cit., page 309.

Quote from Newsweek on vulnerable homosexuals: "Assassination: History or Headlines?" *Newsweek*, March 13, 1967.

Paul Hoch quote on Garrison's homophobic persecution: Echoes of Conspiracy, Volume 13. Number 1.

Quote of Mrs. Lawrence Fischer: James Kirkwood, *American Grotesque: An Account of the Clay Shaw—Jim Garrison Kennedy Assassination Trial in New Orleans* (Simon & Schuster, 1970), page 27.

Garrison telling Richard Billings it is a sadist plot: Dave Reitzes, "Assassination a Homosexual Thrill Killing" http://mcadams.posc.mu.edu/jimloon5.htm

Jim Phelan and Garrison's homosexual plot: Phelan, op. cit., page 150—151.

Jim Garrison telling Newsweek that he was looking for a "gay boy": Hugh Aynesworth, "Assassination: History or Headlines," *Newsweek*, March 13, 1967.

Merriman Smith telling the FBI that Garrison claimed "high-status" fags killed Kennedy: Carpenter, op. cit., page 317.

Northshield contacts the FBI regarding Shaw portrayal as sadist: Carpenter, op. cit., page 313.

Pearson diaries: Unreleased segment Drew Pearson Diaries, Volume 2 1960—1969, (University of Nebraska Press) Page 470—470.

Paese Sera: Max Holland has written extensively about the Paese Sera article and Clay Shaw. See for example, "The Power of Disinformation: The Lie That Linked CIA to the Kennedy Assassination," May 19, 2007, http://www.washingtondecoded.com/site/2007/05/the_power_of_di.html; "The Demon in Jim Garrison," Wilson Quarterly, Spring 2001; "Was Jim Garrison Duped by the KGB?" February 11, 2002, http://www.washingtondecoded.com/site/2002/02/was-jim-garriso.html.

Le Devoir article on Clay Shaw: "La Pravda: la CIA avait sous ses ordres Clay Shaw, accuse d'avoir complote contre J.F.K." *Le Devoir*, May 8, 1967; "L'enquete du procureur Garrison sur l'assassinat de Kennedy conduira-t-elle a Montreal?" *Le Devoir*, March 16, 1967.

Ramparts references Le Devoir: William Turner, "The Garrison Commission," *Ramparts*, January, 1968.

Kondrashev comment to Tennent Bagley regarding Paese Sera: Tennent Bagley, *Spymaster: Startling Cold War Revelations of a Soviet KGB Chief* (Skyhorse Publishing, 2015), page 208.

Diaries of Richard Billings: "The Demons in Jim Garrison," op. cit.

Jim Phelan on Jim Garrison's switchboard lighting up like a pinball machine: "Rush to Judgment in New Orleans," op. cit.

Garrison's conspiracy included: Edward Jay Epstein, "Epitaph for Jim Garrison: Romancing the Assassination," *The New Yorker*, November 30, 1992. http://www.edwardjayepstein.com/archived/garrison2.htm

Warren Hinckle quote on Garrison phone call: Hinckle, op. cit., page 198.

James Phelan limerick: Kirkwood, op. cit., page 79.

Lee Odom in Clay Shaw's address book: Wardlaw & James, op. cit., page 10.

Lee Harvey Oswald's entry in his notebook 19106: Warren Commission Volume XVI, page 58.

Sylvia Meagher sending registered letter to Jim Garrison and his reply: Kelin, op. cit., page 401.

Jim Garrison telling Playboy about Oswald's code: "Playboy interview: Jim Garrison," *Playboy*, October, 1967.

Garrison's code to link Oswald to Ruby: Posner, op. cit., page 447; Associated Press, "Garrison Says 'Code' Links Oswald, Shaw, Ruby," *The Evening Star*, May 13, 1967.

Garrison decoding the local CIA office: Edward Jay Epstein, *The Assassination Chronicles: Inquest, Counterplot and Legend* (Carroll & Graf, 1992) page 188.

David Lifton story from Open City, an L.A. underground newspaper: David Lifton, "Is Jim Garrison Out of His Mind?" http://mcadams.posc.mu.edu/lifton1.htm

Lee Harvey Oswald entry in his notebook for Fort Worth TV station: Warren Commission Volume XVI, page 40.

Jim Garrison repeats story of Oswald's notebook: Jim Garrison, *On the Trail of the Assassins* (Warner Books, 1988), page 171.

Jim Garrison quote on Spiesel testimony: Garrison, op. cit., page 277.

Testimony in Clay Shaw trial: http://www.jfk-online.com/shawtest.html

Reporter writing in his notebook about the Zapruder film playing continuously at Shaw trial: Kirkwood, op. cit., page 332.

Kirkwood quote on the poor case against the Warren Report: Kirkwood, op. cit., page 324.

New York Times quote on prosecution of Shaw: Lambert, op. cit., page xiv.

Aaron Kohn quote on the Jim Garrison investigation: Brener, op. cit., page 49.

Judge Christenberry quote on the prosecution of Clay Shaw: http://www.jfk-online.com/christenberry1.html

Paul Hoch newsletter on Garrison letter about homosexuality: Echoes of Conspiracy, Volume 8, #2, July 17, 1986.

Tights pants testimony in Clay Shaw trial: Adrianne Quinlan, "After JFK Assassination, DA Jim Garrison ripped into life of Clay Shaw," *The Times-Picayune*, November 21, 2013; Questions were asked about tight pants to Lloyd Cobb, Goldie Moore, Clay Shaw, and Jeff Biddison. You can read their testimony here: https://www.maryferrell.org/php/showlist.php?docset=1016

Vincent Salandria quote on Jim Garrison's beating: Kelin, op. cit., page 450.

Plaque for Clay Shaw: Will Fellows, *A Passion to Preserve: Gay Men as Keepers of Culture* (University of Wisconsin Press, 2005), page 227.

Chapter Three: I Was a Teenage JFK Conspiracy Freak

Good Night America show with the Zapruder film: https://www.youtube.com/watch?v=nxCH1yhGG3Q

History of Zapruder film: Richard Trask, *National Nightmare on six feet of film* (Yeoman Press, 2005); Alexandra Zapruder, *Twenty-Six Seconds: A Personal History of the Zapruder Film* (Twelve, 2016).

Newspaper stories on Good Night America: John J. O'Connor, "TV: Two Programs Exploit Subjects," New York Times, March 27, 1975; Earl Golz, "Shooting Gory Sight." *Dallas Morning News*, 7 Mar. 1975, A1.

Ron Rosenbaum quote on the showing of the Zapruder film: Ron Rosenbaum, "What Does the Zapruder Film Really Tell Us?" *Smithsonian* magazine, October 2013.

Geraldo Rivera quote on the Good Night America show: Geraldo Rivera, *Exposing Myself* (Bantam, 1991), page 247.

Ralph Schoenman at the University of Cincinnati: "60s Assassinations Called 'Executions," Barb Zigli, *Cincinnati Enquirer*, May 21, 1975.

Hinckle quote on assassination industry experiencing a recession: Hinckle, op. cit., page 210.

Neil Sheehan review of Mark Lane's Vietnam book: New York Times Book Review, December 27, 1970, http://mcadams.posc.mu.edu/smearing.htm

Harvey Yazijian & Sidney Blumenthal, *Government by Gunplay* (New American Library, 1976); see also Max Holland, "Grassy Knoll Sid: Hillary's Personal Conspiracy Theorist," June 11, 2015, http://www.washingtondecoded.com/site/2015/06/blumenthal.html

Dick Gregory wrong on the changing of the parade route: http://mcadams.posc.mu.edu/route.htm

Mark Lane quote on the confiscation of the autopsy X-rays and photographs: Lane., op. cit., page 61.

Articles on the examination of the JFK autopsy X-rays and photographs: Gary Lattimer, John Lattimer, & Jon Lattimer, "The Kennedy-Connally One Bullet Theory: Further Circumstantial and Experimental Evidence," Medical Times, November 1974; Cyril Wecht and Robert Smith, "The Medical Evidence in the Assassination of President John F. Kennedy," *Forensic Science*, 3 (1974).

Student newspaper article on Rusty Rhodes: Fred Litwin, "Rusty Rhodes sensationalist," *The Georgian*, January 9, 1976.

Montreal Gazette account of Rusty Rhodes talk: Eric Johnson, "Dallas Man reopens JFK 'file'": *Montreal Gazette*, December, 1975.

Secret Service document #767: Document can be found on Mary Ferrell website, https://www.maryferrell.org/showDoc.html?docId=10721&search=secret_service+767#relPageId=116&tab=page; in addition, Schoenman claimed that Oswald's CIA number was 110669. CIA documents show that that number was associated with an Austrian who was in Shanghai in the 1940s, and had nothing to do with Oswald.

Hugh Aynesworth story on Lonnie Hudkins: Aynesworth, op. cit., page 108.

Lonnie Hudkins story on Oswald as an informant: Lonnie Hudkins, "Oswald Rumored as Informant for US," *Houston Post*, January 1, 1964.

Lonnie Hudkins admitting to the Dallas Morning News that he fabricated the story: John Geddie, "Did Oswald Tell Truth?" *Dallas Morning News*, March 11, 1975.

Jack Ruby testimony to the Warren Commission: Warren Commission Volume XIV, page 504—569.

Psychiatric report of Dr. Werner Tuteur based on an examination of Jack Ruby of July 12 -15, 1965; see also Peter Watson, "Ruby told doctor of 'plot' to kill Kennedy," The Sunday Times, August 25, 1974. Schoenman got his information from this article which misspells Tuteur's name. But the text of the article refutes the headline—and includes the information that Ruby referred Dr. Tuteur to Thomas Buchanan's book on the assassination.

Jack Ruby autopsy: "Eight Tumors in Ruby Brain, Doctors Report," *The Tuscaloosa News*, February 5, 1967.

Ramparts description of Dick Gregory lecture: Barry Farrell, "Running with Dick Gregory," *Ramparts*, Aug/Sept, 1975.

Mark Lane & Dick Gregory, Code Name "Zorro": The Murder of Martin Luther King, Jr. (Prentice-Hall, 1977).

HSCA impression of Mark Lane: House Select Committee on Assassinations Final Report, Page 424.

Dick Gregory on NPR: Transcript of NPR News & Notes, July 12, 2005.

Dick Gregory's conspiracies: Ed Wiley III, "The 9/11 conspiracy: Rubbish or reality," NBC News, September 11, 2006.

Dick Gregory on danger of malt liquor at NAACP convention: Randy Hall, "Dick Gregory Blasts 'Insane, Racist System' in America," CNS News, July 7, 2008.

Dick Gregory article for Global Research: Dick Gregory, "WTC 1 and 2: Justice and 9/11 Demands Accountability. Forensic Evidence Indicates Presence of Controlled Demolition Material," September 10, 2010. https://www.globalresearch.ca/wtc-1-and-2-justice-and-9-11-demands-accountability-forensic-evidence-indicates-presence-of-controlled-demolition-material/20979

Dick Gregory on Alex Jones: https://www.youtube.com/watch?v=gubWGmRdcnw

Dick Gregory on Walmart: "ADL Says Dick Gregory Comparison between Walmart and Nazi Regime "Inappropriate and Offensive," September 24, 2013 http://dc.adl.org/news/adl-says-dick-gregory-comparison-between-walmart-and-nazi-regime-inappropriate-and-offensive/

Ralph Schoenman submission to the Rockefeller Commission dated March 26, 1975.

Schoenman's article in 1992 on the Kennedy murders: Ralph Schoenman, "Who killed Kennedy and why," *The Organizer*, January, 1992.

Paul Johnson on Ralph Schoenman: Paul Johnson, *Intellectuals: From Marx and Tolstoy to Sartre and Chomsky* (Harper Perennial, 1988), page 220.

Bernard Levin, "Bertrand Russell: Prosecutor, Judge and Jury," *New York Times*, February 19, 1967.

William Galeota, "Ralph Schoenman: Silhouette," *Harvard Crimson*, March 19, 1968.

"Russell Disavows American Ex-Aide," *New York Times*, December 10, 1969.

Bertrand Russell, "Private Memorandum Concerning Ralph Schoenman," Reproduced in Ronald Clark *The Life of Bertrand Russell* (Alfred Knopf, 1976), pages 640-651; see also Chapter 22, "The Rise of Ralph Schoenman," Chapter 23, "The Enigmatic Friendship," and Chapter 23, "Once More His Own Man."

Warren Hinckle quote on Ralph Schoenman: Hinckle, op. cit., page 211.

Ralph Schoenman, *The Hidden History of Zionism* (Veritas Press, 1988).

Ralph Schoenman venom on Israel in 1994: Alfred Rosenfeld, *Resurgent Antisemitism: Global Perspectives* (Indiana University Press, 2013).

Ralph Schoenman in the Organizer: Ralph Schoenman, "Blood on their Hands—Official Murder in America," *The Organizer*, June, 1995.

Ralph Schoenman on 9/11: Ralph Schoenman, "Who are the Real Terrorists?" http://www.kenrahn.com/JFK/The_critics/Schoenman/Who_Are_the_Real_Terrorists.html

Ralph Schoenman's radio show: https://www.indybay.org/news-items/2010/11/09/18663709.php?show_comments=1

Robert Groden allegation that JFK autopsy photos had been doctored: Comments on the Panel's Report by Robert Groden, Consultant to the Committee, HSCA Volume VI, page 294.

Robert Groden, *The Killing of a President: The Complete Photographic Record of the JFK Assassination* (Studio, 1993).

Groden in the O.J. Simpson civil trial: http://mcadams.posc.mu.edu/groden1.htm

Groden and Bruno Magli shoes: Dale Myers, "The Soothsayer of Dealey Plaza," April 3, 2008, http://jfkfiles.blogspot.com/2008/04/soothsayer-of-dealey-plaza.html

Chapter Four: Oliver Stone's Excellent Homosexual Adventure

1995 documentary on homosexuals in the movies: *The Celluloid Closet*, 1995 written by Vito Russo.

Norman Mailer on the characterization of homosexuals: Norman Mailer, "The Homosexual Villain," contained in *Norman Mailer: Mind of an Outlaw* (Random House, 2014), page 14.

Tom Clancy in Newsweek: Cover story, "Tom Clancy, Bestseller," August 8th, 1988.

Overall gross of JFK film: http://www.boxofficemojo.com/movies/?id=jfk.htm

Michael Kurtz on significance of JFK: Michael Kurtz essay "Oliver Stone, JFK, and History," contained in *Oliver Stone's USA: Film, History, and Controversy* (Culture America, 2000) page 166.

Jim Garrison, *A Heritage of Stone* (G.P. Putnam & Sons, 1970).

Ralph Schoenman letter to Jim Garrison: See Holland, "The Lie That Linked CIA to the Kennedy Assassination," op. cit.

Oliver Stone buys rights to "On the Trail of the Assassins": Bugliosi, op. cit., page 1352.

Oliver Stone likens Garrison's book to a Dashiell Hammett whodunit: "On The Trail of the Assassins": Richard Bernstein, "Film; Oliver Stone, Under Fire Over the Killing of J.F.K." *New York Times*, July 28, 1991.

Stone purchases rights to Crossfire by Jim Marrs: Paul Hoch on Oliver Stone and Jim Garrison, Excerpt from Paul Hoch, Echoes of Conspiracy, Volume 13, Number 1, Note 38.

Stone's belief that Garrison tried to "force a break in the case": Bugliosi, op. cit., page 1381.

Stone's quote on the film being "worth the sacrifice of one man": Ibid.

Quote "At times, however, we had to put words in Ferrie's mouth to write the scene": Oliver Stone & Zachary Sklar, *JFK: The Documented Screenplay*, (Applause Books, 1992), page 88.

Screenplay charge regarding Permindex raising money to assassinate Charles de Gaulle: Stone & Sklar, op. cit., page 83; see also Steve Dorril, "Permindex: The International Trade in Disinformation," Lobster, #3, 1983, http://mcadams.posc.mu.edu/lobster.htm; see also Dave Reitzes, "Fair Play for Clay Shaw?" http://mcadams.posc.mu.edu/fairplay.htm

Scene with "X" in JFK: Stone & Sklar, op. cit., pages 105—114.

Kennedy and Vietnam: National Security Memorandum #273, http://mcadams.posc.mu.edu/viet16.htm; See also Stanley Karnow, "JFK:

Oliver Stone and the Vietnam War," http://mcadams.posc.mu.edu/karnow.htm

Kennedy quote to Walter Cronkite: Ibid.

Kennedy quote to Chet Huntley: Ibid.

Kennedy's planned speech in Dallas: "Context: Kennedy and Foreign Policy," http://mcadams.posc.mu.edu/context1.htm

Quote from Secretary of State Dean Rusk: David Reitzes, "JFK Conspiracy Theories at 50: How the Skeptics got it wrong and Why it Matters," *Skeptic* magazine, March, 2013; https://www.skeptic.com/reading_room/jfk-conspiracy-theories-at-50-how-the-skeptics-got-it-wrong-and-why-it-matters/

Robert Kennedy oral history interview on Vietnam: http://mcadams.posc.mu.edu/vietnam.htm

112th Military Intelligence group and security on November 22, 1963: "L. Fletcher Prouty, Fearless Truth Teller or Crackpot," http://mcadams.posc.mu.edu/prouty.htm

Kennedy's planned speech for Austin, Texas: See "Context: Kennedy and Foreign Policy," cited above.

L. Fletcher Prouty as a consultant to the Lyndon LaRouche organization: Edward J. Epstein, "The Assassination Chronicles," op. cit., page 578.

L. Fletcher Prouty consulting for lawyers working for the Church of Scientology: Ibid.

L. Fletcher Prouty speaking at the 1990 Convention of the Liberty Lobby: Ibid.

L. Fletcher Prouty book: *The Secret Team: The CIA and its Allies in Control of the United States and the World* was published by the Institute for Historical Review (IHR) in 1991. The IHR was founded by David McCalden and William Carto, the head of the Liberty Lobby.

L. Fletcher Prouty presenting at the Liberty Lobby's annual Board of Policy convention: Epstein, op. cit., page 579.

Prouty's remark about the Holocaust: Robert Sam Anson, "The Shooting of JFK," *Esquire*, November, 1991.

Jim Garrison's introduction of L. Fletcher Prouty to Oliver Stone: "Oliver Stone Discusses His Film JFK and Introduces the Real "Man X," L. Fletcher Prouty, *The CIA, Vietnam, and the Plot to Assassinate John F. Kennedy* (Carrol Publishing Group, 1992), page xvii, http://www.prouty.org/stone/stone_x.htm

Leonard C. Lewin, *Report from Iron Mountain* (Dial Press, 1967).

Report from Iron Mountain as a hoax: Victor Navasky, "Conspiracy Theory Is a Hoax Gone Wrong," *New York* magazine, November 17, 2013; https://web.archive.org/web/20120419001730/http://www.silverbearcafe.com/private/Navasky.html

Lewin admits to hoax in the New York Times Book Review: Leonard Lewin, "Report from Iron Mountain: The Guest Word," *New York Times Book Review*, March 19, 1972.

Prouty's quote on the Iron Mountain Group Report: L. Fletcher Prouty, *The CIA, Vietnam, and the Plot to Assassinate John F. Kennedy* (Carrol Publishing Group, 1992), page 5.

Prouty's quote about the power elite: Ibid, page 4.

Stone's introduction to Prouty's book: "Oliver Stone Discusses His Film JFK and Introduces the Real "Man X," op. cit.

Clay Shaw's relationship with the CIA: Max Holland, "The Lie That Linked CIA to the Kennedy Assassination: The Power of Disinformation," op. cit.

New Orleans investigation of Clay Shaw's death: http://mcadams.posc.mu.edu/death9.htm

The Advocate on JFK: David Ehrenstein, "JFK—A New Low for Hollywood," The Advocate, January 14, 1992.

Oliver Stone reply to the David Ehrenstein of The Advocate: Stone & Sklar, op. cit., page 511; see also the exchange of letters between David Ehrenstein and Zachary Sklar in Cineaste, December 1992.

Quote on gratuitous orgy scene: John Weir, "FILM: Gay-Bashing, Villainy and the Oscars," *The New York Times*, March 29, 1992.

George Will on Oliver Stone: George Will, "Is Oliver Stone an intellectual sociopath, indifferent to truth," *Milwaukee Sentinel*, December 20, 1991.

George Lardner, Jr. on JFK: George Lardner, Jr., "On the Set: Dallas in Wonderland," The Washington Post, May 19, 1991; George Lardner, Jr., "The Way It Wasn't: In 'JFK,' Stone Assassinates the Truth," *Washington Post*, December 20, 1991.

Charles Krauthammer on JFK: Charles Krauthammer, "'JFK': A Lie, But Harmless," *The Washington Post*, January 10, 1992.

Oliver Stone discussion with Christopher Hitchens: Tad Friend, "Oliver Stone's Chaos Theory," *The New Yorker*, October 22, 2001.

Oliver Stone at Brown University: George Rush, Joanna Malloy, Kasia Anderson, Lauren Rubin, "Stone Rolls Out a Few New Theories," *New York Daily News*, January 14, 2002.

Stone's documentary "Commandante" and interview with Anne Louis Bardach: Anne Louis Bardach, "Oliver Stone's Twist: Is the director's latest film soft on Castro?" http://www.slate.com/articles/news_and_politics/interrogation/2004/04/oliver_stones_twist.html, April 14, 2004.

Oliver Stone on Jewish control of media: "Oliver Stone: Jewish control of the media is preventing free Holocaust debate," Haaretz, July 26, 2010.

Oliver Stone quote "Israel has f***** up American foreign policy": 'Ben Child, "Oliver Stone apologizes for 'antisemitic' remarks," *The Guardian*, July 27, 2010.

Oliver Stone quote that "I had to apologize": Andrew Goldmannov, "Oliver Stone Rewrites History—Again," *The New York Times Magazine*, November 22, 2012.

Oliver Stone quote on Scientologists: William Drozdiak, "U.S. Celebrities Defend Scientology in Germany," *The Washington Post*, January 14, 1997.

Foreign Policy magazine on "South of the Border": Elizabeth Dickinson, "The Oliver Stone Show," *Foreign Policy*, June 24, 2010.

Ron Radosh on "South of the Border": Ron Radosh, "More on Oliver Stone's latest Travesty, South of the Border," *Pajamas Media*, June 26, 2010.

Oliver Stone & Peter Kuznick, *The Untold History of the United States* (Gallery Books, 2012).

References within "The Untold History of the United States": Yassir Arafat rejecting terror (page 463); Osama bin Laden as part of the CIA (page 488); US 'obtuseness and inflexibility' regarding Taliban handover of bin Laden (page 506); Iraq under Saddam Hussein (page 518); AIPAC (pages 518-519).

Quote in "The Untold History of the United States" on the so-called grand bargain with Iran: (page 534).

The truth about the so-called grand bargain with Iran: Steve J. Rosen, "Did Iran Offer a 'Grand Bargain' in 2003?" *American Thinker*, November 16, 2008.

Quote from Zbigniew Brzezinski in "The Untold History of the United States: Stone & Kuznick, op. cit., (page 545).

Oliver Stone in St. Louis for the 50th anniversary of the JFK assassination: https://www.youtube.com/watch?v=exQcktqeqJM

Foreign Policy magazine on Mi Amigo Hugo: Jeffrey Tayler, "Oliver Stone's Disgraceful Tribute to Hugo Chavez," *Foreign Policy*, May 13, 2014.

Oliver Stone interview of Viktor Yanukovych in Moscow: James Kirchick, "Crazytown: Oliver Stone's Latest Dictator Suckup," *The Daily Beast*, January 5, 2015.

Oliver Stone at Toronto International Film Festival in 2016: Anthony D'Alessandro, "Oliver Stone Remembers 9/11: What The U.S. Government Knew & How We Could Have Prevented That Tragic Day—TIFF," *Deadline Hollywood*, September 11, 2016.

Oliver Stone in Tehran in May 2018: Rohollah Faghih, "Iran's Fajr film festival grabs headlines with Oliver Stone," May 2, 2018, http://www.al-monitor.com/pulse/originals/2018/05/irans-fajr-festival-grabs-headlines.html#ixzz5EorKfGEy; "Director Oliver Stone rips US as 'outlaws' while visiting Iran," Associated Press, April 25, 2018.

Chapter Five: A Conspiracy Too Big?

House Select Committee on Assassinations Final Report, January 2, 1979. Findings begin on page 3.

Steve Barber on the acoustics: Steve Barber, "The Acoustics Evidence—A Personal Memoir," http://mcadams.posc.mu.edu/barber.htm

National Academy of Sciences (NAS): Report of the Committee on Ballistic Acoustics, National Academy Press, 1982. http://www.jfk-online.com/nas00.html

Sabato analysis of acoustics: "The Kennedy Half Century: Acoustical Analysis of November 22, 1963 Dallas Police Recordings, Commissioned by Professor Larry J. Sabato Director, UVA Center for Politics University Professor of Politics," Release Date: October 15, 2013 Washington, DC.

https://www.thekennedyhalfcentury.com/pdf/Kennedy-Half-Century-Audio-Research.pdf

Harrison Livingstone, *High Treason 2* (Carroll & Graf, 1992).

Harrison Livingstone quotes on memory from "High Treason 2": "During periods of great stress…." Page 126); "in the stress and pressure of events…," Page 137; "I am inclined to think that the conflicts…," Page 143; "But it has been so many years..," Page 272.

Quote from High Treason 2 on a massive conspiracy: "High Treason 2," op. cit., page 562.

Quote from High Treason 2 on the "handmaidens of the conspiracy": "High Treason 2," op. cit., page 575.

Paul Hoch quotes: Echoes of Conspiracy, Volume 15, #1, November 3, 1993.

Authentication of Autopsy X-Rays and photos: HSCA Volume VI, page 225; Volume VII, page 37.

HSCA Forensic Pathology Panel: HSCA Volume VII, page 73.

HSCA Photographic Panel: HSCA Volume VI, page 1.

HSCA Earwitness Analysis: HSCA Volume VIII, page 128.

Handwriting and Fingerprint Panel: HSCA Volume VIII, page 223.

Mannlicher-Carcano Firing Test: HSCA, Volume VIII, page 183.

HSCA Firearms Panel: HSCA Volume VII, page 353.

Neutron Activation Analysis: Testimony of Vincent Guinn, HSVA Volume I, page 491.

Wallace Milam quote on "we have identified twelve of the three gunmen,": Paul Hoch, Echoes of Conspiracy, Volume 15, #1, November 3, 1993.

Fred Litwin, "A Conspiracy Too Big?" http://mcadams.posc.mu.edu/toobig.htm

Robert Groden on backyard photographs of Lee Harvey Oswald: Robert J. Groden, "The Killing of a President," op. cit., page 168-171.

Jim Marrs on the backyard photographs of Lee Harvey Oswald: Jim Marrs, Crossfire: The Plot That Killed Kennedy (Revised and Updated Edition), (Basic Books, 2013), page 430.

Scene in the film JFK where intelligence officers are faking the backyard photos: Stone & Sklar, "JFK: The Documented Screenplay," op. cit., page 51.

Robert Groden quote on the single-bullet theory: "The Killing of a President," op. cit., page 125.

Robert Groden's diagrams of the single-bullet theory: "The Killing of a President, op. cit., page 125, page 126, page 128, page 139.

Oliver Stone quote on Robert Groden: "The Killing of a President," op. cit., page x.

Jim Marrs use of faulty single-bullet theory diagrams: Crossfire, op. cit., photo insert after page 302.

Dr. Cyril Wecht use of faulty single-bullet theory diagrams: Dr. Cyril Wecht, Cause of Death: A Leading Forensic Expert Sets the Record Straight (Dutton, 1993). See page 3 of the illustrations. Wecht sources his diagram to Josiah Thompson and captions it as "the remarkable path of the 'magic bullet,' as shown by the Warren Commission." A very misleading caption.

HSCA positioning of Kennedy's neck wound: HSCA Volume VII, page 80.

Dale Myers reconstruction of the single-bullet theory: http://www.jfkfiles.com/jfk/html/intro.htm

Crossfire chapter on convenient deaths: Jim Marrs, Crossfire, op. cit., page 529.

Robert Groden's 43 sidebars on mysterious deaths:

Quote from Crossfire on the "well of paranoia": Jim Marrs, Crossfire, 1993 edition, op. cit., page 558.

Jacqueline Hess testimony about Earlene Roberts death: HSCA, Volume IV, page 466.

Robert J. Groden, *JFK: Absolute Proof, The Killing of a President, Volume III* (Conspiracy Publications, 2013).

Groden quotes on convenient deaths from JFK: Absolute Proof: Page 245.

Quote from Raymond Marcus on the photographic evidence: John Kelin, op. cit., page 123.

Mary Moorman #2 photograph: HSCA Volume VI, page 125.

David Lifton buying a commemorative magazine: John Kelin, op. cit., page 220.

David Lifton quote on "an act of photo interpretation": Ibid, page 220—221.

David Lifton showing pictures to Raymond Marcus: Ibid.

Maggie Field quote on a "monumental discovery": Ibid, page 221.

Sylvia Meagher in a "state of shock": Ibid, page 223.

Leo Sauvage quote on photos being symptomatic of "desperate and dishonest" people: Ibid, page 233.

Vincent Salandria seeing a man he believed was wearing headphones: Ibid, page 237.

Sylvia Meagher quote "said she thought she could see the figure but wasn't sure": Ibid, page 365.

CBS producer Leslie Midgley "said she could not see anything resembling a man in any of the pictures": Ibid, page 366.

James Kirkwood story of Bill Gurvich and Raymond Marcus: Kirkwood, op. cit., page 536-537.

Raymond Marcus testimony before Jim Garrison grand jury: https://www.maryferrell.org/showDoc.html?docId=1194

David Lifton known as "Blowup" in the Ramparts office: Hinckle, op. cit., page 214.

Quote on "a man wearing a Prussian helmet": Ibid.

Size of the Moorman photograph: http://www.jfkfiles.com/jfk/html/badgeman_3.htm

HSCA sending a high-quality negative to the Rochester Institute of Technology: HSCA Volume VI, page 126.

Letters to the editor in response to "A Conspiracy Too Big": Dallas '63: The British Forum for Views and Research into the Assassination of President John F. Kennedy, Volume 2, Number 1, June 1995.

Rebuttal from Harrison Livingstone: Ibid.

The "Who Killed Kennedy" conference in Liverpool: Andrew Rosthorn, "JFK killing: the Liverpool angle," *The Independent*, July 6, 1996.

John Rudd on his talk being similar to Fred Litwin's "A Conspiracy Too Big": "John Rudd Reflects on the Conference," Dallas '63, November, 1996.

Chapter Six: Did the CBC Solve the JFK Assassination?

1983 CBC Memo from a Ouija board session: Internal CBC Memo from Maxine Sidran to Brian McKenna, September 13, 1983. Retrieved from the Brian McKenna archives at Concordia University in Montreal.

Who Killed JFK?, CBC Fifth Estate documentary first broadcast on November 22, 1983.

Fifth Estate documentaries on the JFK assassination produced by Brian McKenna: *Dallas & After*, 1977; *Crossfire*, late 1970s; *The Casket was Empty*, 1981; *Who Killed JFK?*, 1983; *The Conspiracy Files: JFK and 9/11*, 2013; *The JFK Files: The Murder of a President*, 2017. There was also a

I Was a Teenage JFK Conspiracy Freak   263

Fifth Estate documentary in 1975 with Sylvia Meagher and Mark Lane, but I do not know if Brian McKenna was the producer.

Most-watched Fifth Estate show: Internal memo from Ron Haggart, Senior Producer, to Brian McKenna dated January 27, 1984 noting an audience of 2.4 million. Attachment of shire of all viewing on CBC English language stations for January 27, 1984, with a notation that "this is the largest audience in the fifth estate's history."

Brian McKenna winner of 2007 Pierre Berton Award: https://www.newswire.ca/news-releases/film-and-television-writer-director-brian-mckenna-to-receive-2007-pierre-berton-award-534559091.html

Ombudsmen report on "The Valour and the Horror": Stephen Godfrey, "CBC tied for ways to mollify veterans," The Globe & Mail, November 11, 1992.

Pioneer Award from JFK Lancer: http://jfklancer.com/awards.html

Brian McKenna acceptance speech at JFK Lancer event in Dallas: DVD available from JFK Lancer, http://www.jfklancer.com/catalog/nidmedia/dvd2010.html

CBC Press release for "Dallas and After": retrieved from the Harold Weisberg archives, http://jfk.hood.edu/index.shtml?search.html

Canadian Press wire story: "CBC show asks if Oswald victim of fake photo," November 23, 1977.

HSCA contact with Major J.M. Pickard: HSCA Volume II, page 347; https://www.maryferrell.org/showDoc.html?docId=81&relPageId=351

Letter from Major J.M. Pickard to the HSCA: JFK Document #004572, referenced In HSCA Volume VI, page 316.

HSCA conclusions about the backyard photographs: HSCA. Volume VI, page 179.

Trajectory analysis by Thomas Canning of NASA: HSCA Volume II, page 177.

Claims of Dallas and After: Transcript of the show retrieved from the Weisberg Archive. The CBC did not respond to requests for a copy of the transcript.

Oswald qualified as a sharpshooter in the U.S. Marines: Warren Report, page 681.

Testimony of Sgt. James Zahm: Warren Commission Volume XI, page 306.

Oswald's U.S. Marine score book: http://parishotelboutique.blogspot.com/2008/08/john-lattimer-true-collector-of.html; Physician John Lattimer bought the score book from Oswald's mother, Marguerite; http://www.icollector.com/Lee-Harvey-Oswald-s-US-Marine-Corps-Rifle-Score-Book_i17516240; See also Warren Commission Exhibit 239.

HSCA report on earwitness accounts of shots fired in Dealey Plaza: HSCA Volume II, page 122.

Itek Corporation computer analysis of the Zapruder film: https://www.maryferrell.org/showDoc.html?docId=60448#relPageId=1&tab=page

Ruby phoning people to help with the American Guild of Variety Artists: HSCA Final Report, page 155.

Peter Dale Scott letter to the New York Review of Books: Peter Dale Scott, "The CIA's Mystery Man," *New York Review of Books*, April 3, 1975.

Gaudet told investigators that he didn't see Oswald: Warren Commission Document #75—FBI DeBrueys Report of December 2, 1963.

Gaudet contacting the FBI regarding Jack Ruby buying paintings: Warren Commission Exhibit 2880.

Borenstein telling the FBI that Ruby bought paintings in 1959: Ibid.

HSCA information on William Gaudet and possible CIA connections: HSCA Final Report, page 218-219.

HSCA conclusion about Lee Harvey Oswald and the CIA: HSCA Final Report, page 225.

HSCA and the Congressional Research Service investigation of mysterious deaths: HSCA Volume IV, page 466—467.

L. Fletcher Prouty, "The Guns of Dallas," *Gallery* magazine, October, 1975.

Quotes from L. Fletcher Prouty: "The Guns of Dallas," op. cit.

Adrienne Clarkson interview of Gerry Patrick Hemming: from a transcript retrieved from the Harold Weisberg archive. Brian McKenna sent the transcript to Weisberg in April 1978.

Hemming testimony before the HSCA: https://history-matters.com/archive/jfk/hsca/unpub_testimony/Hemming_3-21-78/html/Hemming_0001a.htm

1996 JFK Lancer conference with Hemming: John Kelin, "The Gerry Patrick Hemming Panel," http://www.whokilledjfk.net/gerry_patrick_hemming.htm

Hemming hanging out on JFK bulletin boards: http://educationforum.ipbhost.com/topic/5781-familiar-faces-in-dealey-plaza/?page=5&tab=comments#comment-53407

CBC Memo to publicists: CBC Internal memo from Karen Flanagan-McCarthy to Wyona Shields, Telex supervisor dated November 15, 1983. Retrieved from the Brian McKenna archives at Concordia University in Montreal.

Memo highlighting "responsible sensationalism": CBC internal memo from Ron Haggart, Senior Producer to Brian McKenna dated October 20, 1983. Retrieved from the Brian McKenna archives at Concordia University in Montreal.

David Lifton, *Best Evidence* (MacMillan, 1981)

FBI report by James Sibert & Francis O'Neil: http://www.kenrahn.com/JFK/History/The_deed/Sibert-O'Neill.html

Criticism of Lifton's book: Thomas Powers & Alan Rich, "Robbing The Grave," New York Magazine, February 23, 1981; Harrison Salisbury, "JFK and Further Sinister Forces," *New York Times*, February 22, 1981.

Brian McKenna quote calling David Lifton's research "riveting": https://www.amazon.com/gp/review/R4KUJ9BGCUI8C?ref=pf_vv_at_pdc-trvw_srp

Ulric Shannon on potential CBC documentary in the 1990s: http://mcadams.posc.mu.edu/shannon.htm

Dr. Cyril Wecht on David Lifton's body alteration theory: Gerald Posner, op. cit., page 297.

Brian McKenna's discussion with Dr. Michael Baden: Notes from McKenna's interview of Dr. Baden on September 29, 1983, retrieved from the McKenna archives at Concordia University in Montreal.

Dallas doctors confirm authenticity of autopsy X-rays and photos: http://mcadams.posc.mu.edu/novadocs.htm

Supposed J. Edgar Hoover document about convincing the public that Oswald was the assassin: https://www.archives.gov/files/research/jfk/releases/docid-32263509.pdf

Testimony of FBI inspector James Malley to the HSCA: HSCA Volume 3, page 467.

Thomas Powers on Jefferson Morley: Thomas Powers, "The Monster Plot," *London Review of Books*, May 10, 2018.

Quote from author Max Holland on Jefferson Morley: E-mail to Fred Litwin.

McKenna story of Fidel Castro and Oswald and the CIA: Transcript of Fifth Estate, November 17, 2017.

What's next for Brian McKenna and the Fifth Estate: https://www.amazon.com/gp/review/R4KUJ9BGCUI8C?ref=pf_vv_at_pdctrvw_srp

James Douglas, *JFK and the Unspeakable: Why He Died and Why it Matters* (Touchstone, 2008).

Yoko Ono review of "JFK and the Unspeakable" on Amazon.com: https://www.amazon.com/JFK-Unspeakable-Why-Died-Matters/dp/1439193886/ref=sr_1_1?s=books&ie=UTF8&qid=1529076163&sr=1-1&keywords=jfk+and+the+unspeakable

Chapter Seven: The Quest for the Holy Document

Jim Garrison closing remarks in the Clay Shaw trial: http://www.jfk-online.com/garrisonclosing.html

Marrs quote about locking up evidence: Jim Marrs, *Crossfire*, op. cit., page 542.

Earl Warren comments on secrecy: Vincent Bugliosi, "Reclaiming History," Op. cit., Endnotes, page 134.

John McAdams list of recently declassified documents: http://mcadams.posc.mu.edu/context3.htm

Documents on "secret inks": Bill Miller, "The Very Visible Battle Over Invisible Ink," *Washington Post*, June 13, 2000.

Exchange of gifts between the US and China in 1972: Editorial Board, "Too many government documents are kept secret," *Washington Post*, December 25, 2012.

Secrecy of documents in Canada: Dave Seglins & Jeremy McDonald, "Government accused of hoarding Canadian history in 'secret' archives," CBC News, May 25, 2017.

Secrecy in the UK: Ian Cobain & Richard Norton-Taylor, "Files that may shed light on colonial crimes still kept secret by UK," *The Guardian*, April 26, 2013.

Warren Commission Exhibit 917: Warren Commission Volume XVIII, page 115.

Paul Hoch attending Mark Lane lecture in August 1966: E-mail to Fred Litwin.

Paul Hoch finding a document with a shorter redaction: Commission Document 1114; https://www.maryferrell.org/showDoc.html?docId=11510&relPageId=752

Mark Lane, *A Citizen's Dissent* (Holt Rinehart & Winston, 1968), page 127.

Garrison quote on Oswald's "possible intelligence role,": Jim Garrison, "On The Trail of the Assassins," op. cit., page 54-55.

Garrison's list of "unavailable" Warren Commission documents: Ibid.

Jim Garrison and Playboy magazine: "Playboy interview: Jim Garrison," *Playboy*, October, 1967.

Warren Commission Document 931: https://www.maryferrell.org/showDoc.html?docId=11327

Warren Commission Document 692: https://www.maryferrell.org/showDoc.html?docId=11090

The President John F. Kennedy Assassination Records Collection Act of 1992: https://www.congress.gov/bill/102nd-congress/senate-bill/3006

Harold Weisberg letter to Kevin Costner: Harold Weisberg, "Beware the Tainted Stone: Letter to actor Costner on the Corruption of Oliver Stone," December 26, 1991, retrieved from the Harold Weisberg archive.

History of secrecy of Warren Commission documents: Vincent Bugliosi, "Reclaiming History," op. cit., Endnotes page 132; See also "Final Report of the Assassination Records Review Board," 1998; https://www.archives.gov/files/research/jfk/review-board/report/arrb-final-report.pdf; Dale Myers, "How the upcoming JFK assassination file release came to be,"

May 20, 2017, http://jfkfiles.blogspot.com/2017/05/october-surprise-how-final-upcoming-jfk.html

CIA memo on Cambridge News: https://www.archives.gov/files/research/jfk/releases/docid-32352381.pdf

Dale Myers blog post on newly released documents: "Scraping the Bottom of the Barrel," http://jfkfiles.blogspot.com/2017/10/scraping-bottom-of-barrel.html

Newsweek article on Cambridge News report: Melinda Delkic, "JFK Files: UK Paper Received Curious Tip about Half an Hour Before the Kennedy Assassination," *Newsweek*, October 27, 2017.

Michael Eddowes, *The Oswald File* (Outlet, 1997).

Quotes from reporters at Cambridge News: Anna Savva, "Did Cambridge News reporter really take a call before the JFK assassination?" *Cambridge News*, October 27, 2017.

Dale Myers quote on "unsubstantiated clairvoyance,": Dale Myers, "Scraping the Bottom of the Barrel," op. cit.

Document with truncated answer from Richard Helms of the CIA: https://www.archives.gov/files/research/jfk/releases/docid-32113033.pdf

Headline in the Sun Newspaper on Helms truncated answer: Neal Baker, "Cover Up? JFK Files CUT OUT CIA Director's reply to whether Lee Harvey Oswald was a secret agent…so will we ever know the truth?" *The Sun*, October 27, 2017.

Coverage in the Washington Post and Huffington Post: Dale Myers, "Scraping the Bottom of the Barrel," op. cit.

Helms' full testimony: https://www.maryferrell.org/showDoc.html?docId=1386#relPageId=20&tab=page

Tariq Tahir, "FBI Informant claimed Dallas police officer J.D. Tippit was the REAL JFK assassin—not Lee Harvey Oswald, secret files reveal," *Daily Mail*, 27 October, 2017.

FBI document on FBI informant who was actually Vincent Theodore Lee: http://www.dailymail.co.uk/news/article-5023235/Dallas-police-officer-JD-Tippit-JFK-s-REAL-assassin.html

FBI document that shows this is all similar to Mark Lane's allegation from Rush to Judgment: https://www.archives.gov/files/research/jfk/releases/docid-32187226.pdf

Relevance of international files on the assassination: Kevin Hall, "Documents haven't quelled JFK conspiracy theories. Do the answers lie abroad?" McClatchy DC Bureau, February 16, 2018; See also "Final Report of the Assassination Records Review Board," op. cit., page 140.

CIA document found in Mark Lane's FBI file: ODYSSEY document found in Mark Lane's file, it is an extract from a foreign document; https://www.archives.gov/files/research/jfk/releases/2018/104-10332-10004.pdf

Letter from Lee Harvey Oswald to Mr. Hunt: HSCA Volume VIII, page 357.

Special to the New York Times, "F.B.I. Studying Report of Oswald Letter to Hunt," March 3, 1977.

HSCA on the Hunt note authenticity: HSCA, Volume VIII, page 235.

Mitrokhin story on the Hunt note: Christopher Andrew & Vasili Mitrokhin, *The KGB in Europe and the West: The Mitrokhin Archive* (Penguin Book, 1999), page 298.

JFK Library's collection of Robert Kennedy's files: Dale Myers and Gus Russo, "Drums of Conspiracy," August 30, 2013; http://jfkfiles.blogspot.com/2013/08/drums-of-conspiracy.html

McKinney Tweet: Eileen Fleming, "Trump Reneges on JFK Assassination File, Former House Rep. Responds with a reminder of Vanunu Mordechai," Arab Daily News; https://thearabdailynews.com/2018/04/30/trump-reneges-on-jfk-assassination-file-former-house-rep-responds-with-a-reminder-of-vanunu-mordechai/

McKinney Tweet: https://thearabdailynews.com/wp-content/uploads/2018/04/CynthiaMcKinneysJFKVanunu-Tweet.png

Postscript

Sixth Floor Museum: https://www.jfk.org/

Gallup Polls on JFK conspiracy: https://news.gallup.com/poll/165893/majority-believe-jfk-killed-conspiracy.aspx; See also https://fivethirtyeight.com/features/the-one-thing-in-politics-most-americans-believe-in-jfk-conspiracies/

James DiEugenio, *The JFK Assassination* (Skyhorse Publishing, 2018).

Oliver Stone quote in *The JFK Assassination:* op. cit., page IX.

InfoWars on Zapruder film: Paul Joseph Watson, "Oliver Stone: Zapruder Film Was Altered," InfoWars, November 6, 2013; https://www.infowars.com/oliver-stone-zapruder-film-was-altered/

Zavada report on the authenticity of the Zapruder Film: http://rochester.nydatabases.com/story/zavada-report-jfk-assassination-evidence

Printed in Great Britain
by Amazon